Markets in their Place

Markets are usually discussed in abstract terms, as an economic organising principle, a generalised alternative to government planning, or even as powerful actors in their own right, able to shape local and national economic destinies. But markets are not abstract. Even as the idea of the market seduces politicians around the world to take advantage of their abstract qualities, they constantly run up against material reality. Markets are always somewhere, in place, and it is in place that the smooth theories of markets falter and fail. More than simply being embedded in particular places, markets necessarily emerge in the various political, social, cultural and environmental relations that exist in and between places. Markets shape places, but the reverse is also true.

This collection of essays approaches markets from the ground up, and from a part of the world often still regarded as peripheral to global capitalism: the South Pacific. With a wide variety of case studies, including on indigenous economies, childcare, agriculture, wine, electricity metering, finance, education and housing, the authors show how complex local, social and cultural politics matter to how markets are made within and between places, and the insights that can be gleaned from studying markets in this part of the world. They explore the way in which superficially similar markets work out differently in different places, and why, as well as examining how market relations are constructed in places outside and on the edges of the centres of Western capitalism, and what this says about how markets are understood in those centres.

The book will be of particular interest to scholars and students working in and between economic geography, cultural economy, political economy, economic sociology and more.

Russell Prince is a Senior Lecturer in Human Geography at Massey University in the School of People, Environment and Planning.

Matthew Henry is an Associate Professor in Planning at Massey University in the School of People, Environment and Planning.

Carolyn Morris is a Senior Lecturer in Social Anthropology at Massey University in the School of People, Environment and Planning.

Aisling Gallagher is a Senior Lecturer in Human Geography at Massey University in the School of People, Environment and Planning.

Stephen FitzHerbert is a cultural economic geographer with the National Institute of Water and Atmospheric Research (NIWA).

Routledge Frontiers of Political Economy

Markets in their Place

Context, Culture, Finance

**Edited by
Russell Prince, Matthew Henry,
Carolyn Morris, Aisling Gallagher and
Stephen FitzHerbert**

Routledge
Taylor & Francis Group

LONDON AND NEW YORK

First published 2021
by Routledge
2 Park Square, Milton Park, Abingdon, Oxon OX14 4RN

and by Routledge
605 Third Avenue, New York, NY 10158

Routledge is an imprint of the Taylor & Francis Group, an informa business

British Library Cataloguing-in-Publication Data
A catalogue record for this book is available from the British Library

Library of Congress Cataloging-in-Publication Data
A catalog record has been requested for this book

ISBN: 978-0-367-27340-8 (hbk)
ISBN: 978-1-032-04195-7 (pbk)
ISBN: 978-0-429-29626-0 (ebk)

DOI: 10.4324/9780429296260

Typeset in Bembo
by Taylor & Francis Books

Contents

vi   *Contents*

Illustrations

Figures

Tables

Contributors

Christian Berndt is Professor of Economic Geography at the University of Zurich.

Alana Brekelmans is a sessional academic and anthropologist at the University of Queensland. Her research examines narratives of time and space in post-settler Australia. In particular, she explores the intersection between settler-colonial grand narratives and lived experience in representations of belonging in Outback Australia.

Stephen FitzHerbert is a cultural economic geographer with the National Institute of Water and Atmospheric Research (NIWA). His main interests include: postcolonial economisation, diverse economies and engaged research methodologies.

Aisling Gallagher is a Senior Lecturer in Human Geography at Massey University in the School of People, Environment and Planning. Her research focuses broadly on the geographies of care, welfare and social reproduction, with a special interest in the marketisation of childcare. She has published in Progress in Human Geography; Environment and Planning A and Urban Geography.

Matthew Henry is an Associate Professor in Planning at Massey University in the School of People, Environment and Planning. His research focuses on the historical technopolitics of agri-food systems and environmental knowledge.

Dan Hikuroa (Ngāti Maniapoto, Waikato-Tainui, Ngāti Whanaunga) is a Senior Lecturer in Te Wānanga o Waipapa, University of Auckland. He employs Earth Systems-Environmental Humanities approaches in his research and is an established world expert on weaving indigenous knowledge and science to realise the dreams and aspirations of the communities that he works with. He is UNESCO NZ Commissioner for Culture, Tumuaki of Ngā Kaihautū Tikanga Taiao (Chair of the Statutory Māori Advisory to the Environmental Protection Authority), performs key roles within New Zealand's National Centres of Research Excellence and National Science Challenges and advises national and regional government, communities and philanthropic trusts. Dan has been spearheading alternative ways of assessing sustainability, including weaving indigenous knowledge and epistemologies into legislation, assessment frameworks and decision-support tools.

Gabriel C.M. Laeis is a Professor of Hospitality Management at IUBH International University, Germany, where he enjoys lecturing on hospitality, gastronomy, sustainability and business strategy. Previously, he worked for a number of hospitality companies and studied Hotel Management (BA) and Organic Agriculture and Food Systems (MSc). For his PhD in Development Studies at Massey University, he looked at the role of cuisine in tourism-agriculture linkages in Fiji.

Alexandra (Zannie) Langford is a Postdoctoral Research Fellow at the University of Queensland, researching changing dynamics of rural agriculture in Indonesia with the Partnership for Australia-Indonesia Research. Her PhD research explored how local actors negotiate financial investments in agriculture in northern Australia. She has previously worked on both applied and academic projects exploring land, livelihoods and rural development in Vanuatu and Indonesia, as well as in chemical engineering.

Geoffrey Lawrence is Emeritus Professor of Sociology at The University of Queensland. His work spans the areas of agri-food restructuring, neoliberal globalisation, financialisation and food security. He was President of the International Rural Sociology Association from 2012 to 2016. He is a Life Member of the Australian Sociological Association and an elected Fellow of the Academy of Social Sciences in Australia.

Erena Le Heron is Principal Researcher with Le Heron Leigh Consultancy. Her research is informed by critical socio-cultural, economic and feminist geography and interdisciplinary socio-ecological theory. Her interests are wide-ranging, but are all connected through a focus on narrative, land-coast-sea and the temporal and spatial relationships between them. Her broad research portfolio includes work on: Aotearoa New Zealand filmmakers and their relationship to landscape; agri-food systems and regenerative economies of land-based production; and the transformative potential of marine spaces, blue economy initiatives and enactive participatory processes in multi-use contested marine spaces. Theoretical contributions focus on re-imagining, re-assembling and re-mediating collectively inspired economy-environment relations and the co-development of situated knowledge principles and practices for sustainability transitions.

Richard Le Heron is Emeritus Professor of Geography in the School of Environment at the University of Auckland, a past Chair of the International Geographical Union Research Commission on the Dynamics of Economic Spaces and a former Vice President (Humanities and Social science) of the Royal Society of New Zealand. His early research drew on the geography of political economy literature to explore capitalist accumulation under globalising conditions and investigate restructuring in pastoral, forestry and horticultural industries and organisations in New Zealand. This research was reinvigorated and redirected as he engaged deeply with the provocations of the governmentality, Actor Network, assemblage and other post structural literatures. His recent research, as part of the Biological Economies project and the Sustainable Seas National Science Challenge is trans-disciplinary, across science and social sciences. It includes co-imagining and applying socio-ecological knowledge in conditions of the Anthropocene, the co-governance potential of enactive knowledge under uncertainties, rural and marine economies as sites of progressive experimentation, transitioning challenges to a blue-economy, imagining decolonisation of research practices and new generation institutions and co-agency capacities to embrace land–coast–marine interactions, interdependencies and challenges.

Nicolas Lewis is a political and economic geographer at the University of Auckland. He is interested in the emergence and formalisation of economic formations in diverse fields of cultural and economic life, and the economisation of new fields. He has worked in the areas of agri-food, education, fashion, innovation and the blue economy.

Heather Lovell is Professor of Energy and Society at the University of Tasmania, Australia. She is a human geographer with research interests in energy, climate change and the environment. The scholarship that she has helped to develop concerns the politics, policies and practices of innovation in response to environmental problems, focused on three empirical strands: smart grids, low-energy housing, and carbon markets. Heather has previously held positions at Edinburgh, Durham and Oxford Universities in the UK. Over the course of her career she has published two books and over 40 journal papers.

Carolyn Morris is a Senior Lecturer in Social Anthropology at Massey University in the School of People, Environment and Planning. Her research interests are in the politics of food and farming in Aotearoa New Zealand.

Warwick E. Murray is Professor of Human Geography and Development Studies at Victoria University of Wellington. He has particular expertise in Latin America and the geography of globalisation. He is currently working, with John Overton and others, on a book on ethical value networks.

Laurence Murphy is Professor of Human Geography at the University of Auckland, New Zealand where he was formerly a Professor of Property. His primary interests address housing and urban dynamics and he has published on issues relating to homeownership, mortgage securitisation, social rented housing, calculative practices and housing affordability, gentrification, and commercial property markets and urban change.

John Overton is a geographer at Victoria University of Wellington. As well as teaching and research in Development Studies, and development aid in particular, he has maintained a research interest in the geography of wine for over two decades.

Russell Prince is a Senior Lecturer in Human Geography at Massey University in the School of People, Environment and Planning. His research focuses on the geography of policy mobility and expertise, and he has also published on the economic geography of wine and alternative proteins. His research has been published in Progress in Human Geography, Environment and Planning D: Society and Space, and Economic Geography.

Donna Wynd is an independent activist researcher with expertise in health, education and social development. She has a background in economics and geography. Donna has worked extensively on questions of child poverty.

Acknowledgements

This book had its origins in a workshop run in February of 2016 in the School of People, Environment and Planning at Massey University, Palmerston North, New Zealand. This event was funded by the generous support of the College of Humanities and Social Sciences at Massey. Many of the chapters featured in a session on 'Making Markets' run at the 2018 New Zealand Geographical Society – Institute of Australian Geographers Conference held at the University of Auckland in July of that year. It was there that the possibility of a book was first aired, and this is the result. We would like to thank all of those who participated in those workshops and sessions for their various contributions and engagements, not all of which are represented here.

We would like to thank our contributors for their commitment to the production of the book. It would not have been possible without their support for the project, and we are very grateful, particularly given that so much was asked of us all in 2020, the year of the COVID-19 pandemic, when much of the work for this book has occurred. In this regard, we are very grateful to Andy Humphries at Routledge for supporting the project and for his infinite patience as we pulled the final manuscript together. We are also grateful to Emma Morley for providing technical assistance and editorial support.

Our thanks go to Christian Berndt who has also supported the project from afar and made a keynote contribution to the first workshop, and who generously provided a preface for the book. We would also like to thank the following people who generously gave their time to review chapters: Tom Baker, Glenn Banks, April Bennett, Hugh Campbell, Tony Carusi, Alexander Dobeson, Margaret Forster, Colin McLay, Michael Mouat and Chris Roisin.

Preface

Whether we look at 'experts' – including both academic economists and 'economists in the wild' as Callon (2007) put it – or lay people, just about everybody has some understanding of what the term 'market' means, how markets work and what their key characteristics are (Berndt & Boeckler, 2020, p. 72). If we were to conduct a short, random survey, we would probably get a surprisingly coherent list of responses: supply and demand, prices, competition and perhaps individual interest. But this is surprising only at first sight. After all, this is how market exchange has been defined ever since economic behaviour has been a subject of academic study. And it was this imagination of a perfect market that formed the basis of the famous 'pact' that Talcott Parsons is said to have struck with the discipline of economics more than 50 years ago. In the words of David Stark (2009, p. 7): "You, economists, study value; we, the sociologists, will study values. You will have claim on the economy; we will stake our claim on the social relations in which economies are embedded".

Today this pact is history. This is the work of a diverse set of heterodox perspectives that in their own particular ways shifted the emphasis from the ideal-type capital-M Market towards the multitude of actually existing lower-case-markets. An interdisciplinary movement towards a critical study of markets emerged whose protagonists contributed to de-fetishise the market as prescribed by orthodox economics. This volume is an important contribution to a particular strand of this project. This approach is inspired by Michel Callon's adaption of Science and Technology Studies and Actor-Network Theory to the study of economic processes, under the label of 'social studies of economization' (Çalışkan & Callon, 2010). Putting this perspective into a productive dialogue with the 'diverse economies' framework put forward by J.K. Gibson-Graham and collaborators (e.g. Roelvink, St Martin & Gibson-Graham, 2015), this alternative view on 'the' market shares a number of common insights (for the following, see Berndt & Boeckler, 2020).

The first is the conviction that it is marketisation as a process that matters, and not markets as self-contained entities. Accordingly, the focus is on markets 'in the making' – a process that is necessarily incomplete and instable. As such, marketisation is the performative work of a large number of actors, human and non-human, who form market assemblages or agencements in a delicate double play of entanglement and disentanglement. These framing processes are never complete and regularly evade control. The 'entities' in question exceed the various frames, there are overflows that cause friction and irritation. It is crucial for the smooth functioning of economic orders to veil these contradictions and 'overflows'. Markets, their rules and boundaries, have to appear as pre-given in the eyes of those who are subject to them. The crucial link is this: as long as overflows can be contained and controlled and as long as an appearance of market purity can be maintained, it is possible to realise a range of asymmetrical economic orders that diverge from the pure world of the model. As long as the status of the seemingly neatly framed entities is not challenged, we can create all kinds of hybrids, whether in the realm of the 'economy' or elsewhere.

Second, there is the tricky relationship between the orthodox model of the Market and real markets. By reading marketisation from below, that is, from the vantage point of concrete, actually existing market settings, prescriptive orthodox representations lose their overshadowing hegemony. There are always additional logics and rationalities at work. The ideal-type understanding of the market – however defined – is always only one of these logics. With Karl Polanyi (1957) one might point to well-known institutional forms, each associated with a particular social pattern: price-making markets, grounded in what he called 'market society'; reciprocity, stabilised by symmetrical ties of kinship and community; redistribution, undertaken by collection into and allocation from a centre (usually, the state, but also potentially a business firm); and householding, autonomous allocations within family units. With convention theory one may highlight various 'orders of worth' that are mobilised to legitimise particular practices and to make sense of the (economic) world (Boltanski & Thévenot, 2006). But these are only examples, there are potentially unlimited possibilities, giving form to institutionally diverse markets that can only adequately be mapped with careful empirical analysis: Markets are institutionally diverse and have to be studied in their diversity.

Third, there is increasing acknowledgement that there has been an over-emphasis in the critical literature on the neoclassical Market as economic model performing actually existing markets. But markets can be framed with the help of a wide array of market scripts. The increasingly influential alliance between behavioural and experimental economics is a case in point, playing an enormously important role in the marketisation of social and environmental policies globally (Berndt & Wirth, 2019). Another example is the framing of markets as spatially and organisationally fragmented chains, performed by practice disciplines such as supply chain management, global value chain analysis or logistics. Rather than representing the market as a 'flat' interface where supply meets demand, the idea of the 'market as chain' invokes a much more complex picture of rugged landscapes of production, exchange and distribution.

Fourth, in response to criticism of a perceived apolitical thrust of the arguments advanced by the protagonists of social studies of economisation/marketisation, a productive dialogue between cultural economy and political economy has been initiated that affords more careful attention to the struggles around marketisation. Starting with the insight that marketisation can never be fully successful because nothing can be commodified 'all the way down' (Fraser, 2014), there is greater acknowledgement of how misfires and overflows set limits and provide openings for resistance and alternatives. There are obvious connections with the work of Polanyi and his forceful argument that the expansion of "market organization in respect to genuine commodities was accompanied by its restriction in respect to fictitious ones" (1957, p. 79). For Polanyi, the market was checked on the terrain of labour, land and money. As elements not originally produced for sale these are responsible for what he famously referred to as 'double movement'. But it is necessary to go further and expand this argument to 'normal' commodities. As Margaret Jane Radin (2001) pointed out, these can also never be completely commodified, highlighting the hesitancy, the irritation and the ambivalence of all commodification processes. Such a decentred notion of the commodity is open to a wider range of social relations and regimes of value. This reminds us that marketisation always emerges as the effect of political struggles that inscribe new social differences onto existing ones, throwing into sharp relief that marketisation is gendered, racialised and immersed in class relations and that there is a need to centre categories of difference in processes of marketisation.

Such an understanding of markets as continuously in the making (*marketisation*), as being institutionally variegated (*diverse markets*), as not being solely performed by neoclassical economics (multiple *market scripts*) and as involving incomplete commodification processes that are shot through with inequalities and power asymmetries (*market struggles*) can be considered as an emerging consensus within critical market studies. This volume and its individual contributions are perfect examples for this, offering valuable state-of-the-art studies that illustrate perfectly what theoretically informed empirical analysis of marketisation processes is capable of achieving.

What makes this volume unique in my view, however, is that it additionally addresses an issue that can still be considered as a blind spot in the interdisciplinary project: the tricky question of the *geographies* of marketisation. It should obviously be the task of geographers to shed light here, but it is fair to say that economic geographers widely understood have so far been relatively silent to this end. There have been attempts to remedy this omission recently (see, for instance, Berndt, Peck & Rantisi, 2020), but there is still much to be done to really get to terms with the intricate spatialities of marketisation.

As a contested process, marketisation cannot but play out in uneven ways, not least spatially. There is consequently a need to be sensitive to the manifold geographies and multi-scalar nature of actually existing markets. We all dismiss the spatial imagination that connects the expansionary and all-encompassing market of orthodox theory with a borderless 'market space'. But offering alternatives is far from straightforward. For instance, just as it is insufficient to point to the social embeddedness of markets, and leave it at that, it would be equally short-sighted to simply counter that actually existing markets are bounded and territorialised. The delicate juxtaposition of marketisation and demarketisation translates into an equally delicate co-existence of debordering and bordering processes, the contingent articulation of diverse institutional logics and the struggles over exclusion and inclusion giving shape to spatially uneven market landscapes.

This is where the individual contributions to this volume come in. The volume is written in a spirit that offers a unique geographical perspective in at least two ways. On the one hand, contributions are written from a liminal position somewhere in the boundary zone between global north and global south that enables the placing of markets in unique ways. All authors write from the vantage point of the 'South Pacific' as a global region whose specific histories are so often neglected not only in the scholarly literature. On the other hand, this position at the planetary margins provides the contributions with the opportunity to mobilise particular notions of geographical place. The volume maps a rich, diverse economic geography that does so much more than simply rehearsing the familiar disciplinary litany of uneven regional development, global production networks, primitive accumulation and neoliberal policies. There is welcome attention to internal heterogeneity that refracts notions of the 'South Pacific' against different colonial and postcolonial histories and complex plurilocal networks that connect thousands of islands of variable size. But the contributions are equally sensitive to the way in which this geographical entity cannot be conceptualised as a self-contained social and cultural island in a sea of global market relations. Instead the contributions to the volume map a diverse global-local assemblage, in so doing adding a particular post/colonial twist to the institutional diversity of marketisation processes, offering new ways to provincialise 'northern' market models and complicating the stubbornly persistent thinking in established north-south boxes, whether pre-fixed with 'global' or not. This is an exciting collection of unique studies of Antipodean marketisation that I am sure will find the wide readership that it truly deserves.

Christian Berndt
Department of Geography, University of Zurich

References

Berndt, C.& Boeckler, M.(2020). Geographies of marketization: Performation Struggles, Incomplete Commodification and the "Problem of Labour". In Berndt, C., Peck, J. & Rantisi, N.(Eds.), *Market/place: Exploring spaces of exchange*(pp. 69–88). Newcastle:Agenda Publishing.

Berndt, C., Peck, J. & Rantisi, N. (Eds.). (2020). *Market/place: Exploring spaces of exchange*. Newcastle: Agenda Publishing.

Berndt, C. & Wirth, M. (2019). Struggling for the moral market: Economic knowledge, diverse markets, and market borders. *Economic Geography*, 95(3), 288–309.

Boltanski, L. & Thévenot, L. (2006). *On Justification: Economies of Worth*. Princeton, NJ: Princeton University Press.

Çalışkan, K. & Callon, M. (2010). Economization, part 2: A research programme for the study of markets. *Economy and Society*, 39(1), 1–32.

Callon, M. (2007). What does it mean to say that economics is performative? In D. MacKenzie, F. Muniesa & L. Siu (Eds.), *Do Economists Make Markets? On the Performativity of Economics* (pp. 311–357). Princeton, NJ: Princeton University Press.

Fraser, N. (2014). Can society be commodities all the way down? Post-Polanyian reflections on capitalist crisis. *Economy and Society*, 43(4), 541–558.

Polanyi, Karl. (1957). *The Great Transformation*. Boston, MA: Beacon Press.

Radin, M.J. (2001). *Contested Commodities: The Trouble with Trade in Sex, Children, Body Parts and Other Things*. Cambridge, MA: Harvard University Press.

Roelvink, G., St Martin, K. & Gibson-Graham, J.-K. (Eds) (2015). *Making Other Worlds Possible: Performing Diverse Economies*. Minneapolis, MN: University of Minnesota Press.

Stark, D. (2009). *The Sense of Dissonance: Accounts of Worth in Economic Life*. Princeton, NJ: Princeton University Press.

1   Putting markets in their place

Russell Prince, Carolyn Morris*, Matthew Henry*,
Aisling Gallagher* and Stephen FitzHerbert***

*SCHOOL OF PEOPLE, ENVIRONMENT AND PLANNING, MASSEY UNIVERSITY
**NATIONAL INSTITUTE OF WATER AND ATMOSPHERIC RESEARCH (NIWA),
AOTEAROA NEW ZEALAND

The problem of markets

We live in a world of markets. News websites report the latest fluctuations in financial markets as they happen. We hear of commodities markets 'surging', watch share markets undergoing a 'sell-off', and worry about a 'bloodbath' in the bond market. The global financial crisis of 2008 taught many people about the existence of markets for financial products and 'securities' that proved less than secure. Elsewhere we learn about the promise and peril of supposedly 'emerging markets' in parts of the world with long histories of human habitation. And when we hear about these markets, they seem to have agency: how will 'the markets' react to the latest government policy, severe weather event or global pandemic? For many of us, these markets seem distant and opaque, but we encounter other markets every day ourselves. The housing market, the labour market, the super-market – markets grounded in the particular places in which we live. These more quotidian markets make up what some people call the 'real economy', yet events like the crisis of 2008 can reveal how 'local' markets are connected to those far-away markets. It should also remind us that these other markets, too, are located in places with people and particularities of their own.

Markets are sites for exchange. We might immediately imagine the kind of space where the term first came from – the marketplaces in town centres where you could go to buy food and goods directly from a seller. But most modern marketplaces have a far more complex geography than this image implies. Consider the labour market most of us participate in at various points in our lives. There is no single site where this occurs. We 'sell our labour' in a more or less regular fashion on a daily or weekly basis, or at least we strive to, usually to the same purchaser/employer. But this occurs at all the different sites of employment across the city or region in which we live. 'The labour market' becomes the collection of potential workers available across that place. Or consider a commodities market, such as at the Global Dairy Auction in Singapore. Here commodities like milk powder and butter are traded, but not in the same way as they would in a traditional town marketplace. The commodities are not in the building. Instead, what is traded are contractual obligations to move the commodities stored some-where else around the world in particular ways. In futures markets, these contracts

DOI: 10.4324/9780429296260-1

do not even necessarily lead to this outcome, either now or in the future. Even the town marketplace is not really contained in the market's location: it rests on often vast production networks that get the goods to the market for sale, while both the buyers and the sellers rely on intricate banking networks to make money, the usual medium of exchange, available for an exchange to be enacted. Markets are always somewhere, but this belies their diverse and dynamic geographical underpinnings.

It is important to study markets for at least two reasons. The first is that markets have expanded in almost every sense over the past few decades under the conditions of globalisation and neoliberalism (Harvey, 2005; Robinson, 2004). As trade barriers have gradually and unevenly lowered, international markets in commodities and manufactured goods have expanded and deepened linkages between farmers, workers, consumers, and investors across the planet (Dicken, 2015). Global corporations have flourished, with supply chains and production networks that extend into every human-occupied territory (Coe & Yeung, 2015; Gereffi & Korzeniewicz, 1993). After being partly tied down for a few decades following World War Two, financial markets reach out from Wall Street and the City of London into the lives of more and more households and communities worldwide (Aitken, 2010; French, Leyshon & Wainwright, 2011; Hall, 2018; Krippner, 2005; Lapavitsas, 2013; Pike & Pollard, 2010). It is through markets that our lives and fates often come to be tied up with the lives and fates of distant others.

The growth of markets has been enabled by neoliberal restructuring at different scales. Globally, structural adjustment programmes across the so-called 'developing' world and the former communist bloc saw increased privatisation of large state-run producers and the opening of borders to trade and capital flows (Bello, Cunningham & Rau, 2008; Robinson, 2008; Springer, 2010; Stiglitz, 2002). Many wealthier capitalist countries embraced similar neoliberal prescriptions voluntarily after the 1970s, following the ascendant policy orthodoxy of the time (Brenner & Theodore, 2012; Kelsey, 1995; Macartney, 2010; Swarts, 2013). National neoliberal projects have also seen markets increasingly called upon to provide social services, in everything from health and education to elder care and prisoner rehabilitation (Baker, Evans & Hennigan, 2020; Cohen, 2017; Frankel, Ossandón & Pallesen, 2019; Gallagher, 2018; Hall, 2015). Scratching the surface of the kinds of activities that we normally associate with the domain of the state, such as policymaking, infrastructure provisioning and health-and-safety standard setting, we even find markets proliferating here too (Berndt, 2015; Birch & Siemiatycki, 2016; Reverdy & Breslau, 2019). Arguably neoliberalism was never about the state giving way to the market; it was about the use of the market to achieve various political goals (Harvey, 2005; Mirowski, 2013; Mirowski & Plehwe, 2009; Peck, 2010). As markets have expanded in size and scope, the market model has extended its reach into more domains.

The second reason it is important to study markets now is that they are often treated as spontaneous, natural, and desirable. These assumptions are baked into the ideologies that have underpinned neoliberal reform. In his history of the idea of the market, Matthew Watson (2018) argues that the academic version of the market emerged from the discipline of economics in the 19th century at around the same time as its more political variant. He argues that while the latter often leans on the language of efficiency and equilibrium that preoccupy economists, this is merely to justify political action or inaction. For Watson, the figure of the market associated with economics is evacuated of social content and is really just an object of formal mathematical investigation. Political discourse about 'the market', even when it comes from economists, exists in a different register. Nevertheless, it is this historical duality in the figure of the market that allows for what Berndt and Boeckler (2009, pp. 535–536) call the 'sleight of hand' that separates 'an abstract perfect *Market* from concrete imperfect *markets*'. This position holds that markets would tend towards a kind of universal efficiency, so long as they were left to their own devices. Invoking Adam Smith, it is argued it is our natural propensity to 'truck, barter, and exchange' that is the driving force of history. Everything else, culture and society namely, come after, or can be cast as conjectural.

One of the starting points of this book is the rejection of the idea that there can be a universal, abstract market outside of economics textbooks. All this idea really does is provide a political concept with a philosophical and scientific sheen. But *markets* are real. They vary considerably in size and scope. They are endlessly diverse. They are wrapped up with all sorts of livelihoods, identities, intentions, and meanings. There is no need to assume that they are somehow natural or desirable, or indeed to assume that they are inherently bad: that they are always exploitative or destructive. It is important, however, to recognise that the *ideas* we have about markets are also real, including the idea that they are spontaneous, natural and desirable. It was the *idea* that markets are more productive, efficient, and balanced that encouraged the development of neoliberal philosophy and policy prescriptions. Many of the markets that exist today have been created by governments and institutions drawing on economic theories about markets, such as derivatives markets (MacKenzie, 2006) and carbon trading markets (Doganova & Laurent, 2019). While the figure of the abstract market is illusory, it remains powerful. If we do indeed live in a world of markets, as we have argued here, it is because it has been actively made this way.

Market studies

Orthodox economics is of little use for studying markets as actively produced. Its threadbare notions of supply and demand assume the existence of markets rather than asking how they came to be. But there are a range of other possible guiding literatures for this endeavour. We will briefly summarise these here, emphasising those that make an appearance in the chapters of this book. These overlapping literatures include economic sociology, economic geography, political economy, cultural economy, studies of marketisation and economisation, and assemblage.

Economic sociology is a large and diverse sub-discipline that is fundamentally concerned with the sociological aspects of economic institutions, such as the market (Fligstein, 2002; Granovetter & Swedberg, 2018; Smelser & Swedberg, 2005; Swedberg, 1991, 1997). The economic sociology that has taken shape since the 1970s is a result of the rejection of the earlier division of labour between economics and sociology proposed by Talcott Parsons where the former would study the scarcity of means in relation to wants and the latter the attitudes underpinning societal common ends: often finessed as 'value' and 'values'. A key figure here was Karl Polanyi (1957) who claimed that the Industrial Revolution in Europe involved a 'double movement' of a shift to a market economy followed by a shift to a market society. This idea that the economy is societally embedded was developed by Mark Granovetter (1985), among others, to argue for an economic sociology that accounted for the social networks in which economic activity occurred. In this 'new economic sociology', markets were increasingly conceived as networks in themselves made up of real actors, whether people or firms. The stronger the network within and between firms vis-à-vis consumers, the higher their profits (Swedberg, 1994). Other economic sociologists have argued for a greater consideration of culture and politics beyond social network structures. Viviana Zelizer (1994, 2013, 2017), for example, has long argued for attending to the way that meaning is attached to objects, including money itself, and the way that these meanings shape how markets work and how they draw the line between the acceptably 'marketable' and that which should remain beyond its reach. There are class, gender and racial politics played out in and through market spaces (e.g. Underhill-Sem et al., 2014).

Some strands of economic geography have taken inspiration from economic sociology to engage with the market in ways that also move beyond the economics toolkit. One example is the growing literature on global production networks, which pick a path between the sociological approach to the market-as-network and the political economy of global capitalism to construct geographically and sociologically rich depictions of the inter-firm and firm-to-consumer relations that exist in different industries (Coe & Yeung, 2015; Glassman, 2011; Henderson, Dicken, Hess, Coe & Yeung, 2002; Yeung & Coe, 2015). Markets here are understood in a much wider network context than just around the site of exchange. Global production networks are global systems that are nonetheless embedded in different places and the particular social, cultural and political dimensions layered there (Hess, 2004; Hess & Yeung, 2006; Hughes, Wrigley & Buttle, 2008; Weller, 2006). Another example is the literature on food regimes, which also recognises the globally dispersed but interconnected character of mass food production and the way these have transformed over the 19th and 20th centuries (Friedmann & McMichael, 1989; Le Heron, 2002; Tilzey, 2019). Both these literatures recognise that markets do not exist in isolation, and that the production and consumption 'sides' of a market are often links in a chain that join it up to other sites of exchange.

This insistence on the systemic context of markets is typical of political economy renditions of global capitalism (Panitch & Gindin, 2012; Robinson, 2004). Political economy will emphasise how markets are not spontaneous or natural institutions but are necessarily constructed features of systems of production and distribution that require other forms of power, such as the state, to maintain stability. More radical and Marxist variations of political economy argue that while certain markets are central to capitalism, such as the labour market, they need to be understood and analysed in relation to the productive system (Cahill, 2020). So consumer goods markets exist to supply workers with the necessities of life – and even occasional luxuries – so that they are able and willing to return to work, where they often produce those very goods in exploitative conditions. The antagonistic and destructive social relation at the heart of this production-consumption circle is by turns enforced and ameliorated by the state (Jessop, 2002). Meanwhile, the ideological construction of the abstract market and its 'freedom of choice' apparently realised in consumer markets serves to cover over this reality (Harvey, 2005). For political economy, the analysis of markets is necessarily subservient to the analysis of capitalism more generally (Christophers, 2014, 2015).

Another perspective, which also claims the mantle of Marxism occasionally, would dispute the totalisation of this characterisation of markets. This is work that studies and theorises alternative and 'diverse' economies. Taking inspiration from the work of Gibson-Graham (1996, 2006), this challenges the tendency of Marxist and political economy work to see capitalism everywhere. They argue for accounts of economies that recognise that wage labour is not the only form of work and the market not the only site of exchange (Gibson-Graham and Dombroski, 2020). Apart from the oft-cited role of domestic and unpaid labour in the home and in care, they point to co-operating, gifting, self-provisioning, tithing, volunteering and theft, among other things, as alternative ways through which viable economic lives are made. Here markets are not necessarily subservient to a larger system, but may be part of alternative systems, or hooked into more than one (Bargh, 2012; Gibson-Graham, Cameron & Healy, 2013). The anthropologist Anna Tsing (2009, 2012, 2015) has a similar project, calling attention to the forms of labour, production and exchange that spring up, like mushrooms, in the cracks and crevices of supply chains and among the 'ruins' of failed capitalist development.

While its Marxist heritage points back to political economy, work on diverse and alternative economies often comes under a different sign: cultural economy. Distinct from 'the' cultural economy that describes the characteristics of the collection of cultural industries, such as music and theatre (Pratt, 2009), cultural economy describes a set of approaches that emphasise the performative dimension of economic knowledge (Amin & Thrift, 2003; Bennett, McFall & Pryke, 2008; du Gay & Pryke, 2002). It is particularly interested in the way theoretical and lay economic knowledges shape how markets function by guiding calculative human action (Callon, 1998; MacKenzie, Muniesa & Siu, 2007). Moreover, it has sought to expand the purview of markets by including the agency of the non-human and materiality, such as rapid machine calculation or the perishability of organic matter (Callon, Millo & Muniesa, 2007). This literature pays attention to all the little and large ways that people become market subjects when they enter into relations of exchange. And by bringing the analytical gaze down to the level of the market it attempts to stay true to their complexity and variety, demonstrating their constitutive role in the making of capitalism, rather than assuming that all markets somehow conform to the logic of the latter.

The performativity of economics, which is a reworking of an idea borrowed from Judith Butler (1990), does not mean economics is 'performative' in the sense that it is disingenuous. Rather, to talk about the performativity of economics is to say that the knowledge it produces does not simply describe the world, but remakes it. Donald MacKenzie (MacKenzie, 2006; MacKenzie & Millo, 2003), for example, has written extensively on the way that a particular type of economic knowledge – financial models – reshape activity in financial markets as financiers act on its claims. This can have the effect of making the model 'true', up to a point, not because of a supposed correspondence between the model and 'reality', but because the model is being performed by the actors and materials it describes. Financial models are part of the world of finance, not a reflection of it. This is an approach that takes seriously the work that knowledge, including knowledge of markets, does in the world, remaking it not in its own image, but in a multiplicity of expected and unexpected ways. This opens up avenues for investigating the role of economic models in the structural reform of developing and developed economies along neoliberal lines that does not reduce them to the workings of capitalism and ideology (Ouma, 2015).

Michel Callon (2007a, 2007b, 1998, 2002) has been at the forefront of this project since turning his pioneering work in actor-network theory (ANT) towards economics in a project that has been loosely labelled as the study of economisation and marketisation (see Çalışkan & Callon, 2009; 2010). Callon's emphasis is on the way that markets are achieved through the work to produce what he calls calculative agencies that come together as willing parties to an exchange. He refers to 'framing' as a process whereby objects or services have clear lines drawn around them that demarcate them from their context and make them exchangeable. Ripping a plant from the patch of earth that was its home and placing it in a plastic pot, defining the extent of a cleaning service to be provided by a person in a written contract, and constructing the legal basis for a family to own their home, are all examples of framing. These objects, services, and pieces of land are rendered passive and transferrable, while the humans that exchange them are rendered active, making calculated exchanges of the former by the latter possible. While these acts of framing are necessary to create the stability required for exchange to occur, they also result in overflows. This includes the kinds of things that economists call externalities, such as the pollution that a factory produces which is dumped into a river and not accounted for in the framing and exchange. But it also includes other kinds of outcomes, such as the independent formation of user communities for particular products, the emergence of 'communities of concern' regarding the impact of a particular technology or production process, or the transformation of the place where the market is located (Callon, 2007a). These overflows can lead to new social forms emerging, including new markets. Berndt and Boeckler (2012) provide a particularly geographical twist on these ideas with the notion of b/ordering, highlighting the ways that market-making often involves practices of bordering and de-bordering that open up, close down, and generally direct various flows through particular markets. Free trade agreements, for example, usually involve not the simple 'opening up' of borders, but their reconstruction to allow certain flows through. But this reconstruction often involves reaching beyond borders geographically to alter certain production practices, such as the requirements of certain codified health and safety standards, hence the play on the notion that bordering is also ordering.

Callon's ANT approach to markets overlaps with, if not entirely contained by, what has loosely come to be called assemblage theory (DeLanda, 2006, 2016; Anderson et al., 2012; Anderson and McFarlane, 2011). This translation of a Deleuzean idea plays off the dual meaning of assemblage as both a noun and a verb. In common with ANT, it seeks to transcend structure-agency accounts. So Callon argues that calculative agency is not something simply conducted by humans, but performed via various technological prostheses that are arranged in ways that make particular calculations possible. This includes the market devices that are central to the operation of many current markets, such as calculators, stock tickers, weighing scales and metrological systems (Callon *et al.*, 2007). These socio-technical assemblages are what enable exchange to occur. They are central to the work of framing described above and constitute the distributed object we call the market (Jones, 2013). This consideration of material technologies extends to materiality more generally, and emphasises the importance of the non-human world in making markets possible. How markets work, indeed, whether they work at all, and what they look like will be shaped by the insistent materiality of the world. The biology of organic commodities (Legun, 2016), the liveliness of livestock (Henry & Roche, 2013; McGregor & Houston, 2018), and the distribution of certain metals to hidden pockets around the world (Bridge, 2004) are all material factors that will shape the market assemblage, and thus what markets look like and what overflows they produce.

While we may be back, in some ways, to the figure of market-as-network that we encounter in economic sociology, the ANT and assemblage approaches have some radically different implications. By giving equal ontological status to the non-human, agency is distributed through the assemblage rather than held by human actors. Markets are not simply social networks but assemblages of people, things and ideas, in which certain performances, such as exchange, can be expected to produce certain effects, such as the general acceptance of the transfer of ownership of a particular object. While economic sociology is concerned with what the nature of the market can tell us about the social structures in which it is embedded, an assemblage analytics is more concerned with how the market is stabilised and why it falls apart. From an assemblage perspective, markets are not deviations from an ideal-type, but the real socio-technical arrangements we name as markets. Moreover, the focus on assemblage rejects the pre-given categories that economic sociology and political economy lean on, such as society and economy. Rather than see markets as 'economic' institutions embedded in 'society', it argues that what we call 'the economy' and 'society' are essentially effects caused by analyses that try to separate out the economic and the social (Latour, 2005; Mitchell, 1998). Analysis should not be focused on these illusory categories, but on the real assemblages in which they are produced. The study of 'market societies' and 'market economies', then, becomes the study of the kinds of transformations in historical assemblages that occurred to make these into meaningful descriptions.

Place-ing markets

The contribution of this volume to the study of markets is to deepen its engagement with geography. It does this in two related ways. One, the studies discussed in the book all come from a particular part of the world, with a particular history: the South Pacific. And two, they use the study of markets to engage with the geographical notion of place in different ways. This responds to a number of recent calls in geography to take more seriously the question of markets against a history of focusing much more on regional development, production systems, accumulation regimes and political projects whenever economic questions are at stake (Berndt & Boeckler, 2009; Berndt & Boeckler, 2011, 2012; Birch & Siemiatycki, 2016; Boeckler & Berndt, 2013; Christophers, 2015; Cohen, 2018; Jones, 2013). Jamie Peck (2012) made the case almost a decade ago in a reflective piece on the relationship between the 'island life' of economic geography and the 'continent' of mainstream economics. The second of these, he argues, has dominated the study of 'the market' and is unlikely to broach its geographically variegated nature in a way that does not bury the sensibilities and concerns of geographers under the weight of its dominant epistemology. He argues geographers need to branch out and study markets, concluding that there are 'both intellectual and normative reasons for taking markets more seriously – in all their relativized, plural, and mongrel forms; and across the broadest range of constitutive contexts and cohabitative arrangements – in the service of economic geography's continuing project of rethinking economy' (Peck, 2012, p. 128). The geographical concern for questions of space and place and how these relate to markets has now yielded a number of studies and volumes (Berndt, Peck & Rantisi, 2020; Berndt, Rantisi & Peck, 2020; Muellerleile & Akers, 2015). The rest of this section will expand on the contribution of this collection, before this introduction concludes by outlining the organisation of the chapters.

The studies in this book are all located in that part of the world we call the South Pacific, although they are also concentrated in Aotearoa New Zealand, with two in Australia, and one in Fiji. What value does a set of studies located here add? This is a question that has been grappled with by a range of 'antipodean' scholars (see in particular the special issue of *Dialogues in Human Geography* led by Felicity Wray and Rae Dufty-Jones (Wray *et al.*, 2013), from which much of the following argument takes its cue). One possible answer is that this part of the world has a distinctive history. But is this a case of simply applying predominantly 'Northern' ideas about markets to places outside the North? A first response to this is to question whether certain South Pacific countries, most obviously Aotearoa New Zealand and Australia, are really 'outside' the North (Wray *et al.*, 2013; Gibson, 2009). As settler states colonised by the United Kingdom (UK), these places remain connected to the economic, cultural, social and intellectual networks of the Global North. Both economies are market-centric, governed by the kinds of neoliberal political ideologies which transformed the global economy from the 1980s, and tightly integrated into the global economy. And they are wealthy. Both are part of the Organisation for Economic Cooperation and Development (OECD) – a club for the richest countries and a *de facto* list of comparative peers.

In other ways, Australia and Aotearoa New Zealand are profoundly different from most of the nations that constitute the Global North. Critical to that difference is colonialism: that they are colonised (and sometimes colonising) nations. The difference that colonialism makes is not only the outcome of the goals and strategies of the colonisers, but of the ceaseless struggles of the indigenous peoples for sovereignty (Walker, 2004; Mikaere, 2000). The fact that settler colonialism was the form that colonisation took in Australia and Aotearoa New Zealand is the critical point for understanding the role of place in making markets in the Pacific, but that the contemporary situations in Australia and Aotearoa New Zealand are so very different shows that 'settlerness' alone cannot account for the present state of affairs. Māori and Indigenous Australian societies at the point of colonisation were profoundly different, resulting in different engagements between indigenous peoples and colonising peoples, generating different histories and presents.

One critical factor key to the structuring of current indigenous/coloniser relations is the presence or absence of treaties. In 1840 Māori signed a treaty (Te Tiriti o Waitangi) with the British Crown, in which they were guaranteed "te tino rangatiratanga o o ratou wenua o ratou kainga me o ratou taonga katoa",[1] i.e. "the unqualified exercise of their chieftainship over their lands, villages, and all their property and treasures".[2] Although Te Tiriti was repeatedly violated resulting in widespread dispossession of Māori, that there was a treaty provided the basis for the reestablishment of Māori sovereignty with the result that Aotearoa New Zealand is now a bicultural state with Māori as equal, governing partner with non-Māori. Moreover, Māori corporations are major economic actors, especially in ocean and land-based enterprises (Pawson & Biological Economies Team, 2018; Petrie, 2006; Rata, 2011; Bargh, 2007, 2011, 2012; Lambert, 2008; Reid and Rout, 2016). To make a market in Aotearoa New Zealand is by necessity to make it in some way in relation to Māori.

Australia, by contrast, was claimed unilaterally by Britain under the doctrine of *terra nullius*, the false and useful assumption that the land was unoccupied, unowned wasteland. This act resulted in the dispossession of the Indigenous Australian peoples, making them "intruders in their own homes and mendicants for a place to live" (*Mabo*, 1992: in Dominello, 2009, p. 9). Politically they were excluded from the polity in any way other than as objects of control and/or concern. The landmark *Mabo* decision of 1992 rejected the *terra nullius* doctrine, ruling that "a form of Indigenous native title was found, not only to exist, but also to have predated and to have survived the acquisition of British sovereignty" (Dominello, 2009, p. 2). This law reinstated native title to land and "signalled the potential transformation of the nation by providing a new foundation for the relationship between Indigenous and non-Indigenous peoples" (Dominello, 2009, p. 9). However, the hopes for transformation generated by *Mabo* have not come to fruition, with subsequent court rulings delimiting the scope of native title to rights emanating from traditional "arising out of traditional laws and customs" (Dominello, 2009, p. 17), namely spiritual rights. The effect of this has been to severely delimit Indigenous Australian peoples' economic rights to land. As a result, native title remains "an inferior property entitlement" (Dominello,

2009, p. 20) and Indigenous Australian sovereignty has not been recognised or realised.

But while Australia and Aotearoa New Zealand are integrated into the Global North, they are also engaged in Pacific networks (Stevens, 2018; Levy, 2018; Rapaport, 1995; Teaiwa, 2015; Stead and Altman, 2019; Bennett, 2018; Faleolo, 2019; Mar, 2019; Marsters, Lewis and Friesen, 2006). Both are in the Pacific but are not commonly thought of as Pacific Island nations. That label is applied instead to the approximately 17 nations[3] made up of thousands of islands scattered across the vast expanse of the Pacific Ocean. They are grouped in such a way on the basis of their commonalities: geographic isolation, small size, small populations, small economies and status as "underdeveloped" or "developing". Their primary economic relations (trade, development and so on) are with Australia and Aotearoa New Zealand. And despite the supposed promises of development in the 20th century, urban marketplaces made up primarily of small stallholders remain important in these nations as a vital centre for the distribution of food and provision of work for urban dwellers in the Pacific Islands, even as they express gender and other social inequalities (Underhill-Sem *et al.*, 2014).

Despite these commonalities the Pacific Islands are remarkably ethnically, culturally and linguistically diverse (Rapaport, 2013). They have differing histories of colonisation and colonialism including, as examples, planter colonialism (sugar in Fiji), extractive colonialism (phosphate mining of Nauru), transport colonialism (American air bases on Vanuatu in World War Two), not-in-my-back-yard colonialism (French nuclear testing on Mururoa Island in the Tuamotu archipelago), and postcolonial colonialism, where former colonies remain powerfully shaped by the particular legacies of their colonial histories and/or their on-going entanglements with their former colonisers (Shoemaker, 2015). What they have in common in terms of colonisation, is that none are settler states, i.e. their lands and polities remain under the control of the indigenous people. Writing from the South Pacific is continually refracted through the lens of heterogenous colonialisms. Intricate and contested colonial relationships continue to produce social worlds, policy responses, and market relationships whose effects cannot be discerned, let alone understood, without reference to entwined histories and geographies.

Land is a critical passage point though which many of these understandings flow. Land and its relations of imagination, control, and use is the ontological bedrock of indigenous Pacific people's identities and sustenance (Bargh and Wevers, 2019). At the same time, however, land and the almost magical ability to morally uplift and sustain prosperity that flows from its ownership is also deeply embedded in the origin stories of the Pacific's settler states. Tom Brooking (1996), for example, writing about the settling of Aotearoa New Zealand argued that the land had the misfortune to be settled by two peoples that granted its ownership metaphysical properties. Early encounters between Europeans and the Pacific's indigenous peoples, focused on the former's search for extractable resources, could be, and were, managed within customary use frameworks (Stokes, 2013; O'Malley, 2012; Petrie, 2006; Harris et al., 2014; Salmond, 1991, 1997). As periodic extraction shaded into settling in Aotearoa New Zealand and Australia, land became the source of intense material and ontological conflict. This conflict took different paths in both these places, and the differences are important. However, land that had been imagined and used within intricate indigenous cosmologies was by the late 19th century largely imagined and used within European cosmologies (Campbell, 2020). Core to this shift was the legal transformation of land, and the technopolitics of tenure that placed freehold land at the pinnacle of a hierarchy of tenure types (Byrnes, 2001). Unlike in Australia where the doctrine of *terra nullius* erased customary title from the law until the *Mabo* case, in Aotearoa New Zealand Māori collective title was recognised, but only to the extent to which it was a problem to be solved through its transmutation into individualised fee simple tenure within the framework of British law (Stokes, 2013; Boast, 2017; Kāwharu, 1977; Binney, 2009). Via colonial technopolitics rather than spontaneous eruption, the making of markets for land across Australia and Aotearoa New Zealand and its non-making in many of the Pacific islands could not and cannot be untangled from the ontopolitics of settling. Far from an invisible hand, land and its (non)markets were, and continue to be, a site for the very visible hand of settler states and their shifting projects (Hill, 2004).

European explorers across the South Pacific did not encounter a bucolic wilderness. Hundreds, thousands, and in the case of Australia, tens of thousands of years of indigenous resource use and trade had created deeply modified physical and biotic landscapes (Gammage, 2011; Garden, 2005; Pascoe, 2018; Rapaport, 2013). However, this paled against the changes wrought by the insertion of the South Pacific's places into the increasingly globalised commodity flows of the 18th and 19th centuries (Stevens, 2018). The extraction of timber for naval ships and whales for lighting and lubrication created markets for iron and sex across the Pacific (Stevens and Wanhalla, 2017). But it was agriculture and globalised food circuits that centred upon distant marketplaces like Smithfield in London that would generate the most irrevocable changes. Demand for food, fibre and a host of other commodities generated by swelling European industrial cities transformed landscapes across the Pacific, and the speed of change was staggering (Levy, 2018; Rapaport, 1995). In Aotearoa New Zealand, for example, land that had been legally transformed into freehold title was materially transformed by cycles of clearing, burning and sowing to create the grasslands of empire (Brooking, Pawson & Star, 2010), while similar processes occurred across Australia (Muir, 2014). Writing in the early 1940s the geographer Kenneth Cumberland observed (in admiration rather than despair) that the changes wrought in New Zealand had accomplished in less than a century, 'what in Europe took twenty centuries, and in North America four' (Cumberland, 1941). There was a deep moral economy involved in the remaking of these landscapes that positioned an uninterrupted and growing flow of food as an obligation linking settler states to 'home'. However, the connections, like the colonialisms that sustained them, were intricate. Plant materials such as pasture grasses, sugar cane, coconuts and pine criss-crossed the Pacific (Bennett, 2018). Migrants, both forced and voluntary, likewise did the same (Stead and Altman, 2019; Mar, 2019; Faleolo, 2019). The desire for sugar, for example, saw the introduction of planation agricultures to both Fiji and

Queensland. Plantations that in turn required labour extracted from indentured labourers from places such as the Solomon Islands and India (Garden, 2005). Agricultural productivity was ensured through the mining of phosphate from Makatea, Nauru and Banaba (Teaiwa, 2015). These islands were stripped (figuratively and literally) of their land, to replenish the soils of Australia and Aotearoa New Zealand so that farmers were able to supply agricultural commodity markets in London and elsewhere. Through these intricate connections markets made and remade imaginative and material landscapes across the Pacific.

So this is a part of the world with a complex and longstanding range of connections to the 'North' and a variety of shared characteristics with both 'North' and 'South'. But there is a deeper problem with this frame of reference. The trouble with trying to work out how much or how little this part of the world is a part of 'the North' is that it reinscribes that North–South hierarchy. Raewyn Connell (2007) has pointed out that the people of the South are producers of theory, not simply its objects, and treating theory from the South as just a response or reaction to Northern theory maintains the artificial elevation of the latter (see also Smith, 1999; Wray *et al.*, 2013). Reducing market studies in the South Pacific to just its application elsewhere falls into this trap. Moreover, trying to fit the South Pacific into the North–South binary does a disservice to the particularity of this region of the globe.

But there are other options for how we might frame this research. In a response to Peck's call for more studies of markets in economic geography, Wendy Larner (2012, p. 160) reflected that she is an 'islander', not just as an economic geographer in the sense Peck used the term, but 'by birth and by academic inclination'. She argues that 'island scholarship' is often 'based on bricolage and borrowing, inflected with homegrown innovation and ingenuity' (Larner, 2012, p. 159) alongside a good dose of parochialism. This suggests an ethic of 'provincialising' Northern ideas to make sense of processes and struggles here and now (wherever that might be), alongside whatever else might help, and seeing what lessons this might hold. So rather than try to fit the region into 'Northern' narratives or frame it as a space of exceptions and alternatives, we ask how we might extend, adapt and change the research narrative.

The situation of the research in this volume in the South Pacific, then, is not a case of "'applying' Northern research programmes and their associated ideas to a new non-North, or at least less-North, site. Nor would we just put it down to the hunt for difference in order to 'trouble' Northern accounts of markets (Morris and FitzHerbert, 2017; Wray *et al.*, 2013), although this is certainly a desirable and desired outcome. Rather, in the project of expanding our understanding of the geography of markets, to which we hope to contribute, this site serves to underline what geography can offer because it can help us to bring a key geographical idea that emphasises particularity within a wider context to the forefront of this research: the concept of place. These chapters demonstrate that it is empirically true that places shape markets and, conversely, markets shape places. But this is also a conceptual relationship. How can we refine our understanding of place to take account of markets, and vice versa? Understanding the different histories that make places outside of, and peripheral to, the North, and the difference markets make to them, is vital for fully answering this question.

In geography, place refers to the arrangement of territory, people, objects, and materials that come together in dynamic economic, cultural, social and political formations at a specific location. A classic definition of place points to three aspects: location, locale and sense of place (Agnew, 1987). Location refers to the fact that places are somewhere on earth. They have a longitude and a latitude and usually some kind of fuzzy territorial boundary around them, even if not everyone agrees on exactly where this is. Locale refers to the structure of a place. This is both material and social. It includes its terrain and how it is constructed, with buildings, roads, parks, hills, trees and so on. It has a climate with a particular seasonal pattern. Its social structures include its political structure, its economic structure, its demographic make-up, its non-human inhabitants, its institutions and so on. Finally, sense of place describes the ineffable 'feel' of the place. As Tim Cresswell (2020, p. 117) explains it, sense of place:

> refers to the more nebulous meanings associated with a place: the feelings and emotions a place evokes. These meanings can be individual and based on personal biography or they can be shared. Shared senses of place are based on mediation and representation. When we write "Calcutta" or "Rio" or "Manchester" for instance, even those of us who have not been to these places have some sense of them—sets of meanings produced in films, literature, advertising, and other forms of mediation.

Places are all sorts of different sizes and usually overlap or contain other places. What actually constitutes a place as such is a product of the other two aspects. Places are a site and product of struggle over these aspects: the politics of place.

While places are unique, they are simultaneously interconnected to differing extents with other places in ways that are mutually influential and constitutive. Doreen Massey (1993) provides an image of this with her rendition of the global sense of place that exists anywhere:

> What gives a place its specificity is not some long internalised history but the fact that it is constructed out of a particular constellation of social relations, meeting and weaving together at a particular locus. If one (holds) all those networks of social relations and movements and communications in one's head, then each 'place' can be seen as a particular, unique, point of their intersection. It is, indeed, a meeting place. Instead then, of thinking of places as areas with boundaries around, they can be imagined as articulated moments in networks of social relations and understandings, but where a larger proportion of those relations, experiences and understandings are constructed on a far larger scale than what we happen to define for that moment as the place itself, whether that be a street, or a region or even a continent. And this in turn allows a sense of place which is extroverted, which includes a consciousness of its links with the wider world, which integrates in a positive way the global and the local.
>
> (pp. 67–68)

This captures the way that places cannot be understood in isolation from other places and not simply with those they overlap. They are linked to other, often distant places in material and ideological ways through various networks and flows of people, commodities, money and ideas. Places are caught between the local and the extra-local.

Markets exist in and between places. They will be one set of the institutions that make up the economic and social structure of a place – a feature of its locale – and in many places a contributor to sense of place. Markets are often central to the interconnections between places. And yet they are usually analysed by economists and cognate disciplines as if they are not. In these analyses, places are treated as little more than the location of market activities. Dan Cohen (2018, p. 910) defines markets as 'sites of struggle over the networks, institutions and/or ideas and technologies through which the exchange of commodities is organised'. This definition is useful because it captures the dynamism of markets and the fact that there are social and political stakes in them, as well as economic stakes. In places where exchange occurs, the networks, institutions and ideas that Cohen refers to are part of the locale and 'sense of place' that operates there. This highlights the importance of particular place-based social, political, cultural, technical and material arrangements to the making and functioning of particular markets. The struggle that also constitutes the market will be part of the dynamics and politics of place as they reshape or affirm the networks, institutions and ideas: they are connected to the politics of place.

The resilience and centrality – or fragility and contingency – of market relations is a result of their interweaving with other social, political, cultural, technical and material relations in particular places and the depth of interdependencies in within-market and between-market relations that pertain in particular places. But sometimes, indeed often, the struggle is beyond a place and yet shapes it in important ways. As anyone who has purchased anything online would know, markets themselves are rarely contained in one geographic location: markets often exist 'in-between' places. This is where Massey's sense of global place is useful. It recognises that places are 'meeting points' where various networks, 'each full of power', come together. Places can also be understood as layered over by various constructed scales of power. Most places are within nation-state systems that construct hierarchical political systems in which towns, cities and regions end up with political structures that are beholden to decisions made at other administrative scales. Place-ing markets requires more than just talking about how a market is located in a particular place – it means taking the complex geography of places seriously and the dynamics of its interweaving with the geography of the market.

This brief foray into the intersections between how we theorise place and how we theorise markets is not intended to foreshadow each of the chapters to come, like the 'theory' section of a thesis. Each of the authors uses some combination of the market theories discussed above, and have their own approach to the question of place in relation to these. Rather, here we are opening up the question of what an engagement between markets and place allows for, which is an intellectual space the chapters in this volume will help to fill. So, viewing markets as always 'placed' means that they are not treated as abstract, even if abstract ideas about markets are present. This is obviously important because it means we analyse 'real' markets, but it also allows for a more agnostic view of them. Markets are often praised as saviour and sinner in equal measure, and to recognise that, as Berndt and Boeckler (2009) suggest, markets are multiple in their concrete form means recognising that their outcomes will necessarily be an object of struggle.

Furthermore, viewing markets 'from place' allows for a particular contribution to theories about markets to be made. Places, like markets, exist. They are not themselves abstractions, even if abstractions and ideas are central to their identity and functioning. They are a useful starting point for thinking about what abstract entities actually look like on the ground, whatever ontological status we give to those entities. For example, political economy tends to critique the cultural economy and social studies of markets literature for failing to recognise structure and the importance of organisational architectures in shaping markets (Christophers, 2014, 2015; Nik-Khah & Mirowski, 2019). Damien Cahill (2020) calls this 'market fetishism'. He argues we first need to understand the specifically capitalist nature of the global economy before we can understand markets. But the places that markets are in and between, so long as they are sufficiently theorised, provide the context for markets. Places, like markets, are historically produced and dynamic. This, too, is why there is value in studying markets outside of the 'core' Northern economies of global capitalism. These other places are products of historical processes of capitalism and colonialism, among other things, not just some 'alternative' site that sits outside (Morris and FitzHerbert, 2017; Wray *et al.*, 2013). Insisting on studying markets 'with place' allows us to avoid dropping pre-given theoretical edifices on them that crush their particularity, while recognising that these places are indeed shaped by global capital in important ways. The idea and reality of place is an opportunity to think differently (Horrocks and Lacey, 2016).

Finally, Roscoe and Loza (2019) talk about the responsibilities of 'market studies'. They argue that we need now to consider the work that market studies does in imagining and making new markets:

> If our central claim is that market knowledge is performative – that it participates in bringing markets into being – and if economics offers *just one kind of market knowledge*, it follows that the economists' markets – the markets of high modernity – are *just one kind of market*, and there are as many others possible as we can conjure in our writing.

> (p.216)

Diverse markets exist in diverse places. Furthering our understanding of this will contribute, as Peck (2012, p. 128) suggests, to the project of 'rethinking economy'.

The organisation of this book

The essays in this volume demonstrate how place is pivotal in the making of markets. Moreover, as markets become more ubiquitous, they are increasingly pivotal to the transformation of place as well. The chapters themselves, however, are diverse in their subject matter, the questions that they ask, the theoretical and methodological approaches that they use, and the kinds of conclusions that they draw. Rather than try to box them into distinctive sections, we summarise the chapters below according to a variety of cross-cutting themes. Chapters appear in more than one theme and so are ordered in the book alphabetically by first author. The reader can read them in this order, or if they are interested in a particular theme, they might read those chapters suggested below.

Colonialism, culture, multi-culturalism/biculturalism

One of the themes underpinning a number of the chapters is the ongoing work of colonial histories in the making of markets and the work of markets in the reworking of colonial legacies. These chapters all drive home the point that 'culture' matters in market-making in places where cultural difference is a salient axis of social, economic and political distinction and action. This contrasts with more conventional analyses of culture and economy, where the former is 'commodified' in the service of the latter. It demonstrates one of the key ways that place conditions and shapes markets. The chapter by Hikuroa, Le Heron and Le Heron describes shifting relations between Māori and non-Māori in Aotearoa New Zealand that are disturbing the ontological pre-conditions in which market-making is desirable and possible and markets are actually made. They describe the emergence of relational agency, where Māori acknowledge the interconnectedness and shared agency of human and non-human actors as the ground and advocate the concept of re-commoning as a way of making sense of this reorganisation of ecological and economic relations. FitzHerbert's chapter explores the Māori economy, describing the multiple ways in which Māori horticulturalists engaged with a Māori led/state supported experiment in market-making. His work demonstrates that Māori economies are not co-terminus with market economies and are animated by different values and aspirations. However, when Māori choose to also engage in capitalist markets, their articulation of these diverse economies opens up the potential to imagine and enact different economic futures. The chapter by Gallagher describes the cultural politics critical to the making of a market for early childhood education (ECE) in Aotearoa New Zealand. The state's goal in assembling such a market is (in part) to address a social problem generated by colonisation, so the making of this market is inevitably political. Gallagher's argument shows that social and cultural difference are not contexts in which markets are made, but critical to their formation. Laeis and Morris likewise describe a place where the legacies of colonialism continue to shape the making (or actually the non-making) of markets. They show that it is not possible to make sense of the failure to assemble a local market for the supply of fruit and vegetables to resort hotels without attending to the contemporary cultural politics generated by the history of relations between indigenous iTaukei and the descendants of Indian labourers.

Global connections

We pointed our earlier that markets will exist both in and between places. Following Massey's line that places are 'meeting places', we can conceive of a place as the intersection of all kinds of social linkages that exist across vast tracts of space. These topographical networks render places topological: the product of relations that have the effect, in John Allen's (2011, p. 284) terms, of 'draw(ing) distant others within close reach or construct(ing) that close at hand at-a-distance'. These linkages are often a product or a feature of a market, and so global market connections are an integral feature of the topologies of place that make and remake the latter.

Matthew Henry demonstrates such place-making as a feature of the historical construction of (very) long distance trading networks between the UK and New Zealand. He shows that the making of the 'daily miracle' of being able to eat lamb meat – a seasonal and perishable commodity – in the UK all year round depended on the making of a temporal order where farms, freezing works, meat market-places, carcasses and refrigeration technologies were made and mobilised to get lamb meat from New Zealand into the UK during the latter's off-season. This involved the reassemblage of places – in terms of work practices, production processes, shipping schedules and consumer desires, to name a few – in both the UK and New Zealand that made the market possible. However, as Gabriel Laeis and Carolyn Morris show in their chapter on the failure to assemble a market for local produce in the tourist hotels of Fiji, global connections can contribute to the stymying of markets. The business model that requires flows of tourists and, importantly, tourist tastes, into Fijian hotels undermines the demand side of the market, while the ability to trade mass commodities to export markets reduces the willingness of the farmer to supply. Sometimes the market connections that make a place make other markets impossible: as distant tourists and exporters are drawn into a place through particular means, geographically proximate hotels and farmers are respectively pushed apart.

Other kinds of global connections between places are visible in other chapters too, making and facilitating markets, or at least attempting to do so. The international wine markets alluded to by John Overton and Warwick Murray rely on referential connections to places often distant from the place of consumption: Bordeaux, Napa Valley, Marlborough. Place has currency in the global wine market. But this also reflects a cultural economy that the global wine trade depends on: the global circulation of wine-making, consuming and marketing knowledges and practices. 'Knowledge' connections are central to the making of the electricity metering market that Heather Lovell describes as well. Policy networks that stretch between different places, made up of various consultants, policy wonks, researchers and politicians, and their various materials and spaces of policy learning enable the mobilisation of market policy. These often present carefully curated versions of policies from elsewhere, but sometimes with the power to shape a market.

Neoliberalism and market 'solutions'

The proliferation of new state/market relations, (or marketisation – Birch & Sie-miatycki, 2016) to address complex social problems has been a hallmark of more recent versions of after-neoliberal governance (Larner & Craig, 2005; Frankel *et al.*, 2019). Moving beyond the debates of 'roll back' and 'roll out' neoliberalism (Peck and Tickell, 2002), whereby states were seen to withdraw as much as possible from their role in society and economy in order to allow other, non-state actors to flourish, a number of the chapters instead tackle head on the complex and increasingly experimental entanglement of state/market relations, and their related politics. What each of these chapters highlight is the considerable work and challenges involved in deploying markets to meet social concerns. They also show, to varying extents, the central role the state plays as 'midwife' (Ball, 2012) in creating, shaping and guiding these markets as they address social domains that are too important not to.

The chapter by Murphy considers the deployment of markets to meet demand for an everyday, yet crucial human resource: housing. His work focuses on two state-led projects intended to recreate the Aotearoa New Zealand housing market to address the shortage of both social and affordable housing. Despite governmental attempts to operationalise a particular economic model of the housing market to achieve this aim, Murphy demonstrates the limitations of this endeavour as it comes up against the emplaced and 'locked in' nature of existing calculative practices within the housing market, which ultimately cause these interventions to flounder.

Focusing on another crucial part of everyday life, Lewis and Wynd bring our attention to new forms of economisation in education and the creation of schools as distinctive 'marketsites' for teacher professional development and poverty reduction programmes. The chapter highlights the constitutive work of new private, for-profit actors as they situate themselves alongside other, more traditional education actors within emerging 'school-based wellbeing economies'. Tracing the proliferation of these new actors, they show how they work to generate new opportunities to access public funding, to commodify public goods and to reorganise well-being market assemblages such that they become central to them. Ultimately, the authors ask how education is being transformed through the fashioning of schools as new kinds of marketsites. Finally, the chapter by Gallagher examines governmental attempts to marketise another part of the Aotearoa New Zealand education sector, early education, as a means of addressing poor child welfare outcomes, particularly for the children of indigenous Māori. As a country with one of the worst child wellbeing statistics in the Organisation for Economic Co-operation and Development, the government took on board the proliferation of international research on the purported benefits of formal early education as a means of intervening in the cycle of disadvantage and mitigating welfare spending in the future. However, attempts to create an ECE market to achieve this considerable social policy ambition came up against the political challenges of marketisation in a bicultural context. Where young Māori children should be cared for and by whom becomes a fundamental political question in the context of the postcolonial present. As Gallagher describes, the resulting contestation between government and the Māori childcare provider, Te Kohanga Reo, lays bare the epistemological and normative assumptions that underlie the creation of markets for collective concerns.

Place–market–time

The central argument of this book is that markets are locked in a mutually generative embrace with places. This speaks to the intimate spatiality of markets. At the same time, however, a number of chapters in this book demonstrate that the place-market dyad can, and should, be seen as place-market-time. Murphy, for example, in his discussion of housing markets grounds his argument in the moment of crisis that has surrounded Auckland's housing market. The market that he talks about is being fashioned in a particular place, but equally so at a particular point in time that makes it different from what has previously happened in Auckland. In contrast, a theme in Langford, Brekelmans and Lawrence's chapter is the importance of longstanding personal relationships in the making of finance markets in Australia's Northern Territory. These durable relationships are crucial to navigating both the uncertain play of drought and also the rhythms of credit expansion and contraction. The theme of intellectual experimentation and genealogy lie at the heart of Hikuroa's, Le Heron's and their colleagues' argument about generative potential of new metaphors to reshape market relations. Henry also engages with ideas of agricultural seasonality, arguing that the markets for lamb that connected New Zealand farmers and Smithfield merchants was fashioned through the ability to manipulate temporal relations and transform time into an economic quality. In doing this, Henry suggests that rather than time as an independent marker of change, time, like place, is relationally constituted. Temporalities, then, can be seen as assemblages that simultaneously emerge from and give structure to market performances and possibilities.

Placing market subjects

Making markets requires the making of market subjects. Market subjects are those that are able and willing to participate in the market, with the right kinds of capacities, resources and orientations. Lewis and Wynd show how far this can go in their chapter, where schools are shown to be actively constructed as sites for accumulation through actors seeking to respond to governmental imperatives for students to be taught to be resilient and emotionally sound. Schools, and thus students, become consumers of techniques adapted from positive psychology that teach them to be entrepreneurial and yet caring and able to adapt to the demands of a neoliberal society and economy. But market subjects will never only be market subjects. While neoliberal ideology and its critics assume that markets require and produce narrowly economically instrumental rational actors, market actors' relations to other, often place-bound social formations will interact with their market relations. Langford and her colleagues and FitzHerbert demonstrate in their chapters the way that market subjects are produced in the moral economies of place, as well as the narrow confines of market rationality. Langford *et al.*'s bank managers are concerned about the sustainability of the farms and farmers that comprise the disparate community in northern Australia − a place defined by its distance from elsewhere and its harsh environmental conditions. Bank managers are quintessential market actors whom one might expect to be incentivised by the simple arithmetic of the numbers on the page before them, but in this place, their rationality is necessarily redefined according to the reality of its social and environmental context. Meanwhile, in FitzHerbert's study, indigenous Māori identity is central to a market for specifically Māori produce. While the market 'fails' from a certain perspective, for the market subjects, participation in the market-making project was not necessarily just about selling their wares, but supporting and connecting with and through a, in principle, Māori-centred economic experiment with reverberations beyond exchange. Subjectivity is a key site where the relations of the market, place and culture come together.

The uses of place

A particular place is, as much as anything, an idea. Most places have associations with them that are part of their 'sense of place', conjuring up certain images and ideas: Paris, Marrakesh, Hong Kong. These place associations circulate well beyond the geographical confines of the place itself. Markets for tourism and fine goods often operate through these representations, and will in turn operate on the places themselves. This intertwining at the representational level is one of the key ways that markets and places shape one another. Overton and Murray demonstrate this in their chapter on the role of place in the wine industry. They demonstrate the complex relation between place and capital in this industry that has always emphasised the distinctive role of *terroir* − the place-bound conditions that affect the quality of the wine being produced there. They show how wine capital constructs and mobilises place with layered, complex and symbiotic strategies in order to sell it at different price points in the market through the association of certain places with notions of quality. Places are a product of such marketing strategies. But places clearly have agency as well. Their materiality, captured in the idea of *terroir*, shapes the materiality − and taste − of wine. And even the social structures of places shape how they will be used by wine makers, visible in 'old world' regional rule structures, such as the French *appellation* system as opposed to 'new world' geographical indicators like we see in Aotearoa-New Zealand. In the wine industry, markets do not just exist in places, but because of them. Heather Lovell also demonstrates how places are mobilised in her chapter on electricity metering in Australia, where New Zealand's consumer choice electricity metering market was consistently pointed to as a model. As Lovell argues, place is a narrated entity − a product of stories told about it both within and outside its borders. She shows that places are understood in relation to other places − in this case how various electricity market jurisdictions in Australia came to be understood in relation to New Zealand's market. But places are always more than just their (always partial) narrations. While the idea of place played a role on the attempted making of a market in Australia, Lovell shows how it has come unstuck as it has encountered all those other aspects of place that make them different to one another: the 'people, objects, materials, institutions, regulations and governance structures'.

Notes

1 Available at https://nzhistory.govt.nz/politics/treaty/read-the-treaty/maori-text, last accessed 7 December 2020.
2 Available at https://nzhistory.govt.nz/politics/treaty/read-the-Treaty/differences-between-the-texts, last accessed 7 December 2020.
3 What counts as a Pacific Island nation depends on your definition of nation, so the exact number is uncertain.

References

Agnew, J. (1987). *Place and politics: The geographical mediation of state and society*. London: Allen and Unwin.
Aitken, R. (2010). Ambiguous incorporations: Microfinance and global govern-mentality. *Global Networks*, 10(2), 223–243.
Allen, J. (2011). Topological twists: Power's shifting geographies. *Dialogues in Human Geography*, 1(3), 283–298. https://doi.org/10.1177/2043820611421546.
Amin, A. & Thrift, N. (Eds.). (2003). *The Blackwell cultural economy reader*. Chichester, UK: Wiley-Blackwell.
Anderson, B., Kearnes, M., McFarlane, C. & Swanton, D. (2012). On assemblages and geography. *Dialogues in Human Geography*, 2(2), 171–189. doi:10.1177/2043820612449261.
Anderson, B. & McFarlane, C. (2011). Assemblage and geography. *Area*, 43(2), 124–127. doi:10.1111/j.1475-4762.2011.01004.x.
Baker, T., Evans, J. & Hennigan, B. (2020). Investable poverty: Social investment states and the geographies of poverty management. *Progress in Human Geography*, 44(3), 534–554. https://doi.org/10.1177/0309132519849288.
Ball, S.J. (2012). *Global Education Inc; New policy networks and the neo-liberal Imaginary*. London: Routledge.
Bargh, M. (2007). *Resistance: An indigenous response to neoliberalism*. Wellington: Huia Publishers.
Bargh, M. (2011). The triumph of Māori entrepreneurs or diverse economies? *Aboriginal Policy Studies*, 1(3), 53–69.
Bargh, M. (2012). Rethinking and re-shaping indigenous economies: Māori geothermal enterprises. *Journal of Enterprising Communities: People and Places in the Global Economy*, 6(3), 271–283.
Bargh, M. & Wevers, L. (2019). Land is never just land. *Women Talking Politics: A Research Magazine of the New Zealand Political Studies Association*. (November), 32–34.
Bello, W.F., Cunningham, S. & Rau, B. (2008). *Dark victory: The United States, strucutural adjustment and global poverty*. London: TNI/Pluto Press in cooperation with Food First.
Bennett, J.A. (2018). Pacific Coconut: Comestible, Comfort and Commodity. *The Journal of Pacific History*, 53(4), 353–374.
Bennett, T., McFall, L. & Pryke, M. (2008). Culture/economy/society. *Journal of Cultural Economy*, 1(1), 1–7.

Berndt, C. (2015). Ruling markets: the marketization of social and economic policy. *Environment and Planning A*, 47(9), 1866–1872. https://doi.org/10.1177/10.1177_0308518x15598324.

Berndt, C. & Boeckler, M. (2009). Geographies of circulation and exchange: Constructions of markets. *Progress in Human Geography*, 33(4), 535–551. https://doi.org/10.1177/0309132509104805.

Berndt, C. & Boeckler, M. (2011). Geographies of markets: Materials, morals and monsters in motion. *Progress in Human Geography*, 35(4), 559–567. https://doi.org/10.1177/0309132510384498.

Berndt, C. & Boeckler, M. (2012). Geogrpahies of marketization. In T J. Barnes, J. Peck & E. Sheppard (Eds.). *The Wiley-Blackwell companion to economic geography* (pp. 199–212). Chichester: Wiley-Blackwell.

Berndt, C., Peck, J. & Rantisi, N.M. (Eds.). (2020). *Market/place: Exploring spaces of exchange*. Newcastle-Upon-Tyne: Agenda Publishing.

Berndt, C., Rantisi, N.M. & Peck, J. (2020). M/market frontiers. *Environment and Planning A: Economy and Space*, 52(1), 14–26. https://doi.org/10.1177/0308518x19891833.

Binney, J. (2009). *Encircled Lands: Te Urewera, 1820–1921*. Wellington: Bridget Williams Books.

Birch, K. & Siemiatycki, M. (2016). Neoliberalism and the geographies of marketization:The entangling of state and markets. *Progress in Human Geography*, 40(2), 177–198. https://doi.org/10.1177/0309132515570512.

Boast, R. (2017). Māori Land and Land Tenure in New Zealand: 150 years of the Māori land court. *Comparative Law Journal of the Pacific*, 23, 97–133.

Boeckler, M. & Berndt, C. (2013). Geographies of circulation and exchange III: The great crisis and marketization 'after markets'. *Progress in Human Geography*, 37(3), 424–432. https://doi.org/10.1177/0309132512453515.

Brenner, N. & Theodore, N. (2012). Spaces of neoliberalism: Urban restructuring in North America and Western Europe. https://doi.org/10.1002/9781444397499.

Bridge, G. (2004). Mapping the bonanza: Geographies of mining investment in an era of neoliberal reform. *Professional Geographer*, 56(3), 406–421.

Brooking, T. (1996). Use it or Lose it: Unravelling the land debate in late nineteenth-century New Zealand. *New Zealand Journal of History*, 30(2), 141–162.

Brooking, T., Pawson, E. & Star, P. (2010). *Seeds of empire: The environmental transformation of New Zealand*. London: I.B. Taurus.

Butler, J. (1990). *Gender trouble: Feminism and the subversion of identity*. New York, NY: Routledge.

Byrnes, G. (2001). *Boundary markers: Land surveying and the colonisation of New Zealand*. Wellington: Bridget William Books.

Cahill, D. (2020). Market analysis beyond market fetishism. *Environment and Planning A: Economy and Space*, 52(1), 27–45. https://doi.org/10.1177/0308518x18820917.

Çalışkan, K. & Callon, M. (2009). Economization, part 1: shifting attention from the economy towards processes of economization. *Economy and Society*, 38(3), 369–398. https://doi.org/10.1080/03085140903020580.

Çalışkan, K. & Callon, M. (2010). Economization, part 2: a research programme for the study of markets. *Economy and Society*, 39(1), 1–32. https://doi.org/10.1080/03085140903424519.

Callon, M. (2007a). An essay on the growing contribution of economic markets to the proliferation of the social. *Theory Culture & Society*, 24(7–8),139–163. https://doi.org/10.1177/0263276407084701.

Callon, M. (2007b). What does it mean to say economics is performative? In D. MacKensie, F. Muniesa & L. Siu (Eds.). *Do economists make markets? On the performativity of economics* (pp. 311–357). Princeton, NJ: Princeton University Press.

Callon, M. (Ed.). (1998). *The laws of the markets*. London: Blackwell.

Callon, M., Méadel, C. & Rabeharisoa, V. (2002). The economy of qualities. *Economy and Society*, 31(2), 194–217. https://doi.org/10.1080/03085140220123126.

Callon, M., Millo, Y. & Muniesa, F. (Eds.). (2007). *Market devices*. Oxford: Blackwell.

Campbell, H. (2020). *Farming inside invisible worlds: Modernist agriculture and its consequences*. London: Bloomsbury Academic. doi:10.5040/9781350120570.

Christophers, B. (2014). From Marx to market and back again: Performing the economy. *Geoforum*, 57, 12–20. https://doi.org/10.1016/j.geoforum.2014.08.007.

Christophers, B. (2015). Constructing and deconstructing markets: making space for capital. *Environment and Planning A*, 47(9), 1859–1865. https://doi.org/10.1177/0308518x15604971.

Coe, N.M. & Yeung, H.W.C. (2015). *Global production networks: Theorizing economic development in an interconnected world*. Oxford: Oxford University Press. https://doi.org/10.1093/acprof:oso/9780198703907.001.0001.

Cohen, D. (2017). Market mobilities/immobilities: mutation, path-dependency, and the spread of charter school policies in the United States. *Critical Studies in Education*, 58(2), 168–186. https://doi.org/10.1080/17508487.2016.1242507.

Cohen, D. (2018). Between perfection and damnation: The emerging geography of markets. *Progress in Human Geography*, 42(6), 898–915. https://doi.org/10.1177/0309132517729769.

Connell, R. (2007). *Southern theory: The global dynamics of knowledge in the social sciences*. London: Routledge.

Cresswell, T. (2020). Place. In A. Kobayashi (Ed.), *International encyclopedia of human geography* (2nd ed.) (pp. 117–124). Oxford: Elsevier. https://doi.org/10.1016/B978-0-08-102295-5.10997-7.

Cumberland, K. (1941). A century's change: natural to cultural vegetation in New Zealand. *Geographical Review*, 31, 529–554.

DeLanda, M. (2006). *A new philosophy of society: assemblage theory and social complexity*. London: Continuum.

DeLanda, M. (2016). *Assemblage Theory*. Edinburgh: Edinburgh University Press.

Dicken, P. (2015). *Global shift: Mapping the changing contours of the world economy* (7th Ed.). London: Sage Publications.

Doganova, L. & Laurent, B. (2019). Carving out a domain for the market: Boundary making in European environmental markets. *Economy and Society*, 48(2), 221–242. https://doi.org/10.1080/03085147.2019.1624071.

Dominello, F. (2009). The politics of remembering and forgetting native title law and reconciliation in Australia. *Cosmopolitan Civil Societies Journal*, 1(3), 1–34.

du Gay, P. & Pryke, M. (Eds). (2002). *Cultural Economy*. London: Sage Publications.

Faleolo, R.L. (2019). Wellbeing Perspectives, Conceptualisations of Work and Labour Mobility Experiences of Pasifika Trans-Tasman Migrants in Brisbane. In V. Stead & J. Altman (Eds.), *Labour Lines and Colonial Power: Indigenous and Pacific Islander Labour Mobility in Australia* (pp. 185–206). Action, ACT: ANU Press and Aboriginal History Inc.

Fligstein, N. (2002). *The architecture of markets: An economic sociology of twenty-first-century capitalist societies*. Princeton, NJ: Princeton University Press.

24   *Russell Prince et al.*

Frankel, C., Ossandón, J. & Pallesen, T. (2019). The organization of markets for collective concerns and their failures. *Economy and Society*, 48(2), 153–174. https://doi.org/10.1080/03085147.2019.1627791.

French, S., Leyshon, A. & Wainwright, T. (2011). Financializing space, spacing financialization. *Progress in Human Geography*, 35(6), 798–819. https://doi.org/10.1177/0309132510396749.

Friedmann, H. & McMichael, P. (1989). Agriculture and the state system: The rise and decline of national agricultures, 1870 to the present. *Sociologia Ruralis*, 29(2), 93–117. https://doi.org/10.1111/j.1467-9523.1989.tb00360.x.

Gallagher, A. (2018). The business of care: Marketization and the new geographies of childcare. *Progress in Human Geography*, 42(5), 706–722. https://doi.org/10.1177/0309132517702970.

Gammage, B. (2011). *The biggest estate on earth: How Aborigines made Australia.* Crows Nest, Australia: Allen & Unwin.

Garden, D. (2005). *Australia, New Zealand and the Pacific: An environmental history.* Santa Barbara, CA: ABC-CLIO.

Gereffi, G. & Korzeniewicz, M. (Eds.). (1993). *Commodity Chains and Global Capitalism.* Santa Barbara, CA: ABC-CLIO.

Gibson, C. (2009). Australasia. In Thrift, N. & Kitchin, R. (Eds.). *International Encyclopedia of Human Geography* (pp. 225–233). Oxford: Elsevier. https://doi.org/10.1016/B978-008044910-4.00253-4.

Gibson-Graham, J-K (1996). *The end of capitalism (as we know it): a feminist critique of political economy.* Cambridge, MA: Blackwell.

Gibson-Graham, J-K (2006). *A post-capitalist politics.* Minneapolis, MN: University of Minnesota Press.

Gibson-Graham, J-K, Cameron, J. & Healy, S. (2013). *Take back the economy: An ethical guide to transforming our communities.* Minneapolis, MN: University of Minnesota Press.

Gibson-Graham, J.-K.& Dombroski, K.(Eds.). (2020). *The Handbook of Diverse Economies.* Cheltenham:Edward Elgar.

Glassman, J. (2011). The geo-political economy of global production networks. *Geography Compass*, 5(4), 154–164. https://doi.org/10.1111/j.1749-8198.2011.00416.x.

Granovetter, M. (1985). Economic action and social structure - the problem of embeddedness. *American Journal of Sociology*, 91(3), 481–510.

Granovetter, M. & Swedberg, R. (Eds.). (2018). *The Sociology of Economic Life* (Vol. 3). New York, NY: Routledge.

Hall, S. (2015). Geographies of marketisation in English higher education: territorial and relational markets and the case of undergraduate student fees. *Area*, 47(4), 451–458. https://doi.org/10.1111/area.12216.

Hall, S. (2018). *Global finance: Places, spaces and people.* London: Sage Publications.

Harris, A., Binney, J. & Anderson, A. (2014). *Tangata Whenua: An Illustrated History.* Wellington: Bridget Williams Books.

Henderson, J., Dicken, P., Hess, M., Coe, N. & Yeung, H.W.C. (2002). Global production networks and the analysis of economic development. *Review of International Political Economy*, 9(3), 436–464. https://doi.org/10.1080/09692290210150842.

Henry, M. & Roche, M. (2013). Valuing lively materialities: Bio-economic assembling in the making of new meat futures. *New Zealand Geographer*, 69(3), 197–207. https://doi.org/10.1111/nzg.12021.

Hess, M. (2004). 'Spatial' relationships? Towards a reconceptualization of embeddedness. *Progress in Human Geography*, 28(2), 165–186. https://doi.org/10.1191/0309132504p h479oa.

Hess, M. & Yeung, H.W.C. (2006). Whither global production networks in economic geography? Past, present and future. *Environment and Planning A*, 38(7), 1193–1204. https://doi.org/10.1068/a38463.

Hill, R. (2004). *State Authority, Indigenous Autonomy: Crown-Maori Relations in New Zealand/Aotearoa, 1900–1950*. Wellington: Victoria University Press.

Horrocks, I. & Lacey, C. (2016). *Extraordinary Anywhere: Essays on Place from Aotearoa New Zealand*. Wellington: Victoria University Press.

Harvey, D. (2005). *A brief history of neoliberalism*. Oxford: Oxford University Press.

Hughes, A., Wrigley, N. & Buttle, M. (2008). Global production networks, ethical campaigning, and the embeddedness of responsible governance. *Journal of Economic Geography*, 8(3), 345–367. https://doi.org/10.1093/jeg/lbn004.

Jessop, B. (2002). *The future of the capitalist state*. Cambridge: Polity Press.

Jones, A. (2013). (Re)conceptualising the space of markets: The case of the 2007–9 global financial crisis. *Geoforum*, 50, 31–42. https://doi.org/10.1016/j.geoforum.2013.07.010.

Kāwharu, I.H. (1977). *Maori Land Tenure: Studies of a Changing Institution*. Oxford: Oxford University Press.

Kelsey, J. (1995). *The New Zealand experiment: A world model for structural adjustment?* Auckland: Auckland University Press.

Krippner, G.R. (2005). The financialization of the American economy. *Socio-Economic Review*, 3(2), 173–208. https://doi.org/10.1093/SER/mwi008.

Lambert, S. (2008). *The expansion of sustainability through new economic space: Māori potatoes and cultural resilience*. [Unpublished doctoral thesis]. Lincoln University.

Lapavitsas, C. (2013). *Profiting without producing: How finance exploits us all*. London: Verso.

Larner, W. (2012). Reflections from an islander. *Dialogues in Human Geography*, 2(2), 158–161. https://doi.org/10.1177/2043820612449312.

Larner, W. & Craig, D. (2005). After neoliberalism? Community activism and local partnerships in Aotearoa New Zealand. *Antipode*, 37, 402–424.

Latour, B. (2005). *Reassembling the social: An introduction to actor-network theory*. Oxford: Oxford University Press.

Legun, K. (2016). Ever-Redder apples: How aesthetics shape the biology of markets. In R. Le Heron, H. Campbell, N. Lewis & M. Carolan (Eds.). *Biological economies: Experimentation and the politics of agri-food frontiers* (pp. 127–140). London: Routledge.

Le Heron, R. (2002). Globalisation, food regimes and 'rural' networks. In I.R. Bowler, C.R. Bryant & C. Cocklin (Eds.), *The sustainability of rural systems (The GeoJournal Library*, vol. 66, pp. 81–96). Dordrecht: Springer. https://doi.org/10.1007/978-94-017-3471-4_5.

Levy, J. (2018). Ideal Coconut Country: Commodified Coconuts and the Scientific Plantation in Pohnpei, Micronesia. *The Journal of Pacific History*, 53(4), 436–453.

Macartney, H. (2010). *Variegated neoliberalism: EU varieties of capitalism and international political economy*. London: Routledge. doi:10.4324/9780203836347.

MacKenzie, D. (2006). *An engine, not a camera: How financial models shape markets*. London: TheMITPress.

MacKenzie, D. & Millo, Y. (2003). Constructing a market, performing theory: The historical sociology of a financial derivatives exchange. *American Journal of Sociology*, 109(1), 107–145.

MacKenzie, D., Muniesa, F. & Siu, L. (Eds.). (2007). *Do economists make markets? On the performativity of economics*. Princeton, NJ: Princeton University Press.

Mar, T.B. (2019). 'Boyd's Blacks': Labour and the making of Settler Lands in Australia and the Pacific. In V. Stead & J. Altman (Eds.), *Labour Lines and Colonial Power: Indigenous and Pacific Islander Labour Mobility in Australia* (pp. 57–74). Action, ACT: ANU Press and Aboriginal History Inc.

Massey, D. (1993). Power-geometery and a progressive sense of place. In J. Bird, B. Curtis, T. Putnam, G. Robertson & L. Tickner (Eds.), *Mapping the future: local cultures, global change* (pp. 59–69). London: Routledge.

Marsters, E., Lewis, N. & Friesen, W. (2006). Pacific flows: The fluidity of remittances in the Cook Islands. *Asia-Pacific Viewpoint*, 47(1), 31–44.

McGregor, A. & Houston, D. (2018). Cattle in the Anthropocene: Four propositions. *Transactions of the Institute of British Geographers*, 43(1), 3–16. https://doi.org/10.1111/tran.12193.

Mikaere A (2000). Māori and Self-Determination in Aotearoa/New Zealand. Working Paper, no. 5/2000. University of Waikato, Hamilton.

Mirowski, P. (2013). *Never let a serious crisis go to waste: How neoliberalism survived the financial meltdown*. London: Verso.

Mirowski, P. & Plehwe, D. (2009). *The road from Mount Pelorin: The making of the neo-liberal thought collective*. Cambridge, MA.: Harvard University Press.

Mitchell, T. (1998). Fixing the economy. *Cultural Studies*, 12(1), 82–101.

Morris, C. & FitzHerbert, S. (2017). Rethinking 'alternative': Māori and food sover-eignty in Aotearoa New Zealand. In M. Wilson (Ed.), *Postcolonialism, indigeneity and struggles for food sovereignty: Alternative food networks in the Subaltern world* (pp. 15–33). London: Routledge.

Muellerleile, C. & Akers, J. (2015). Making market rule(s). *Environment and Planning A*, 47(9), 1781–1786. https://doi.org/10.1177/0308518x15610950.

Muir, C. (2014). *The broken promise of agricultural progress: An environmental history*. Abingdon: Earthscan.

Nik-Khah, E. & Mirowski, P. (2019). On going the market one better: Economic market design and the contradictions of building markets for public purposes. *Economy and Society*, 48(2), 268–294. https://doi.org/10.1080/03085147.2019.1576431.

O'Malley, V. (2012). *The Meeting Place: Maori and Pakeha Encounters*. Auckland: Auckland University Press.

Ouma, S. (2015). *Assembling export markets: The making and unmaking of global food con-nections in West Africa*. Oxford: Wiley Blackwell.

Panitch, L. & Gindin, S. (2012). *The making of global capitalism: The political economy of American empire*. New York: Verso.

Pascoe, B. (2018). *Dark Emu*. Broome, WA: Magabala Books.

Pawson, E. & Biological Economies Team (Eds). (2018). *The new biological economy: How New Zealanders are creating value from the land*. Auckland: Auckland University Press.

Peck, J. (2010). *Constructions of neoliberal reason*. Oxford: Oxford University Press.

Peck, J. (2012). Economic geography: Island life. *Dialogues in Human Geography*, 2(2), 113–133. https://doi.org/10.1177/2043820612443779.

Peck, J. & Tickell, A. (2002). Neoliberalizing space. *Antipode*, 34(3), 380–404.

Petrie, H. (2006). *Chiefs of Industry: Māori Tribal Enterprise in Early Colonial New Zealand*. Auckland: Auckland University Press.

Pike, A. & Pollard, J. (2010). Economic geographies of financialization. *Economic geography*, 86(1), 29–51.

Polanyi, K. (1957). *The great transformation*. Boston, MA: Beacon Press.

Pratt, A.C. (2009). Cultural economy. In R. Kitchin & N. Thrift (Eds.), *International Encyclopedia of Human Geography* (pp. 407–410). Oxford: Elsevier. https://doi.org/10.1016/B978-008044910-4.00146-2.

Rapaport, M. (1995). Oysterlust: Islanders, entrepreneurs, and colonial policy over Tuamotu lagoons. The Journal of Pacific History, 30(1), 39–52.

Rapaport, M. (Ed.). (2013). *The Pacific Islands: Environment and society* (Rev. ed.). Honolulu, HI: Unversity of Hawai'I Press.

Rata, E.(2011). Encircling the commons: Neotribal capitalism in New Zealand since 2000. *Anthropological Theory*, 11(3), 327–353. doi:10.1177/1463499611416724.

Reid, J. & Rout, M. (2016). Maori tribal economy: Rethinking the original economic institutions. In T. Anderson (Ed.). *Unlocking the Wealth of Indian Nations* (pp. 60–83). London: Lexington.

Reverdy, T. & Breslau, D. (2019). Making an exception: Market design and the politics of re-regulation in the French electricity sector. *Economy and Society*, 48(2), 197–220. https://doi.org/10.1080/03085147.2019.1576434.

Robinson, W.I. (2004). *A theory of global capitalism: Transnational production, transnational capitalists, and the transnational state*. Baltimore, MD: Johns Hopkins University Press.

Robinson, W. I. (2008). *Latin America and global capitalism: A critical globalization perspective*. Baltimore, MD: Johns Hopkins University Press.

Roscoe, P. & Loza, O. (2019). The –ography of markets (or, the responsibilities of market studies). *Journal of Cultural Economy*, 12(3), 215–227. https://doi.org/10.1080/17530350.2018.1557730.

Salmond, A. (1991). *Two worlds: first meetings between Maori and Europeans, 1642–1772*. Auckland: Viking Press.

Salmond, A. (1997). *Between worlds: early exchanges between Maori and Europeans, 1773–1815*. Auckland: Viking Press.

Shoemaker, N. (2015). A typology of colonialism. *Perspectives on History*. 1 October, www.historians.org/publications-and-directories/perspectives-on-history/october-2015/a-ypology-of-colonialism.

Smith, L.T. (1999). *Decolonizing Methodologies: Research and Indigenous Peoples*. Dunedin: University of Otago Press.

Smelser, N.J. & Swedberg, R. (Eds). (2005). *The handbook of economic Sociology* (Vol. 2). Princeton, NJ: Princeton University Press.

Springer, S. (2010). *Cambodia's neoliberal order: Violence, authoritarianism, and the contestation of public space*. London: Routledge. https://doi.org/10.4324/9780203848968.

Stead, V. & Altman, J. (Eds). (2019). *Labour Lines and Colonial Power: Indigenous and Pacific Islander Labour Mobility in Australia*. Action, ACT: ANU Press and Aboriginal History Inc.

Stevens, K. (2018). *Wasting Coconuts?*Consumption Versus Commerce in Colonial Wallis and Futuna. *The Journal of Pacific History*, 53(4), 478–501.

Stevens, K. & Wanhalla, A. (2017). Intimate Relations: Kinship and the Economics of Shore Whaling in Southern New Zealand, 1820–1860. *The Journal of Pacific History*, 52(2), 135–155.

Stiglitz, J. (2002). *Globalization and its discontents*. London: Penguin.

Stokes, E. (2013). Contesting resources: Māori, Pakeha and a tenurial revolution. In E. Pawson & T. Brooking (Eds). *Making a new land: Environmental histories of New Zealand* (pp. 52–69). Dunedin: Otago University Press.

Swarts, J. (2013). *Constructing neoliberalism: Economic transformation in Anglo-American democracies*. Toronto, ON: University of Toronto Press.

Swedberg, R. (1991). Major traditions of economic sociology. *Annual Review of Sociology*, 17, 251–276.

Swedberg, R. (1994). Markets as social structures. In N. J. Smelser & R. Swedberg (Eds.). *The Handbook of Economic Sociology* (Vol. 1, pp. 255–282). Princeton, NJ: Princeton University Press.

Swedberg, R. (1997). New economic sociology: What has been accomplished, what is ahead? *Acta Sociologica*, 40(2), 161–182.

Teaiwa, K.M. (2015). *Consuming Ocean: stories of people and phosphate from Banaba*. Bloomington, IN: Indiana University Press.

Tilzey, M. (2019). Food regimes, capital, state, and class: Friedmann and McMichael revisited. *Sociologia Ruralis*, 59(2), 230–254. https://doi.org/10.1111/soru.12237.

Tsing, A. L. (2009). Supply chains and the human condition. *Rethinking Marxism*, 21(2), 148–176. https://doi.org/10.1080/08935690902743088.

Tsing, A.L. (2012). Empire's salvage heart: Why diversity matters in the global political economy. *Focaal*, (64), 36–50. https://doi.org/10.3167/fcl.2012.640104.

Tsing, A.L. (2015). *The mushroom at the end of the world: On the possibility of life in capitalist ruins*. Princeton, NJ: Princeton University Press.

Underhill-Sem, Y., Cox, E., Lacey, A. & Szamier, M. (2014). Changing market culture in the Pacific. *Asia-Pacific Viewpoint*, 55: 306–318. https://doi.org/10.1111/apv.12063.

Walker, R. (2004). *Ka Whawhai Tonu Matou: Struggle Without End* (2nd ed). Auckland: Penguin Books.

Watson, M. (2018). *The Market*. Newcastle-Upon-Tyne: Agenda Publishing.

Weller, S. (2006). The embeddedness of global production networks: The impact of crisis in Fiji's garment export sector. *Environment and Planning A*, 38(7), 1249–1267. https://doi.org/10.1068/a37192.

Wray, F., Dufty-Jones, R., Gibson, C., Larner, W., Beer, A., Le Heron, R. & O'Neill, P. (2013). Neither here nor there or always here and there? Reflections on antipodean reflections on economic geography. *Dialogues in Human Geography, 3(2)*, 179–199. https://doi-org.ezproxy.massey.ac.nz/10.1177/2043820613493158.

Yeung, H.W.C. & Coe, N.M. (2015). Toward a dynamic theory of global production networks. *Economic Geography*, 91(1), 29–58. https://doi.org/10.1111/ecge.12063.

Zelizer, V.A. (1994). *Pricing the priceless child: The changing social value of children*. Princeton, NJ: Princeton University Press.

Zelizer, V.A. (2013). *Economic lives: How culture Shapes the economy*. Princeton, NJ: Princeton University Press.

Zelizer, V.A. (2017). *The social meaning of money: Pin money, paychecks, poor relief, and other currencies*. Princeton, NJ: Princeton University Press.

2 Making a diverse Māori economy market

Economic experimentation with digital platforms for Māori produce

Stephen FitzHerbert

NATIONAL INSTITUTE OF WATER AND ATMOSPHERIC RESEARCH (NIWA),
AOTEAROA NEW ZEALAND

Introduction

Māori economies have specific dimensions – technical, political and moral – in which the values, practices and objects of Māori economies and economic exchange are situated in Māori cultural worlds. Māori economy and economy-making projects will not, and cannot, be bounded in mainstream economic accounts (Bargh 2012, 2018; FitzHerbert, 2016). They are shaped by cultural economic aspirations for keeping Māori resources alive and generating improved Māori livelihoods (Smith, Tinirau, Gillies & Warriner, 2015; Amoamo, Ruwhiu & Carter, 2018). Economy-making projects are qualified and measured across multiple trajectories of value, even if some of these are capitalist and must perform in capitalist worlds of joint-ventures and required rates of return, or in state worlds of new public management. It is crucial to be attentive to the articulation and translation work across different projects of Māori economy-making and actualised Māori economies and between them and broader economic circulations.

A vast majority of Māori economy-making projects are situated in expectations of regional economic development and enterprise in marginal contexts. The state has a major presence, commonly in partnership with Māori economic and political actors and new forms of policy intervention and investment. Conceptions of Māori economic development are shifting, unstable and subject to new shaping by favoured resources and new 'experts' (many themselves Māori) who exhort different ways of being economic (see Rata 2011; Bargh, Douglas & Te One, 2014; O'Sullivan, 2018). Together with state agencies and tribal authorities, these new experts (entrepreneurs, investment analysts, business incubators and mentors) are at work mobilising and capitalising on the significant Māori economic asset base. Māori economy and its subjects are arguably being rationalised and made orthodox.

In recent years, the increasing prominence of iwi (tribal) Trust Boards and associated corporate entities as investors and entrepreneurial actors in Aotearoa New Zealand economies has been coined the rise of the 'Taniwha Economy'[1] (Minister of Māori Affairs, 2012). Mobilising assets returned through the Treaty of

DOI: 10.4324/9780429296260-2

Waitangi settlement process, iwi organisations have become major actors in resource-based and other economies.[2] Named to suggest its unknown and potentially disruptive qualities as well as its emergence, the Taniwha economy is increasingly being made calculable by Māori, economists and state actors to ramp-up the Māori economic development agenda. Valued in capitalist terms at approximately $42 billion (Nana *et al.*, 2015), yet claimed to be underperforming, the Taniwha economy is managed largely by Māori asset holding tribal trusts. The five largest each have assets over NZ$500 million. It is an assets-driven, consultancy-supported, largely capitalist assemblage of Māori ownership, development governmentalities, iwi aspirations, and ready capital and is often narrated by Māori, government and corporate interests alike as the great hope for Aotearoa New Zealand's economic future.

Operating under deeds of trust that commit their executives to produce better livelihoods for their people through sustainable use of resources and long-term multigenerational management horizons, Māori entities are neither capitalist nor alternative (Smith *et al.*, 2015). Rather, they negotiate the cultural political economy of their articulations in innovative ways (Durie, 2003; Bargh & Otter, 2009; Bargh, 2011; FitzHerbert, 2016; Amoamo *et al.*, 2018) and economise Māori-held resources (cultural, social, physical and economic) in non-standard ways. The economies that they actualise are conceptualised, framed, categorised and managed as 'Māori'. They are understood as holistic assemblages of social, cultural, moral and political practices and aspirations as well as economic concerns, and include non-human actors (mountains, rivers, flora and fauna, and creatures like the taniwha) as well as humans. Notable investments include seafood corporations, industrial scale dairy agriculture and forestry, geothermal investments, and major tourism initiatives.

While generally used to refer to the conjunction of corporate capitalism, Māori investment and state interest, the Taniwha economy intersects with Māori-led agricultural projects that utilise Māori land and indigenous knowledge to cultivate cash or community crops (Roskruge, 2004; Lambert, 2008; FitzHerbert, 2016; Stein, Mirosa & Carter, 2018). What is produced is a range of diverse Māori economies and a hybridised sense of 'Māori economy' that positions and shapes them. However, questions about how such hybridised economies are made and actualised or interpreted and represented are rarely asked. Composed as they are of Māori aspirations, practices and values as well as capitalist techniques and logics and market institutions, such economies are different and not all exchanges are market transactions (Bargh, 2012; Amoamo *et al.*, 2018). When deployed instrumentally, as in much public and policy discourse, the notion of the market consciously or otherwise occludes the complexity and richness of Māori economy and the cultural embeddedness of exchange, entrepreneurial activity and meanings/values.

Discourses of 'the Market' and 'the Economy', then, marginalise many of the activities and discount the values of many economy-making experiments in Māori horticultural enterprise. They hide, for example, the experience of Māori vegetable networks, the practices that constitute economy-making, the richness of their social relations of exchange and much of their cultural and political economy

(McFarlane, 2007; Lambert, 2008; Morris & FitzHerbert, 2017; FitzHerbert, 2016). This is a pivotal issue for Māori seeking to mobilise assets for new forms of enterprise. It restricts opportunities and silences aspirations as well as weakening our understandings. Questions about how to engage critically have been asked for many years in different academic literatures (Bargh *et al.*, 2014; Underhill-Sem & Lewis, 2008) but are now being posed in new more constructive ways (Bargh & Otter, 2009; FitzHerbert & Lewis, 2010; Amoamo *et al.*, 2018). To address these issues, this chapter will demonstrate the breadth and depth of Māori economy-making and expose the opportunities that lie in a deeper understanding of the mobilisation of economic experimentation (by Māori) through the case of a Māori market-making project. Empirical research of this type promises to invigorate new thinking in this field (Barr & Reid, 2014; Reid & Rout, 2016), extend understandings of diverse economies and economisation, and give hope to new groups in different places around the world.

This chapter illustrates how economic experimentation and articulation is put to work in making-Māori economies. The project was a Māori-state collective market-making experiment to connect small-scale Māori producers with Aotearoa New Zealand consumers, it sought to get things (Māori products) moving in and between different economies. In the first section, I bring together Michel Callon's notion of economic experimentation and J-K Gibson-Graham's diverse economy thinking to investigate and make sense of the constitutive actors, practices, moments and relations of Māra Kai. Second, I provide an overview of the methodological approach for an ethnographical knowing of the market-making project. Next, I present the key empirical moments of the project's proliferation, to trace its conception, pilot experiment, and post-pilot stages. Lastly, I conclude with an analysis of the experiment and its significance for understanding articulation and market-making. The narrative of this chapter is developed for the purpose of learning to know and do economy differently, and to explore the un-explored possibilities of Gibson-Graham *et al.*'s diverse economy project. It allows me to see and come to know diverse economies as both emergent yet not neatly bordered or contained. My project is, like that of Gibson-Graham and colleagues (2013), one of taking back, but one in which I engage enactively in is that of taking back an economy in articulation with others, to understand the possibilities of performing hopeful economic futures through re-articulation of the multiple circulations of objects and values that constitute them. This project is situated in Māori economy, and thus in imagining, enacting and reproducing diverse economies in articulation with capitalist economies, but on terms that open opportunities for diverse economy actors to mobilise multiple relationships.

Economic experimentation and diverse economies

Economic experimentation is understood as means to generate new and/or extend existing articulations and circulations between and across economies. My hypothesis in a sense is that there exists a diverse Māori economy in which economic experimentation is a constant. It is deeply Māori, a diverse and moral economy (but marginal), which articulates with other economies. The question of how Māori mobilise economic experimentation to expand diverse Māori economies requires assembling the theoretical trajectories of Michel Callon and J-K Gibson-Graham to understand economy-making.

Drawing on actor network theory, Callon (with Çalişkan) explores the notion of economisation (Callon, 1998, 2007; Çalişkan & Callon, 2009, 2010). They attend to the networks [agencements] of humans and non-humans and the interaction between them that contributes to the construction of economy (Callon, 1998b; Callon et al., 2007). Callon argues, economy is generated through collectives out of sociotechnical experimentation in/with human and non-human relations, and that economy (and markets) is composed of economic experiments, co-constitutively constructed and regulated, by diverse and multiple actors (human and non-human). Performativity is central to the thesis, in particular the performativity of economic knowledge, models and experiments (Callon, 1998, 2007, 2010; Callon et al., 2007; Çalişkan & Callon, 2009, 2010). Along with other economic anthropologists and sociologists (see, for example MacKenzie *et al.*, 2007; Knorr-Cetina & Preda, 2005; Pinch & Swedberg, 2008; Roscoe, 2013), Callon explores how 'the economy' has been fashioned into a privileged institution by economists and given undue autonomy from social worlds. A particular focus of this approach is economic experimentation.

Callon considers experimentation to be an ongoing dimension of economies and markets that are always in the making in an uncertain world (Muniesa & Callon, 2007; Callon, 2007; Çalişkan & Callon, 2009; Berndt & Boeckler, 2009). No single individual, organisation or institution can impose a fully durable or 'perfect' economic or market form/logic. Experimentation takes the place of the plan in economic coordination and design and facilitates economic adjustment and the search for compromises that enlivens economies (Callon, 2009). Callon refers to *in vitro* (in the lab) and *in vivo* (in the wild) experiments. Experiments bring to bear ideas, practices and technologies in relation to extant agencements and imagined entanglements. The efficiency or success of economic experiments such as market design or organisational restructuring depends to a large extent on the socio-technical agencements of which they are made or into which they are translated (Callon, 2007, 2009;Muniesa & Callon, 2007; Callon *et al.*, 2007; Mitchell, 2007, 2008). Whether in the lab or inadvertently in the wild, they put something to the test (i.e. a new law, new product, a new device etc.), generate insights into the reflexive co-ordination of economic activities, and change things. Experimentation affords human agents a privileged reflexive agency in economy-making, and renders markets reflexive institutions.

Economic experiments are mobilised by what Callon calls confined economists and economists in the wild. This differentiation emerged in Callon's later work, which suggests a broadened categorisation of economic agents – beyond just the neoclassical economist (Callon, 2007, 2009). Economists refer to those economic agents confined (i.e. within universities, think tanks, government institutions), who seek to test ideas produced in the lab in the wild in the name of enhancing economic efficiencies (through for example models) and rendering other worlds 'economic' (for example, assigning neoclassical ideas and individual property rights to areas previously open) (see, for example, Mitchell, 2007, 2008; Weszkalnys, 2011; Mukhopadhyay, 2014). Economists in the wild experiment more or less formally shaped by normative prescriptions, practical knowledge of application in the wild, and socio-technical agencements in which they are embedded in multiple and complicated ways. While experiments in the wild are often more spontaneous, any experiment will involve monitoring and reflexivity in the context of uncertain outcomes, whereby the effects, affects and results can be taken into account and evaluated by the experimenters (and its followers/participants). Taking place in scientific or economic socio-technical agencements (and sometimes in econo-scientific agencements), experiments are necessarily collective (Callon, 2007). This raises the possibility of forms of experimentation that bring those working in labs together with those in the wild to 'multiply the possible worlds of a more thorough collective experimentation' (Callon, 2007, p. 352). This points to the political potential of a Callonistic approach, to enact new formations by collective experimentation and thus rethinking what goes inside and what remains outside an experiment, particularly in the realms of valuation and exchange (see, for example Gibson-Graham & Roelvink, 2010; Berndt & Boeckler, 2012; Kama, 2014). Any experiment will involve processes of both framing and overflowing (Callon, 2007).

As a concept, experimentation highlights the 'in-the-making' nature of markets and economies and the hybridity of agencements, as well as theorising a pivotal process in this dynamism. Multiple actors will be involved in any experiment, such that their design, implementation, evaluation and translation will be contested, and their value and success will be understood differently. The making of markets via on-going experimentation is also a matter of trials of strength. These ideas are being tested (for example, Weszkalnys, 2011; Mitchell, 2007, 2008; Mukhopadhyay, 2014; Cockburn, 2014), with economic geographers attending to their spatialities and spatial effects (Ouma, Boeckler & Lindner, 2013; Berndt, 2011b, 2013). These authors reveal the messy, uncertain and contested translation of experiments in local settings, highlighting collisions (articulations and disarticulations) with historical, cultural, and political contexts. Economic experimentation in the wild or in translation from the lab to the wild is never straightforward. Rather, it is troubling and disruptive.

Gibson-Graham and the Community Economies Collective (CEC) deploy what they term a diverse economy framework to focus attention on what might be considered the agencements of on-going economic activity and purposeful economic experiments beyond capitalist economy. Their work has an explicit praxis – to take back the material practices, being and becoming, collectivity, breadth and ethics of economy from economists and the universalism of all manner of models of economisation. This directs me to attend to the values, practices and exchanges of Māori economy that could otherwise largely be considered as externalities or overflows. As learned in my MSc and PhD research, much of what constitutes production and exchange, and the associated values, in Māori economies involves diverse [more-than-economic] economic practices (FitzHerbert, 2009; see also Morris & FitzHerbert, 2016).

As much an ethical as a theoretical project, the diverse-economy project seeks to theorise and enact more-than-capitalist economies, 'by repopulating the economic landscape as a proliferative space of difference' (Gibson-Graham, 2008, p. 615). In its more recent expressions, the project is situated as a performative ontological politics and ethics for creating (and supporting already existing) alternative economies (i.e. non-capitalist) and generating new economic agencies, identities and more-than-human collectives (Gibson-Graham, 2006, 2008; Gibson-Graham & Roelvink 2010; Gibson-Graham, Cameron & Healy, 2013). A number of CEC members draw on Callon's ideas within their diverse economy work (see, for example, Gibson-Graham, 2008; Roelvink, 2009; Miller, 2014; Roelvink, St Martin & Gibson-Graham, 2015), particularly Callon's notion of economic performativity, economisation more-than- capitalist and more-than-human hybrid economic collectives. These, they suggest, enliven researchers to all the relationships that comprise our 'web of economic life' (Gibson-Graham *et al.*, 2013, p. 192).

Here, I draw on diverse economies to rethink, explore and register the unexplored potential of diverse economies in relation to economic experimentation and in articulation with other economies. In the case of Māori economy, the approach directs attention to articulations among diverse Māori economies with state capitalist economies, science economies and industrial capitalist economies and to how they enact new agentic configurations and institutions for economy-making (FitzHerbert, 2016). Bringing diverse economy sensitivities to Callon's approach highlights the possibilities of thinking and doing (making) economy otherwise. Doing so highlights how actors do and objects can and do move across economies, drawing investment, other actors, knowledges and exchange nodes to marginal economies.

An emergent diverse Māori economy literature exists which demonstrates how Māori think and do Māori economy differently (Underhill-Sem & Lewis, 2008; FitzHerbert & Lewis, 2010; Bargh, 2014; FitzHerbert, 2016; Morris & FitzHerbert, 2016; Amoamo *et al.*, 2018). While always struggling more or less successfully with the perils of essentialism, the shared project is to decolonise economy – to free Māori assets and minds from being 'servants' of the Pākehā capitalist economy (Jackson, 2007, p. 172). The diverse Māori economy project seeks to revitalise and find power in stories of alternative Māori doings, encouraging Māori to do economy on their terms, in both Māori and capitalist worlds (see, for example McCormack, 2010; Lambert, 2008, 2012; Bargh, 2011, 2012). As a result, any economy (and market)-making project mobilised in Māori worlds must be sensitive and enactive of diverse Māori economies. Furthermore, for Māori, the doing of economy does not exclude engaging with and mobilising other ways of being economic in efforts to generate better Māori livelihoods – indeed, as shown in the literature, Māori are well apt at recognising and enrolling capitalist ideas and practices for Māori advantage (Lambert, 2008; Bargh, 2014, 2018; Morris & Fitz-Herbert, 2017; O'Sullivan, 2018).

Diverse Māori economy projects reveal more-than-capitalist values and practices in Māori economies. These offer a counter-narrative to dominant economic imaginaries and fracture expert framings, definitions, and categories of economy and notions of what it ought to be. Decolonising economy requires going beyond adding-in Māori non-capitalist activity to capitalist activity to understanding how Māori (and other indigenous) become to do and think their economic activity (and economic development). In this way 'the economy' is challengeable and open to reconfiguration, something already in-the-making in certain Māori enterprises. Furthermore, although Māori may still draw on state investment, they are increasingly mobilising projects that add value to Māori ways of doing and knowing economy in order to negotiate the articulation of Māori economy with capitalist processes and to generate and return surplus to Māori. The case of the market-making project examined in this chapter demonstrates how Māori mobilised an economic experiment (from the outside) to learn new ways of doing economy.

Callon *et al.* and the CEC's approaches are complementary, in the sense that they share the understanding that economies and markets are made and can be made otherwise. As with Callon's notion of circulation, diverse economy-making (and economy) is friable and permeable, and traversed by actors who move between economic worlds and have relations to capitalist and state economies as well as diverse economies. The emergent diverse Māori economies literature brings forward a politics less disparaging toward engaging with capitalism, so long as its mobilised by Māori on their own terms. These actors do not stop being in one economy as they move and situate the what of their encounters into objects for diverse economy-making in and for Māori cultural political economies (i.e. state investment). This opens both Callon's and CEC's projects up to a concern with how marginal actors can frame and set the boundaries of economy and translate things from elsewhere for Māori economies. There lies in these articulations a fundamental acceptance of relationality and the productive potential of articulations among different economies for supporting and enacting more resilient diverse Māori economies. In particular, framing becomes an act of inclusion rather than exclusion, whereby for enacting diverse Māori economies, articulation is seen as a necessary node which injects resources into them.

The market-making project: Māra Kai an overview

For the purposes of this chapter, the market-making project is given the anonymised name Māra Kai. Information on Māra Kai was gathered between 2010 and 2015 using an ethnographic approach in which the research followed and participated in the activities of Māra Kai. This was supplemented with ongoing expert dialogues with Māra Kai's developers and participants as well as analysis of Māra Kai's commercial documents. Māra Kai was an economic experiment that sought to establish an internet-based market for Māori vegetable producers. It brought together 100 Māori horticulturalists as a collective, constructed a Māra Kai brand, and took Māori vegetables and their growers to the market via the internet. Its supporters, the host Iwi's asset holding company (AHC) and state agencies Te Puni Kōkiri (TPK) and the Māori Economic Taskforce (MET)[3] envisaged Māra Kai as a market-making experiment to bring diverse Māori economies into the orbit of the Taniwha economy. AHC manages iwi (tribal) assets and its corporate activities but retains commitments to fostering multiple small-scale initiatives in the production of vegetables for subsistence and cultural as well as commercial purposes. Māra Kai mixes commitments in this regard to new Taniwha economy imaginaries (commercialisation, entrepreneurialism, innovation, branding, technoscientific innovation, and exporting). It involves AHC, the state, commercialisation, branding web design experts, professional management consultancies, Tāhuri Whenua (a non-profit national Māori horticultural organisation), market devices, growers, and Māori vegetables.

Māra Kai in proposal: a genealogy of diverse economic aspirations, imaginaries, actor relationalities, and experts.

Māra Kai's chief organiser was inspired by an 'Aunty', a female Māori elder who grew Māori vegetables, utilising Māori practices and Māori knowledge on Māori land. On the whole, Māra Kai was largely inspired by small-scale Māori horticulturalists who either produced food for market exchange and/or traditional exchanges (i.e. gifting food, feeding family, and feeding ceremonial centres) and those Māori with an interest in 'returning to their land' to try something. AHC wanted to develop a platform to assist Māori horticulturalists to enter the market. With the support of a public relations consultant (a proclaimed expert at telling stories for the development of brands), the organiser took the Māra Kai proposition to AHC for initial support and investment, and, then the state-funded MET and TPK, who were mobilising a set of economic experiments at the national scale, who would provide additional expertise and investment. The organiser had considerable experience in corporate Māori affairs and was well versed in negotiating relations between key Māori leaders and Māori development agencies. The 'Aunty', herself was well embedded in diverse Māori economies through her role in grassroots Māori vegetable organisations (i.e. Tāhuri Whenua and Te Waka Kai Ora). Together, the organiser, consultant, and Aunty brought into a stable relation Māori economic development, place-based brand-making and marketing, and Māori horticulturalists and organisations. The organiser mobilised her relationships to the AHC, the MET and TPK to create lines of investment, which situated Māra Kai in relation to Māori-state economic projects.

Aligning Māra Kai to AHC, the MET and TPK required the project to be assembled by AHC in line with Taniwha economy aspirations and be given shape by the MET and TPK and underlying economic experts (i.e. BERL and Price-WaterhouseCoopers, PwC). AHC supported Māra Kai as it envisaged it as a commercial project to create additional value for the Iwi's existing businesses. They provided offices and investment. The organiser then connected the Māra Kai proposition to MET and TPK's Māori development initiatives, commercialisation imperatives and associated expertise and the awakening of the Taniwha Economy. Connecting Māra Kai to these projects (i.e. branding, small-scale collectives, and digital technology), established various channels of investment (advice, money and expertise). The MET greeted the Māra Kai idea with enthusiasm, saying 'put something together that's to do with branding and we'll invest'. The proposal was subsequently worked at through a number of meetings with the MET. It was jointly funded by TPK (MET) and AHC. As a condition of TPK investment, MET would mentor Māra Kai in Māori enrolment and commercialisation strategies. Additionally, AHC and the MET required Māra Kai to be assessed by a professional consultancy service (PwC) in regard to its commercial feasibility. PwC stated that it saw value in the Māra Kai proposition and claimed it 'was an exciting opportunity for Māoridom'. This endorsement legitimised AHC and TPK investment.

In summary, the assemblage of Māra Kai from multiple trajectories meant there were different levels of aspirations, expertise and different economic imaginaries at play. Māra Kai came from different places – different somewheres that could (and would) become mobilised 'elsewhere'. The 'elsewheres' were reasonably known to certain actors and this was reflected in many of the project aspirations, but preparation for market remained an economic imaginary with significant traction. These competing imaginaries presented capitalist market economy and diverse Māori economies as seamless.

Constructing Māra Kai: infrastructure, devices, practices and growers

Māra Kai received Iwi and TPK investment in 2010 for a six-month pilot project. According to the pilot proposal document, it would establish Māra Kai, its brand, website and networks. The pilot would determine the viability and any ongoing investment and development. The organiser set about developing the necessary infrastructure (brand and website) and situating Māra Kai in diverse Māori economies. Māra Kai was registered with the New Zealand Companies Office under the New Zealand Companies Act 1993 and had three company directors, all with backgrounds in Māori commercial interests. AHC was the sole shareholder. The following paragraphs outline Māra Kai as a strategic experiment across four key dimensions: the development of the website; the enrolment of Māori personnel; the development of brand expectations and standards; and the enrolment of Māori horticulturalists.

First, the internet was the proposed device to take Māra Kai and Māori to the market. AHC contracted an external web development company to develop the virtual market platform. This virtual platform was considered to provide profile and a relatively low-cost option for Māori participation; provided they had computer, internet access and computer skills. The platform enabled Māori producers to tell their own story, promote their products, contact other producers, while providing consumers a place to locate producers and products. The website acted as an online directory of Māori producers. Second, staff were employed to enrol Māori and support the virtual market-place. The positions were filled by Māori, who eagerly set to work building the profile and credibility of Māra Kai across Aotearoa New Zealand. Third, in order to perform a brand, Māra Kai instituted expectations and standards (of growers and products). Māra Kai was gifted the Māori concept Te

Table 2.1 Connecting demand with Māra Kai producers.

		Current purchase requests			
Date	*Purchase request*	*Date required*	*Purchaser*	*Location*	*Completed*
Jan. 2011	10 tonne Māori potatoes	1 June 2011 (Matariki)	Marae	Waikato	X
Feb. 2011	80kg Watercress	Weekly	Restaurant	Napier	X
Feb. 2011	Avocado	11 May 2011	Organic retail store	Gisborne	X
March 2011	50kg Pikopiko	ASAP	Restaurant	Queens-town	
April 2011	100kg Organic Passionfruit	April 2011	Restaurant	Well-ington	X
April 2011	50kg Kokihi	ASAP	School	Takitimu	
April 2011	80kg Organic Basil	Weekly	Food manu-facturer	Auckland	X
April 2011	1 tonne Organic Apples	ASAP	Juice company	Well-ington	
April 2011	200kg Walnuts	ASAP	Food manu-facturer	Auckland	
April 2011	6 Pigs (Hangi)	1 Jan 2012	Marae	New Plymouth	
May 2011	150kg Kumara	30 March 2012	Marae	Masterton	
May 2011	300kg Māori potatoes	10 Dec 2011	Fish and Chip Store	Tauranga	X
May 2011	300kg Pumpkin	30 March 2012	Individual	Taupo	
July 2011	200kg Kaanga Ma	17 March 2012	Restaurant	Auckland	

Wheke and utilised this as both an overarching principle for Māra Kai and for producers to declare themselves according to Te Wheke. The Te Wheke approach, was envisaged, as a means to situate Māra Kai in Māori worlds as well as a practical metric for Māori and non-Māori to understand the brand, according to story-telling and traceability. Māra Kai was positioned as a premium brand. Lastly, albeit worked at from the conception of Māra Kai, the organisers had to enrol Māori producers. They drew on their relationships with Māori organisations, to present Māra Kai to Māori in Māori spaces (i.e. the marae). These spaces gave Māra Kai access to Māori and situated itself within diverse Māori economies. Māra Kai utilised these spaces to propose how it connected to existing Māori initiatives and was a market-making experiment for all Māori.

Māra Kai spent considerable time producing a relationality between object (Māra Kai) and the wild (diverse Māori economies). This involved a number of situating practices (i.e. Te Wheke and marae-based encounters). Creating Māra Kai involved injecting some familiar and unfamiliar objects into diverse Māori economies. Māra Kai was largely prefaced on the website with supporting infra-structure (i.e. internet, computers, social media). Marae encounters provided a site to embed the experiment within diverse Māori economies – these moments sparked considerable interest among Māori and gave Māra Kai purchase within these worlds. Producers liked Māra Kai as it was 'owned by Māori', which gen-erated an element of trust, it was something new and exciting, yet while many were enthusiastic, translating this into becoming an active Māra Kai member proved difficult. Producers who became a member largely included those who already had some existing circuits of exchange: Māra Kai provided them with an additional circuit of exchange. From this perspective producers also imagined this as an experiment for their own exchange practices and investigated how it could enact new exchange pathways.

Māra Kai goes live: happenings and movements

Māra Kai's virtual market-place went live in May 2011. The launch took place on a marae which was the quasi-home for Māra Kai: the organiser and lead producer had direct connection to this marae. At this point, some 100 producers had been recruited. This section focuses particularly on the devices, producers, movements and rumblings generated as the virtual market place went live. In its simplest, yet arguably most powerful, form, as a device the Māra Kai website assembled toge-ther Māori horticulturalists and their products from across Aotearoa New Zeal-and – it made visible diverse Māori economies. Māori and non-Māori consumers could access information and products from Māori producers (who had been lar-gely invisible previously, in terms of accessibility to those not already in the know). Furthermore, Māori growers could use the site to locate other Māori engaged in horticulture to share advice and support each other. The next paragraphs briefly outline some of the happenings generated by the website.

Upon clicking on 'Producer' it was possible to read about each producer and their Te Wheke declaration, see where they were located, view what products they had available, and make contact directly. The device acted to build attachments between producers and producers, producers and Māori, and pro-ducers and consumers. The website acted as a device for articulation, revealing diverse Māori economies, and building circulations within and between diverse Māori economies and to state capitalist economies by being revealed to other circulations.

The website enacted the movement of Māori products. Similarly, producers reported being contacted by numerous people (previously unknown) who sought their products. The website instituted other devices to facilitate the circulation and exchange of producer's products. One means, was the implementation of a Current Purchase Requests table, in which consumers would contact Māra Kai and lodge their order on the Current Purchase Requests table (Table 2.1) on the website. Table 2.1 illustrates the sorts of products (i.e. traditional Māori vegetables, organic produce and animals) consumers sought and who the purchasers were themselves (individuals, Māori groups, food manufacturers, restaurants) and their location in Aotearoa. Exchanges ranged from one-off purchases to weekly supply arrangements. Produce was requested as available or in advance of the growing season. It reveals that Māra Kai was utilised by both Māori and non-Māori purchasers. Māra Kai staff also directly connected producers if they knew they could immediately fulfil a consumer request.

Māra Kai was in effect a disruption to diverse Māori economies – it constituted new lines of expansion. It stimulated new interest, injected new things, and built new relationships. Going live in the wild helped Māra Kai nudge the Taniwha Economy, and one that was in terms set by its moral economy foundational propositions. The website became an enactive device, revealing diverse Māori economies, and fostering relationships between Māori producers and took Māori producers and their products elsewhere. It assembled and revealed a diverse Māori economy and generated new attachments between Māori producers and consumers. This opened up new lines of expansion from diverse Māori economies into capitalist economies, on terms set largely by, and in terms narrated by, Māori producers. The internet demonstrated new possibilities for circulation and articulation (some overtly capitalist, some provenanced moral economy) – it revealed the elsewhere (i.e. marginal, disparate and remote diverse Māori economies) somewhere (on www.Māra Kai.co.nz). It expanded in a rush into Aotearoa New Zealand's first and largest collective of Māori horticulturalists. They and their products became locatable. It built new connections and pathways along which Māori products might circulate, all within a few clicks on a platform crafted by Māori and co-performative of Māra Kai producers' identities. In this reading Māra Kai was a success, but a deeper set of stories reveal a set of dead ends, obstructions and contradictions among economic imaginaries that became increasingly difficult to silence.

Māra Kai fails: post-failure reflections

At the end of the pilot project the AHC deemed Māra Kai a commercial failure and investment discontinued. The Māra Kai organiser has spent considerable time reflecting upon their experience in terms of what happened, what caused its demise, and what could still become. Lending weight to the notion of Māra Kai being an economic experiment, the organiser (as with others) has produced knowledge about what generated and/or challenged success, and taken these to reconstitute economy (and market)-making going forward. Here I outline these dimensions and illustrates how the experiment was mobilised by multiple (conflicting) interests.

To begin, the organiser discussed how the experiment had been too top-down, being imposed by both the AHC, the MET and the State. The necessary relation to state and iwi projects effectively constructed imaginaries of how Māra Kai would operate and framed what success meant. This assumed that Māori were ready, willing and able to take on new technologies and capitalist practices of exchange. It assumed the idea of a single brand would be unproblematic in assembling Māori together. The brand and the use of technology was presumed to become effective immediately and in turn generate instant commerciality and profitability. Indeed, the pressure to be immediately commercial set the experiment on course for failure. The organiser noted that these top down economic imaginaries and categories did not map onto the diverse Māori economies in which they sought to support, and, that Māori felt weary of projects from elsewhere (especially the state).

Rather than a smooth translation of 'rational economic ideas/imperatives' from project design to real-world practice, these clashed with Māori producers. In terms of Māra Kai's ownership (an AHC), producers had limited investment and stakes (i.e. Māra Kai was free for them to join) in contributing to Māra Kai's success. Had Māra Kai been 'owned' by producers, they might have been more invested in trying to keep it going. Aside from these, the organiser suggested the promised support from the mentoring group (and MET) was patchy, often critical and not always helpful or productive. The organiser speculated that some members had less interest in seeing Māra Kai succeed and more interest in learning from its failures, in order to develop their own market-making experiments. In terms of the producer participants, although interest was high, uptake was slow and participation was limited; approximately 5 per cent of producers regularly utilised the website. Furthermore, many producers only wanted to observe what Māra Kai would make happen: *Māra Kai was only ever a secondary project for them, they concentrated on their immediate exchange projects.* In addition, for many producers located in remote regions, they either had no access to a computer and/or the internet. This was further complicated by the lack of distribution options for fresh produce. To complicate matters, the Māra Kai had no control or input into the creation of the Māra Kai web infrastructure. They were dependent on the web development company, which at best provided partial help and cost money. As funding dried up, this presented a significant challenge, they neither understood the website or how to change/correct errors and for general site maintenance (at one point the web-link took visitors to a porn site). The organiser reflected it would have been preferable had they developed a website themselves, even if it had been 'less flash', at least they would have developed the skills to be independent.

The organiser's reflections demonstrate the difficulties in generating a relationship between Māra Kai and diverse Māori economies. Given that Māra Kai had come from elsewhere (i.e. an AHC and the state) the economic imaginaries and expectations of 'being economic' did not seamlessly fit into diverse Māori worlds. Likewise, the material infrastructure and its integration proved problematic. Producers did not use or have access to technology and distribution logistics were not available. Plus, the website was malfunction prone. And because there were numerous individual projects going on with Māra Kai, a shared sense of Māra Kai as a collective experiment was only partial. The fact that Māra Kai has 'failed' attests the challenges but does not mean the economic experiment was a failure or that its energies have dissipated. Rather, it has taken new lines of expansion. A new Māori market-making project has emerged from a Māori Trust and the MET that takes up many of the ideas of Māra Kai, which was seen all along as valuable by PwC. As the organiser speculated, MET and this Māori Trust saw in Māra Kai their own (less risky) experiment to pilot a web-based Māori marketing initiative. This new project has addressed some of the tensions in Māra Kai: it employs a looser form of Māori branding and only includes enterprises that are sufficiently commercial and have established value-added products (e.g. Manuka honey, beer, wine, mussels). It seeks to maximise the potential of already commercial Māori enterprises (especially China's export markets), but does not provide a platform for participants in more marginal Māori economies (i.e. small-scale Māori producers growing taewa and kumara). This will help it to meet more commercialised performance targets but does not perform the role of cultivating Māori enterprises from the ground up or from pre-enterprise form and thus encouraging marginalised producers to utilise resources to grow a few or plenty of Māori vegetables.

Māra Kai: a failed economic experiment?

Although seen as a failure by the state and capitalist iwi actors, the Māra Kai organiser and numerous participant producers suggest the experiment cultivated new learnings, circulations of exchange, nodes of articulation and opportunities for Māori to perform, make visible and narrate their economy differently. They, and those looking on, learned that the articulation of diverse Māori economies with other economic processes is far from seamless, and furthermore, the challenge of reconciling the heterogeneity of diverse Māori economies is not straightforward. Rather, translation of ideas, objects and actors is fraught with difficulties, which become performative in some expected and unexpected ways. In what follows, I will develop a counter-narrative to that of failure. This presents Māra Kai as an experiment which fostered a diverse Māori economy by learning and doing economy in new ways, bringing together diverse Māori economy actors, and making diverse Māori economies visible to Māori and others. In doing so, it created lines for diverse economy expansion.

Māra Kai faced significant challenges in articulating diverse, state and capitalist economy. These challenges echo other author's accounts of failed attempts to fit the world into particular economic imaginaries in the face of the lived practices and values of peoples who live different economic realities and cannot or will not be *homo economicus* and reduce their lives to 'unlocking' their 'economic potential' (e.g. Mitchell, 2007; Ouma et al., 2013; Radcliffe, 2019). The state and economists failed to understand the situatedness of diverse Māori economic actors and spaces where they sought to roll-out market-making projects. The 'inside' and 'outside' (of) and 'economy' were framed within narrow economic imaginaries and projected onto worlds in order to recreate them. For Māra Kai, the state and economists considered exchange to be 'market exchange' and growers to be 'capitalist entrepreneurs', whereas use of land, growing food and exchange of food had different meanings and values for Māra Kai participants. The experiment demonstrated a tension between projected worlds (from somewhere – the outside) and cultural economic worlds (the here – the inside), and assumed articulation with the outside would happen smoothly. Māra Kai drew on certain practices and relations that were projected onto them from the outside, and then sought to reconcile differences and construct new opportunities for circulation. Producers and the AHC sought to balance Māori diverse economies and capitalist economies rather than seeing a particular world traded-off. This enacted multiple outcomes: a success for producers, as they could continue their practices and learn some new ones; but a failure for the state and AHC, as the experiment did not lead to commercialisation.

The situated experience of Māra Kai and the tensions between outside and inside practices that undermined the experiment is made particularly visible by the counterfactual of the new Māori market-making experiment. Supported by the MET, under many of the same principles 'to create market opportunities for Māori', this new project is championed as 'successful'. However, the inside-outside relations are different, and the articulation of Māori and capitalist economies is premised on different kaupapa (purpose); those that involve capitalist economy-making by Māori rather than Māori economy-making. Participants within the new experiment were already established profit-generating enterprises with ambitions to upscale their business and trade with international markets (i.e. China). The experiment fitted Māori economy into predetermined projects, with pre-prescribed values and ideas. Viewed as a successful experiment in economisa-tion, this new project is economy-making and has created effects and affects of economisation. It has enclosed, narrated and fostered extant projects of *tangata-economicus 2.0* [4] – projects that fitted its established mandate (Māori brand, value-added goods, ready for export). This is not to diminish the value of this new project's achievements, but to recognise that accounts of its success are rendered in the terms of a mandate that is and ought to be seen as different to the kaupapa of Māra Kai. For Māra Kai, success or otherwise looks different.

Rendering accounts of Māra Kai must attend to notions of affect and recognise predetermination of notions of success or failure in the performativity of eco-nomics as a language and practice. Indeed, it is important to recognise not only that the effects cited as success might not have been generated by the experiment or even prove positive in the longer term. While, I have sought assiduously to avoid making outsider comments on affect or drawing judgements in that regard, the comparison of Māra Kai with the new project points to the importance of keeping open the possibility of multiple other experiments that could shift worlds and make economies that do not fit conventional accounting. That is, the new experiment has been, as Mitchell (2008) observes of De Soto's experiment in assigning property rights to Peruvian slum dwellers, one of fashioning an economy that fits into established economic models and produces the empirical fact of its creation as an applied experiment as a demonstration of its success. Māra Kai was a more open and wild experiment with possibilities, and one that has at the very least remained open, fostered other experiments, kept possibilities alive, generated positive affect, and created lines of expansion (articulation) for diverse Māori economies.

As Callon (2007) recognises, economic experiments are performed by collectives that vary in size, nature and scope, including (maybe) professional researchers or experts and experts in the wild. The experts in the Māra Kai experiment included market practitioners and state agencies. The experts in the wild included stakeholders (iwi and iwi asset companies), supporting organisations (Tāhuri Whenua, Te Waka Kai Ora), and the Māori producers. Each had their own expertise, some shared, but mostly divergent when related to Māra Kai. The experts also had differing 'market' and 'market-making' imaginaries, perspectives on the values of commercialisation, views of cyber-technological potential, and how producers would perform as economic beings. The producers' subjectivities assumed by experts (technologically able, profit-motivated, market-ready entrepreneurs with market-ready and available products) clashed with those understood by experts in the wild (Māori experts of Māori cultural economies). Producers themselves proved to be a mixed group, as did their products, and their access to the internet. Some had become a Māra Kai participant to support the initiative but did not participate beyond signing up; while others sat back to see what happened. Who the experts were and where the experiment came from mattered: many of the participants saw experts and the experiment as belonging to a certain iwi (not theirs), shaping who participated and how they participated. Indeed, Māra Kai was seen by many people as an experiment to take part and see what happens to learn about 'the market', see what other Māori are up to and to use it as a means to connect with other Māori (not 'the market'). Māra Kai as an economic experiment was not just about marketisation.

Māra Kai demonstrates that collective economic experimentation is difficult. Constituting the collective from the different trajectories of object, subject, meaning and the target of expectations and aspirations must be worked at. Taking any experiment to the wild performs uncertainty, rearrangement, overflows, messiness and brings them into a risky political light. Some producers used the experiment to practice and demonstrate their support for a Māori project, others wanted to build connections with other Māori, and others saw it as a commercial endeavour. Translation of meanings, values and investment from diverse to capitalist economies is problematic. Not only does it require translators; in this instance, entrepreneurial agents of both economies, but complex exchanges of financial and cultural capital.

Conclusion

Experimentation unsettles diverse Māori economies opening-up possible interventions to learn and do economy in new ways, build new relationships and generate new lines of expansion. This chapter has brought together Callon and J-K Gibson-Graham to explore the unexplored potential of economic experimentation and the possibilities of articulation for (indigenous) diverse economies. The case demonstrates that actors seeking to articulate diverse economies learn the challenges and opportunities of how they might negotiate as they participate in experiments. By enacting an articulation across diverse and capitalist economies, economic experiments have the potential to reveal and cultivate productive tensions that generate new knowing and doing of diverse economies (i.e. trying things, rejecting things, working cultural values and practices and bumping together and negotiating capitalist processes). Economic experiments need to be read across cultural and economic categories in order to open-up value and success to mean different things and produce new aspirations in relation to them – economic experiments are not just the domain of those whom seek to reproduce capitalism.

The account of Māra Kai as an economic experiment in economy-making and the potentiality that resides within it are very much products of the articulation between and across economies that is largely left out of both the economisation and diverse economy literatures. Māra Kai demonstrates the articulation between diverse, capitalist and state economies as actors move between them and objects circulate around them. Practices (such as state policymaking) bind them together, while meanings, qualities and subjects become co-constituted across their border. The case of Māori economy-making as told through this chapter confirms that diverse economies do not exist within neatly bordered separate spaces. Taking back and enacting different economic futures needs to think about processes of articulation and the multiple circulations of objects and values that constitute them, as well as imagining, enacting and reproducing economies outside of capitalism, and encourage their expansion. In fact, thinking Māori economy (re)politicises Gibson-Graham *et al.*'s post-capitalist project and suggests a broader set of possibilities and a richer potentiality than that imagined in the diverse economy literature. At the same time, it de-privileges the capitalocentric nature of Callonistic ideas of economisation as a process restricted to capitalist economy and markets. Thinking and doing diverse Māori economies leads to more-than-markets and to 'more-than-market' imaginaries of what can be economic.

Notes

1 Taniwha are spiritual beings. Many are kaitiaki/guardians and are a conduit to te ao wairua/the spiritual world – so are tohu/messengers. They often manifest to remind Māori to be cautious when venturing into new or risky spaces. Taniwha forms and characteristics vary according to different Māori groups. In much of the Pākehā/non-Māori literature, Taniwha are incorrectly defined as mystical beings associated with analogies like unknown and emerging from the primodial dark depths. Such words as mystical do not make sense from a Māori perspective – Taniwha are known, they only appear under certain circumstances and they are certainly not mystical. Such non-Māori conceptualisations undermine their importance to Māori culture. Furthermore, such word choice plays into the whole privileging of non-Māori/Western knowledge and ways of knowing in which Māori notions are framed as fantastical not fact, thereby the significance of these beings are often ignored. Additionally, the term 'Taniwha economy' as framed by the Minister and Crown is contested among Māori.
2 See Petrie (2006) for an historical account of the dominance of 18th- and 19th-century Māori economies. Māori have always been major players in resource-based economies.
3 The Māori Economic Taskforce was established by the New Zealand Government as a prominent national economic development agency to facilitate Māori economic development in the 'after' neoliberal terms of steerage, guidance and market promotion (Larner & Craig, 2005).

4 People are not born psychologically endowed like the *homo economicus* of neoclassical economics (i.e. endowed with values and skills to operate (capitalise). Rather, even if 'she/he' is a desired subject, 'for markets to exist, homo economicus has to be created, formatted, framed and equipped with prosthesis which help her/him in her/his calculations and which are, for the most part, produced by economics' (Callon 1998: 51).

References

Amoamo, M., Ruwhiu, D. & Carter L. (2018). Framing the Māori economy: The complex business of Māori business. *MAI Journal*, 7(1), 66–78.

Bargh, M. (2011). The triumph of Māori entrepreneurs or diverse economies? *Aboriginal Policy Studies*, 1(3), 53–69.

Bargh, M. (2012). Rethinking and re-shaping indigenous economies: Māori geothermal enterprises. *Journal of Enterprising Communities: People and Places in the Global Economy*, 6(3), 271–283.

Bargh, M. (2014). A blue economy for Aotearoa New Zealand? *Environment, Development and Sustainability*, 16(3), 459–470.

Bargh, M. (2018). Māori political and economic recognition in a diverse economy. In D. Howard-Wagner, M. Bargh & I. Altamirano-Jiménez (Eds.). *The Neoliberal State, recognition and indigenous rights: New paternalism to new imaginings* (pp. 293–308). Canberra, ACT: ANU Press.

Bargh, M., Douglas, S.-L. & Te One, A. (2014). Fostering sustainable tribal economies in a time of climate change. *New Zealand Geographer*, 70(2), 103–115.

Bargh, M. & Otter, J. (2009). Progressive spaces of neoliberalism in Aotearoa: a genealogy and critique. *Asia Pacific Viewpoint*, 50(2), 154–165.

Barr, T. & Reid. J. (2014). Centralized decentralization for tribal business development. *Journal of Enterprising Communities: People and Places in the Global Economy*, 8(3), 217–232.

Berndt, C. (2013). Assembling market b/orders: Violence, dispossession, and economic development in Ciudad Juárez, Mexico. *Environment and Planning A*, 43(11), 2646–2662.

Berndt, C. & Boeckler, M. (2009). Geographies of circulation and exchange: Constructions of markets. *Progress in Human Geography*, 33(4), 535–551.

Berndt, C. & Boeckler, M. (2011b). Performative regional (dis)integration: Transnational markets, mobile commodities, and bordered North – South differences. *Environment and Planning A*, 43(5), 1057–1078.

Berndt, C. & Boeckler, M. (2012). Geographies of marketization. In T. Barnes, J. Peck & E. Sheppard (Eds.). *The Wiley-Blackwell companion to economic geography* (pp. 199–212). Oxford, UK: Wiley-Blackwell.

Cǎlişkan, K. & Callon, M. (2009). Economisation, part 1: Shifting attention from the economy towards processes of economisation. *Economy and Society*, 38(3), 369–398.

Cǎlişkan, K. & Callon, M. (2010). Economisation, part 2: A research programme for the study of markets. *Economy and Society*, 39(1), 1–32.

Callon, M. (1998). *Introduction: The embeddedness of economic markets in economics. In M. Callon (Ed.) The laws of markets* (pp. 1–57). London: Blackwell.

Callon, M. (2007). What does it mean to say that economics is performative? In D. MacKenzie, F. Muniesa & L. Siu (Eds.), *Do economists make markets: On the performativity of Economics* (pp. 311–357). Princeton, NJ: Princeton University Press.

Callon, M. (2009). Civilizing markets: Carbon trading between *in vitro* and *in vivo* experiments. *Accounting, Organizations and Society*, 34(3–4),535–549.

Callon, M. (2010). Performativity, misfires and politics. *Journal of Cultural Economy* 3 (2): 163–169.

Callon, M., Millo, Y. & Muniesa, F. (2007). *Market Devices.* Malden: Blackwell Publishing.

Cockburn, P. (2014). Street papers, work and begging: 'experimenting' at the margins of economic legitimacy. *Journal of Cultural Economy,* 7(2): 145–160.

Durie, M. (2003). *Ngā Kāhui Pou: Launching Māori futures.* Wellington: Huia Publishers.

FitzHerbert, S. (2009). *Following the Peruperu: Geographies of Circulation and Exchange.* [Unpublished master thesis], University of Auckland.

FitzHerbert, S. (2016). *Geographies of economy-making: The articulation and circulation of taewa Māori across Aotearoa New Zealand.* [Unpublished doctoral dissertation], University of Auckland.

FitzHerbert, S. & Lewis, N. (2010). He Iwi Kotahi Tatou Trust: Post-development practices in Moerewa, Northland. *New Zealand Geographer,* 66(2), 138–151.

Gibson-Graham, J.-K. (2006). *A Postcapitalist Politics.* Minneapolis, MI: University of Minnesota Press.

Gibson-Graham, J.-K. (2008). Diverse economies: Performative practices for 'other worlds'. *Progress in Human Geography,* 32(5), 613–632.

Gibson-Graham, J.-K., Cameron J & Healy, S. (2013). *Take back the economy: An ethical guide for transforming our communities.* Minneapolis, MI: University of Minnesota Press.

Gibson-Graham, J.-K. & Roelvink, G. (2010). An economic ethics for the Anthropocene. *Antipode,* 41(s1), 320–346.

Jackson, M. (2007). Globalisation and the colonising state of mind. In M. Bargh (ed.) *Resistance: An Indigenous Response to Neoliberalism* (pp. 167–182). Wellington: Huia Publishers.

Kama, K. (2014). On the borders of the market: EU emissions, trading, energy security, and the technopolitics of 'carbon leakage'. *Geoforum,* 51, 201–212.

Knorr-Cetina, K. & Preda, A. (2005). *The Sociology of financial markets.* Oxford: Oxford University Press.

Lambert, S. (2008). *The expansion of sustainability through new economic space: Māori potatoes and cultural resilience.* [Unpublished doctoral thesis], Lincoln University.

Lambert, S. (2012). Innovation, Māori and the Māori Economy: A flat or lumpy world. International Indigenous Development Research Conference (pp. 248–255), Auckland (27 June-30 June 2012).

Larner, W. & Craig, D. (2005). After neoliberalism? Community activism and local partnerships in Aotearoa New Zealand. *Antipode,* 37(3), 402–424.

MacKenzie, D., Muniesa, F. & Siu, L. (Eds.). (2007). *Do economists make markets? On the performativity of economics.* Princeton, NJ: Princeton University Press.

Massey, D. (2005). *For space.* London: Sage Publications.

McCormack, F. (2010). Fish is my daily bread: Owning and transacting in Māori fisheries. *Anthropological Forum: A Journal of Social Anthropology and Comparative Sociology,* 20(1), 19–39.

McFarlane. T. (2007). *The contribution of Taewa (Māori Potato) production to Māori sustainable development.* [Unpublished masters dissertation],Lincoln University.

Miller, E. (2014). Economization and beyond: (Re)composing livelihoods in Maine, USA. *Environment and Planning A,* 46(11), 2735–2751.

Ministry of Māori Affairs (2012). *Science,* Innovation and Technology to power the Taniwha Economy. Retrieved 16 June 2012, from: www.beehive.govt.nz/release/science-innovation-and-technology-power-taniwha-economy.

48   *Stephen FitzHerbert*

Mitchell, T. (2007). The properties of markets. In D. MacKenzie, F. Muniesa & L. Siu (Eds.), *Do economists make markets? On the performativity of economics* (pp. 244–275). Princeton, NJ: Princeton University Press.

Mitchell, T. (2008). Rethinking economy. *Geoforum*, 39(3), 1116–1121.

Morris, C. & FitzHerbert, S. (2017). Rethinking 'alternative': Māori and food sovereignty in Aotearoa New Zealand. In M. Wilson (Ed.), *Postcolonialism, indigeneity and struggles for food sovereignty: Alternative food networks in the Subaltern world* (pp. 15–33). London: Routledge.

Mukhopadhyay, B. (2014). Taking Callon to Calcutta: Did economist-administrators make market in the colony. *Economy and Society*, 43(2), 183–210.

Muniesa, F. & Callon, M. (2007). Economic experiments and the construction of markets. In D. MacKenzie, F. Muniesa & L. Siu (Eds.), *Do economists make markets? On the performativity of economics* (pp. 163–189). Princeton, NJ: Princeton University Press.

Nana, G., Khan, M. & Schulze, H. (2015). *Te Ōhanga Māori 2013: Māori Economy Report 2013*. Wellington: Te Puni Kōkiri (Ministry of Māori Development).

O'Sullivan, D. (2018). Māori, the state and self-determination in the neoliberal age. In D. Howard-Wagner, M. Bargh, I. Altamirano Jiménez (Eds.), *The Neoliberal State, recognition and indigenous rights: New paternalism to new imaginings* (pp. 241–256). Canberra, ACT: ANU Press.

Ouma, S., Boeckler, M. & Lindner, P. (2013). Extending the margins of marketization: Frontier regions and the making of agro-export markets in northern Ghana. *Geoforum*, 48, 225–235.

Pinch, T. & Swedberg, R. (Eds.). (2008). *Living in a material world: Economic sociology meets science and technology studies*. Cambridge, MA: MIT Press.

Radcliffe, S. (2019). Geography and indigeneity III: Co-articulation of colonialism and capitalism in indigeneity's economies. *Progress in Human Geography* (in press), https://doi.org/10.1177/0309132519827387.

Rata, E. (2011). Encircling the commons: Neotribal capitalism in New Zealand since 2000. *Anthropological Theory*, 11(3), 327–353.

Reid, J. & Rout, M. (2016). Getting to know your food: The insight of indigenous thinking in food provenance. *Agriculture and Human Values*, 33(2), 427–438.

Roelvink, G. (2009). Broadening horizons of economy. *Journal of Cultural Economy*, 2(3), 315–334.

Roelvink, G., St Martin, K., Gibson-Graham, J.-K. (Eds.). (2015). *Making other worlds possible: Performing diverse economies*. Minneapolis, MN: University of Minnesota Press.

Roscoe, P. (2013). On the possibility of organ markets and the performativity of economics. *Journal of Cultural Economy*, 6(4), 386–401.

Roskruge, N. (2004, July 8–9). He kai kei aku ringaringa. In *Proceedings of the Te Ohu Whenua Hui a Tau* (pp. 67–69). Palmerston North: Massey University.

Smith, G., Tinirau, R., Gillies, A. & Warriner, V. (2015). *He Mangōpare Amohia: Strategies for Māori economic development*. Whakatane: Te Whare Wananga o Awanuiarangi.

Stein, K., Mirosa, M. & Carter, L. (2018). Māori women leading local sustainable food systems. *AlterNative: An International Journal of Indigenous Peoples*, 14(2), 147–155.

Underhill-Sem, Y. & Lewis, N. (2008). Asset-mapping and whānau action research: 'New' subjects negotiating the politics of knowledge in Te Rarawa. *Asia Pacific Viewpoint*, 49(3), 305–317.

Weszkalnys, G. (2011). Cursed resources, or articulations of economic theory in the Gulf of Guinea. *Economy and Society*, 40(3), 345–372.

3 Making markets for collective concerns

Childcare in a bicultural context

Aisling Gallagher

SCHOOL OF PEOPLE, ENVIRONMENT AND PLANNING, MASSEY UNIVERSITY

Introduction

On the 25 July 2011 some 1,200 kōhanga reo (a Māori cultural and language immersion service for young children) supporters took part in a hīkoi (a march) through the streets of Wellington, New Zealand's capital (see Figure 3.1). Their intention was to deliver a claim under urgency to the Waitangi Tribunal, a standing commission of inquiry which makes recommendations on claims taken by indigenous Māori against the British Crown in relation to potential breaches of the founding document, the Treaty of Waitangi. A claim was made that the Crown had undermined the work of kōhanga reo, by attempting to bring them in line with a new education framework as part of the creation of a market for early childhood education (ECE). It was claimed that by holding kōhanga reo accountable to the new ECE legislation and standards of provision, the Crown 'had failed to understand the purpose and nature of kōhanga reo and had sought or acquiesced in the assimilation of kōhanga reo as a mainstream ECE service' (Waitangi Tribunal, 2012, p. 3). As a consequence, it was argued that their assimilation had resulted in a steady decline in the number of children enrolling in kōhanga reo, which ultimately threatened the survival of Te Reo Māori (the Māori language) among younger generations.

The primary aim of this chapter is to consider the role of culture in the creation and contestation of markets. Within this context I aim to do two things. The first is to situate the marketisation of ECE within a broader literature which considers the increasing use of markets, in various forms, to address social problems (England, Eakin, Gastaldo & McKeever, 2007; Schwiter, Berndt & Truong, 2018). The neo-liberal restructuring of care since the 1990s in many Western welfare contexts has paved the way for new state-market arrangements in the delivery of care services (Birch & Siemiatycki, 2015). Precipitated in many cases by the retrenchment of the state from a direct hand in service provisioning and the subsequent 'roll out' of new market based solutions to address a range of social problems (Peck & Tickell, 2002), in these emergent 'post-neoliberal' (Simon-Kumar, 2011) assemblages of care there is an increasing trend towards services which are subsidised by government, yet outsourced in much if not all of their delivery. Within this neoliberalised landscape, the rationale is increasingly on 'choice', seeking to proliferate the range of service

DOI: 10.4324/9780429296260-3

Figure 3.1 Kōhanga reo supporters take to the streets of Wellington in 2011
Source: Photograph used with permission of Stuff/*Dominion Post*

options (based on cost and type for example) for care consumers (Milligan & Power, 2010). The result has been significant diversification of services, working under a competitive market-based system.

Set against this narrative of competition and market darwinism, the second aim of the chapter is to consider the challenges of creating a market to address social problems in a postcolonial context, where the legacy of colonisation still shapes the kinds of interventions thought possible, and where the expression of cultural difference plays a significant part in framing market relations. Markets and market interventions are far from neutral. As Berndt and Boeckler suggest, markets are profound sites of struggle, and their realisation is a hard won 'practical accomplishment' (2010, p. 565). Moreover, as Zelizer reminds us, market exchanges are inflected with all sorts of normative understandings and moral assumptions about what is appropriate and 'right' (Zelizer, 2013). Critiquing the widely held notion in neoclassical economics that we are, at heart, ultimately self-maximising calculating agents operating in response to an external economic system, Zelizer illustrates how social and cultural assumptions fundamentally shape all economic practices and behaviours. To that end, there is no such thing as a pre-social market (Peck, 2005; Polanyi, 1944).

One way to read such market contestation is to consider the different epistemologies at work in framing market relations (Pollard & Samers, 2007). As Krippner suggests:

> congealed into every market exchange is a history of struggle and contestation that has produced actors with certain understandings of themselves and the world which predispose them to exchange under a certain set of rules and not another. In this sense, the state, culture and politics are contained in every market act.
>
> (2002, p. 112)

With that in mind, in this chapter I consider attempts to create an ECE market within a postcolonial context in which different epistemologies of care and education contest the legitimacy of the market itself. What I aim to illustrate is not solely another example of 'the market' encountering social mores in society, but rather how culturally different epistemologies of care and education challenge attempts to frame the market. In keeping with the aim of the book then, I attend to the marketisation of ECE in place by considering the social and cultural politics, and the related histories, which have shaped the care and education of young children in Aotearoa New Zealand. Aotearoa is uniquely placed for this work as it has a bicultural, rather than a multicultural, framework underpinning its postcolonial political settlement (Larner, 2006). As a key part of this settlement, the British Crown is obliged to recognise the rights of Māori to preserve their cultural heritage. Since 1975, Māori sovereignty has formally been recognised through the auspices of the Waitangi Tribunal: a non-judiciary permanent advisory board of inquiry and redress, which is charged with upholding the tenets of the foundational document of the state, the Treaty of Waitangi. As such, it represents a key terrain on which political, cultural and economic redress can be sought by Māori. Within this context, the following sections will explore two key attempts to marketise ECE in Aotearoa New Zealand and consider the place of the Māori language immersion service, Te Kōhanga Reo, within the emergent market.

Problematising the care and education of young children

Childcare markets represent what some proponents of SSEM have termed as 'markets for collective concern' (see special issue of *Economy and Society*, 2019). As Frankel, Ossandón & Pallesen (2019, p. 154) suggest these are 'markets that have been constructed as policy instruments because policy makers supposedly expect them to offer the best possible solution to a particular collective problem'. This represents more than the use of markets to reach policy outcomes, but further the commitment that policy making is an exercise in 'continuous market organisation'

(p. 154). The care and education of young children is a politically fraught domain. Over the past 30 years, early childhood education services in Aotearoa New Zealand have come to be relied upon to address many different governmental ambitions. Such is the political malleability of childcare; wavering between its status as an educational resource for young children, and thus part of the broader education system on the one hand, and on the other as a care and social support for working parents, increasingly directed towards children deemed 'at risk' (May, 2009). Central to this growing interest is the purported breadth of benefits which formalised ECE can bring to society: from reducing incarceration and recidivism rates, to breaking the cycle of deprivation. And yet, in more neoliberalised policy contexts like Aotearoa New Zealand, the delivery and governance of ECE has taken place primarily through the market (Brennan, Cass, Himmelweit & Szebehely, 2012), based on an imaginary that is centred around empowering the 'parent consumer' rather than assume state responsibility for ECE as a public good.

Governmental interest in the care of the young child grew internationally from the mid-1980s, in line with the changing understanding of investment in the early years across the OECD (see for example OECD, 2001, 2006). Likened more to a 'third way' approach, investment in ECE became a key part of the shift in international social policy to productive rather than redistributive spending (Esping-Andersen, 2002; Jenson, 2004). Drawing on research from the fields of developmental psychology and neuroscience in particular (see Rose, 1989), the case was made in policy spheres that investment in the early years would reap improved future social and economic outcomes for society as a whole (Mahon, 2010; Schweinhart, Montie, Xiang, Barnett, Belfield & Nores, 2005). Endorsed by the OECD, this thinking was met positively in Aoteraroa New Zealand, a country which continues to have poor child welfare outcomes[1] (UNICEF, 2017), especially for Māori children. Under this new policy emphasis, the child in society became the 'investable child' (Prentice, 2009), reflective of an economic reframing of childhood itself. As Prentice goes on to suggest, for the investable child 'early childhood mutates from a site of economic loss and expense to one of current and future economic growth. Children, formerly conceived of as private parental property and expense, assume the lustre of potential economic returns if carefully handled' (pp. 689–690). It is within this changing political context, that the childcare (subsequently ECE) market in Aotearoa New Zealand became a site of significant governmental interest and intervention. To explore how this instrumentalist thinking framed the emerging market, in the following sections I will focus on two key market making interventions: the *Before Five* reforms (1989) and the '20 Hours free ECE' payment (2007).

Investing in children: Creating a market of collective concern

While a full account of the complex history (and herstory) of the childcare and early education sector in Aotearoa New Zealand is outside the scope of this chapter, what I offer in the following sections is an insight into two key events in order to focus on points of problematisation in the creation of the market. As

Ouma (2015, p.22) reminds us 'marketization is a process of proliferation that hinges on the solution of a distinct set of practical problems'. Set against concerns about poor childhood outcomes, coupled with growing pressure to support female labour force participation, the development of the ECE market was borne from the confluence of these distinct social and economic problems. Childcare in Aotearoa New Zealand has never been considered a 'public good' (Daly, 2002), and always operated through a mixed economy of provisioning, involving volunteer, community not-for-profit, and private for-profit services. Until the 1970s, extra-familial care of young children was located under the separate monikers of 'pre-school' and 'childcare'. In 1984, the incoming Labour government signalled a profound change in how these early childhood services were viewed by the state. As part of an entire review of the education system, to 'put markets to work to achieve new social and educational goals' (Gordon, 1992, p.282), early childhood services were reconceptualised as part of the broader education system. In so doing it became renamed as Early Childhood Education rather than childcare. Prime Minister David Lange, against advice from Treasury, committed for the first time to heavily invest in ECE as a crucial service for children and working families[2]. To that extent, the resulting *Before Five* reforms as they were known, represented 'a philosophical shift by the Government and a recognition that early childhood care and education should have an educational and therefore developmental emphasis' (Waitangi Tribunal, 2012, p. 25).

The *Before Five* reforms set the conditions for the marketisation of early childhood services and laid the terrain on which it continues to operate today. Under the reforms, only services that met newly established minimum requirements for licensing would be eligible for funding from government. Importantly, this was now applicable to both the private for profit and community not for profit providers[3]. In a sector that was already highly diversified, the reforms recommended a funding increase across the board to equalise financial supports between the different types of services. A charter system was introduced to obligate licensed services to meet the new standards of practice as set out in the accompanying regulations (Ministry of Education, 1990). The extent to which licensed services were maintaining standards as set out in their charter was measured by the new Review and Audit Agency (later the Education Review Office – ERO) through an audit-based system.

Occurring at the pinnacle of neoliberal thinking during a period known internationally as the 'New Zealand Experiment' (Kelsey, 1993), Manning (2016) suggests that most government intervention into ECE at the time was rationalised as contracting out service provisioning. The government effectively became a purchaser of ECE, as the Minister of Education later explained, 'under current policies the government buys educational hours of a particular quality from early childhood education centres and overall is neutral in terms of the service type' (Ministry of Education, 1995, p. 3). The newly constituted ECE sector was funded through a bulk-funding system, based on a formula that contributed an amount towards the cost per hour for each child in care dependent on age. Under this system, parents made up the remainder of the cost of care.

Bulk-funding was a game-changer in terms of the amount of money coming in and the way it discursively realigned the governance of the sector around new ideas of 'quality'. As such, it was envisioned as the answer to a range of problems undermining access to ECE, such as cost and accessibility. By the late 1980s the rising cost of care for parents was becoming an election-defining topic. Part of the response by government through bulk-funding was to stimulate an increase in the amount and type of services on offer, thus rebalancing supply to match the growing demand for ECE. Characteristic of government discourse at the time, the Deputy Minister for Education indicated that 'the emphasis has been on raising quality standards, reducing costs to families, and meeting individual needs and preferences, rather than homogenising pre-school education... When we talk about early-childhood care and education we talk about variety' (Shields, 1989, p. 264). By raising the number of available ECE places, the balance of power was anticipated to be tipped towards the parent-consumer in the market. In essence, parents would 'talk with their feet', choosing to relocate their children to services which they deemed to be better, in terms of quality and cost. Empowering the parent consumer was pivotal to the logics of bulk-funding and to the marketisation of ECE in general, as it meant that the state could (in theory) remain distanced from the consumer side of the market as much as possible.

When funding was finally implemented in 1990, almost all services[4] gained about a 50 per cent increase. For centres who accommodated infants under the age of two, many saw their funding double (May, 2009). However, bulk-funding was a challenge to manage for government, as criteria for eligibility was its only control point (Mitchell, 2003). In 1991, the first year of funding, high uptake of the subsidy by services and growing enrolments meant that governmental costs soared by over twice what was budgeted for. Fiscal pressures mounted and saw a change in government that same year. Keen to rein in expenditure, an incoming centre-right National Government executed a deleterious 'mother of all budgets' in 1991, infamous for severe reductions made to social spending including ECE, which put paid to many of the checks and balances which were written into the initial *Before Five* reforms.

Reframing the market: The 20 hours 'free' payment

The second major governmental intervention into the sector came again under a Labour-led government which took office in 1999. The introduction of bulk-funding had led to a significant rise in children participating in ECE and the number of services meeting this demand. However, by the early 2000s the profile of the sector had changed, with stronger growth in private for-profit provision, the proliferation of childcare chains and evidence of more corporatised governance models emerging in the sector (Gallagher, 2017). Cuts made under the intervening government had accentuated a number of problems (Mitchell, 2003). A lack of accountability for how funding was being spent meant that little was flowing through to wages for the care workforce, especially in the for-profit part of the sector, and the anticipated upskilling of staff had not manifested. Questions were being asked as to whether profiteering was becoming apparent on the back of government investment and whether this would set perverse motives for providers to enter the market (Laugeson, 2007; Quirke, 2005). Parental costs were again soaring, despite bulk-funding subsidising the cost of care, which many attributed to the growing presence of private for-profit services.

In the face of growing recognition that the childcare market was working poorly for providers, workers, parents and families, solutions were envisioned to remedy these problems. Importantly as Frankel *et al.* (2019) suggest that, with markets for collective concerns, solutions tend to be found among a range of interventions that aim to make the market work *better*, rather than re-orientate towards another means of meeting the policy goals. With that in mind, a second, demand-side intervention was designed known as the 20 hours 'free' ECE scheme. Introduced in 2007, the scheme covered the cost of care up to 20 hours per week for all three to five-year olds. Crucially, funding was intended as a payment, rather than a subsidy, meaning that a rate was set above which providers were not allowed to charge for those hours. Under the accompanying strategic plan (2002–12) a new distinction began to emerge in government's view of the market: between parent-led and teacher-led services. This was significant as it began to reframe ECE as a totally distinctive sphere from other prominent care services in the sector which relied on parental voluntarism to operate (like Playcentre and Te Kōhanga Reo). While it was claimed to be based on a quality judgement, where quality was equated to the level of trained ECE teachers in the service, it was also an economic decision. The biggest cost driver in ECE is wages, and making the 20 hours available only to teacher-led services was understood as a way of limiting government expenditure. However, the scheme was anticipated to ultimately incentivise providers to hire more teacher qualified staff, as funding was tagged to the level of trained teachers in the service[5]. As a demand-side payment, it was predicted to make a marked difference to the cost of care for parents of three- and four-year-olds (although in many cases the cost of care for the under twos and the hours in attendance outside the 20 hours rose to offset the scheme)[6]. Assuming that the state as a purchaser of education hours rather than a provider of ECE, the 20 hours was intended as a market intervention to standardise quality across the sector and to make what was being 'purchased' more transparent to both government (notably through the work of the ERO) and to parents.

Combined, both of these interventions by government can be seen as clear, but distinct, attempts to marketise ECE in order to reach particular social policy ambitions for young children. Initially bulk-funding sought to produce a more diverse and competitive sector, whereby the state would take a back seat as 'purchaser' of ECE hours. Central to this market imaginary was the parent consumer, who would decipher which services offered the best balance of quality and cost in a proliferating market environment. The social goal was to make ECE as accessible as possible to families, in line with the growing international evidence about the importance of ECE for childhood outcomes. The second intervention was intended to address problems with the market and to work further towards child welfare goals by directly identifying providers and the type of care they offered that met new 'quality' expectations. The imaginary of the knowledgeable parent consumer changed under the 20 hours supplement, as government sought to direct consumer choice to particular kinds of services through the structure of funding itself. Within the context of the changing market for ECE, in the next section I will trace the trajectory of one particular service, Te Kōhanga Reo.

Locating Kōhanga Reo in the Market

Envisioned as culture and language 'nests', the origins of the kōhanga reo movement stem from an activist period of Māori self-determination in the 1970s[7]. On the back of claims for bicultural self-determination, in 1982 the first kōhanga reo was established as part of a Māori educational revolution (Tuiwhai-Smith, 2007). Of pressing concern was the declining ability to speak the Māori language: dropping from 90 per cent of Māori schoolchildren in 1913, to just 5 per cent in 1975 (Waitangi Tribunal, 2012, p. 16). Within this post-colonial context, Donna Awatere, a key advocate for kōhanga reo argued that 'Kindergartens are the first of the educational gates. A bastion of white power, Kindergartens have frightened Māori people off pre-school education. they don't meet their needs' (as cited in May, 2009, p. 179). In response, a key part of Māori language revival was the establishment of distinctive care services for young children, which operated through the medium of te reo. Thus kōhanga were seen as an important step towards decolonisation and a key part of Māori cultural renaissance more generally. It was estimated that in the early years of the movement, whānau (family) covered at least 60 per cent of the cost of running services (Waitangi Tribunal, 2012, p. 23), demonstrating the level of community commitment to the initiative. In keeping with Tikanga Māori, or traditional customary practice, kohanga were a community initiative organised around kaumātua (elders) and whānau (extended family) primarily through voluntary labour. Within Māoridom the remit of kōhanga reo was always understood to be wider than the Crown's expectations around the developmental role of ECE and the 'investable child'. As they define it 'Te Kōhanga Reo means 'the language nest' where we care and nurture our young in a warm and secure environment alongside the whānau. Tamariki (children) in kōhanga are totally immersed in the Māori language, customs and values' (Te Kōhango Reo National Trust website, 2020). In the spirit of localised community engagement, and in the absence of significant capital funding, from the outset services were co-located on marae (Māori meeting houses) or community centres, and for the most part they were not purpose-built under any ECE regulatory framework. This was a radical departure from the increasingly regulated ECE environment which was being discursively signalled as preferable in social policy domains. Despite this, it was hugely successful. In the first three years there was staggering growth, with 377 kōhanga reo established, catering for about 5,800 children nationally. By the introduction of bulk-funding in 1989, te kōhanga reo was the fourth largest provider of ECE in the country, with some 500 centres and over 8,000 children in their charge (May, 2009).

The *Before Five* reforms and related bulk-funding marked a considerable change in the fortunes of kōhanga reo. From a governance perspective, they were moved from the auspices of the Department of Māori Affairs to the Ministry of Education (MoE) in 1989, along with other educational services for young children as part of the government's growing interest in ECE. Change also came in relation to the funding and auditing of the sector. This meant that, like other services, they had to be licensed by 1990 in order to receive funding and to meet new standards as monitored by the ERO. Before the move to the MoE, funding was given to the Kōhanga Reo National Trust as a block grant for them to distribute among services as they deemed appropriate, irrespective of licensing. This was replaced by a bulk subsidy based on hours of attendance. Throughout the 1990s, the relationship between kōhanga reo and the MoE became strained. Their ERO reviews of 1993 and 1997 highlighted faults in the operation of numerous kōhanga and identified a number of services as below minimum standards (as per the regulations and charter)[8], which compounded tensions.

The position of kōhanga reo waned further under the changes introduced around the 20 hours ECE scheme. Until then, they had been part of the single bulk-funding system under the sector. Under the conditions of the 20 hours ECE, and the distinction drawn between teacher-led and parent-led services, they were placed as a lower cost service and not eligible for the new payment. This was a problem in large part as in keeping with its cultural practices they relied on the voluntary work of whanau to operate, but also because the training for kōhanga reo teachers (called kaiako) was not recognised by the New Zealand Teachers Council. After three tense years of debate, most kōhanga became eligible to apply for the 20 hours payment by 2010. Unsurprisingly, by that stage uptake of the 20 hours scheme by kōhanga reo was much lower than the rest of the sector as parental usage of the service had been undermined.

With the introduction of more funding into the sector, expectations around quality also increased. New regulations introduced in 2008 became applicable to all services, including kōhanga reo. From the outset the regulations were problematic, as they were in English only and the MoE were keen to only have the English version legally recognised, an important aspect of the politics of market making (May, 2009). A specific framework was developed in consultation with the ERO to assess kōhanga reo, based around self-assessment and self-audit of compliance. However, the ERO continued to find issues with the operation of kōhanga reo and the Trust became sceptical of its ability to conduct a culturally sensitive assessment. The ongoing debates between the Ministry, the ERO as the primary review body and the Trust were inevitably picked up and reported in mainstream media. These reports portrayed the ERO reviews as indicative of poor practices and an inability for kōhanga reo to meet new quality standards in the emergent market (Harris, 2006). Having been established in marae and community centres, which were not purpose built in line with subsequent regulations, and not having the capital funding to remedy this made them susceptible to criticism under the new regulatory framework. In a market increasingly driven and organised around parental choice, it was inevitable that this would have a negative impact on parental engagement with the service. Between 1995 and 2007 enrolments in kōhanga reo declined by 52 per cent, despite 89 per cent of Māori children participating in ECE by 2006.

The Waitangi Tribunal as market arbitrator

In 2012 a claim was brought by the Kōhanga Reo National Trust under urgency to the Waitangi Tribunal. The claim stated that the cultural work of kōhanga had been severely undermined by government's ongoing emphasis on bringing all early childhood services into the same ECE market and by incorporating kōhanga as just one of a range of services to compete for parents, rather than protecting its unique place in the market. The following section is based primarily on analysis of the 450-page tribunal report which reflects the debate which took place at the hearing. In relying on this document, I acknowledge that I am leaning heavily on the insights of Māori scholars and other Tangata Whenua who work with and have supported the kōhanga reo movement since its inception in the early 1980s.

A key criticism levelled during the tribunal was that governmental emphasis was on encouraging Māori participation in ECE as part of a broader social policy agenda for improving educational outcomes for Māori, as they tended to be overrepresented in the research on poor childhood outcomes, but that this emphasis did not align with encouraging involvement in kōhanga reo or te reo immersion more generally (Waitangi Tribunal, 2012, p. 49). As was made explicit in the ECE strategic plan, 'Māori have a choice of ECE services that best meet their needs' (Ministry of Education, 2002, p. 107). Moving kōhanga reo under the auspices of the MoE and bringing them into alignment with regulations and funding in the sector signalled that they were anticipated to compete alongside other services, even though being part of a market for ECE was never part of their remit. Kōhanga reo became positioned as one among many 'choices' for parents on an ever widening playing field. In essence, they were being mainstreamed into ECE, having instead been intended as an autonomous movement established under the premise of decolonising Māori education (Walker, 2016).

While increasing parental choice was the driving rationale for governmental intervention, the tribunal found that choice was effectively framed towards particular parts of the market, particularly through the 20 hours payment. Those services who could access the higher rates of government funding for parents and as a result were implicitly identified as preferable, were given an advantage in the emergent market. The initial neoliberal funding ambition by government of remaining 'neutral' as to the kinds of service types which proliferated in the market was over-ridden by the subsequent demand side payment, which ultimately prioritised some groups over others. Thus it was argued that government intervention into the market essentially skewed parental choice. Undermining the place of kōhanga within the market ultimately presented a dilemma for parents who wanted to benefit from financial supports like the 20 hours payment, but who could not receive it at a kōhanga. It forced them to make a judgement as to whether they wanted to place emphasis on a westernised model of 'early education' or cultural and language immersion for their children, a division implicitly drawn through the funding model.

Indeed, drawing kōhanga reo into the ECE market through the funding model began to reshape the social and cultural relations on which kōhanga operated, as staff began to aspire for recognition and change their practices. This caused tensions within the organisation itself. As Dame Iritana Tāwhiwhirangi described in the course of a nationwide kaupapa (principles) review of kōhanga reo from 1997 to 1999:

> many kōhanga reo were in fact assimilating to ECE. We found that some whanau had been putting their staff through ECE courses ... In other kōhanga reo, the ECE programme had been invasive and kōhanga were following ECE lesson plans, learning outcomes and assessing children in relation to ECE outcomes
>
> (Waitangi Tribunal, 2012, p. 31)

For those services who were unwilling to meet the kaupapa or principles of practice for kōhanga reo, they had their charter and licence revoked by the Trust. Between 1997 and 2005, a total of 51 services had their licences revoked finding themselves caught adrift within the market and the different epistemologies of care and education shaping how early childhood was being practiced.

After the two weeks of testimony, the tribunal found in favour of the Trust, stating that the Crown had a duty of protection for te reo Māori which it had failed to meet, and had ultimately breached Article three of the Treaty, pertaining to the protection of Māori cultural autonomy. At the time of writing details of the claim remain unsettled and a resolution is ongoing. However, kōhanga reo chose to opt out of conversations for the new Strategic Plan (2019), preferring to distance themselves from the formalised ECE sector and find an alternative governance and funding structure with the MoE.

Discussion: Epistemological difference and market contestation

Processes of marketisation are ambivalent endeavours which are about both incorporating *and* expelling places, people and things (Berndt & Boeckler, 2010). For some, the significant decline in enrolment for kōhanga reo, despite the steady increase in Māori children in ECE overall, could be read as a reflection of the market working 'well'. Where parental choice is signalled as the central tenet around which the market is constructed, some services will be winners and others losers. However, this reading of the situation misses much of the cultural politics on which the ECE market has been created in Aotearoa New Zealand. The initial desire for neutrality by government for providers in the market was a crucial first step leading to the problems for kōhanga reo today, as such a position directly contradicts Treaty obligations to Māori and the preservation of their cultural heritage. Under the treaty and the bicultural political settlement, all services are not equally positioned to compete in the market. The legacy of colonial relations between Māori and the British Crown and the ongoing battle to redress the longstanding social and economic inequities mean that this can never be read as a simple case of the market deciding. The prioritisation of the neoliberal aspiration of parental choice, mobilised in justification of the different government interventions into the market, comes up against the cultural politics of the care and education of young children *in* place.

The discursive framing of the ECE market around notions of quality has been a powerful means of differently situating providers within the market. It is also a discourse that is very hard to speak back to, as it has a self-evident 'truth' which depoliticises conversation as to what exactly prefigures the notion of 'quality' in the first place (Walters, 2004). The heightened regulations and their associated expectations of practice have shaped the market to favour particular kinds of services (notably teacher-led services). At the heart of this normative process of differentiation and valuation is the work of the ERO. Although its role was originally intended as a place of last resort (May, 2009), the balance of power changed to the point that they increasingly acted as an 'apparatus of control' (Lewis, 2004, p. 149) around the funding models, governing the market from a distance through processes of audit and self-regulation. To that extent, their work sought to equalise and smooth out perceived differences in quality across the sector, and at the same time played a crucial role in framing the market by indicating who did not meet regulations. However, as highlighted at the tribunal, the knowledge base on which their judgements are made has been influenced by particular understandings of ECE and child development. Notably, ideas of 'quality' have been shaped by Westernised understandings of child development through the growing prominence of disciplines like neuroscience and development psychology, and the work of international fora like the OECD. Consequently, in the process of the tribunal the work of the ERO was criticised for their failure to appropriately evaluate the work of kōhanga for the children in their care, stating 'Whether or not proficient in te reo, most reviewers either did not have sufficient understanding of the kaupapa, or applied a mainstream ECE perspective in identifying areas for improvement' (Waitangi Tribunal, 2012, p. 225).

Early childhood interventions for Māori children in Aotearoa New Zealand have been shaped around two distinct political projects, which have quite different intended outcomes and rationales. As was apparent from the evidence presented at the Tribunal hearing, increasing Māori children's participation in ECE was a primary governmental ambition, in keeping with international recommendations about its long term benefits for improving the outcomes of vulnerable children. As a result, from the perspective of government the participation of Māori children in ECE falls part of a broader social investment logic, where particular kinds of ECE environments are deemed more appropriate than others in order to achieve these purported benefits. However, while the kōhanga reo movement have the same ambitions for the life chances of their youth, their approach to achieving these goals is embedded in Tikanga Māori, which is ultimately forged from a project of decolonisation.

In Aotearoa New Zealand the work of the Waitangi Tribunal has been critical for helping to lay bare the logics which frame the ECE market and for contextualising governmental aspirations for ECE within a longstanding history of relations between the Crown and Māori. The Tribunal acts as an arbitrator to redress cultural, social and economic grievances conducted in this case in the name of creating a more efficient market, but to also provide a terrain in which to consider the particular epistemologies on which the market itself is legitimised. Within this light we see that market interventions into ECE, despite the discursive semblance of 'neutrality', are far from neutral. Framing market relations around a westernised epistemology, one which is based on relatively recent normative understandings of child development, is shown through the tribunal to be only *one way* to frame the marketisation of ECE. Although not legally binding, the tribunal forces government to reflect on the assumptions underpinning its decisions and to view them not merely as attempts to address a problem (such as increasing Māori participation in ECE for example), but as culturally specific interventions in their own right. These interventions into the market and the particular form that they take are shaped within the post-colonial present – one that is concerned with improving outcomes for Māori children but at the expense of te reo revitalisation and the preservation of Tikanga Māori.

Conclusion

All markets are deeply social and relational, making them prime sites for contestation. This is especially the case with regards to the marketisation of services that provide an ostensible public good, like care or education, and even more fraught when pertaining to vulnerable groups such as children. As I have illustrated in this chapter, ECE markets, as markets of collective concern, are inflected with normative assumptions about the most appropriate ways of caring for and educating young children. These norms are socially produced and culturally embedded, reflective of particular understandings about the role of childhood and the place of the child in society. Speaking back to the theme of the book, this chapter has sought to consider ECE markets as sites of social struggle within a postcolonial political context, where the exigencies of the market are situated against the broader political commitment to biculturalism. The fortunes of the kōhanga reo movement and the care and education of Māori children remains closely entangled with the ECE market, even as it tries to step away from being associated with it in the wake of the Tribunal hearing. Current demographic predictions indicate a significant growth in the number of Māori children over the coming years, to the point that they will make up about one-third of children in Aotearoa New Zealand by 2038. Where they spend their pre-school years and the kind of educational care that they receive will have significant long-term implications for the future of te reo and tikanga āori.

Notes

1 In 2017 Aotearoa New Zealand was ranked 34th out of 41 countries by UNICEF on an index of child wellbeing, with 27 per cent of children estimated to be living in income poverty.

2 It was not a co-incidence that government investment coincided with the publication of a key report on prison reform (Roper Report 1989), which extolled the benefits of investing in the early years as a means of mitigating imprisonment rates in the future, a theme which was shaping the nature of ECE spending across the OECD

3 Some funding was already present but it was primarily for community based providers of Kindergarten and Playcentre services.

4 Except kindergartens.

5 This also went alongside a push to have 100 per cent teacher-led services by 2012. As Mitchell (2013) has suggested, funding to support this progressive initiative went from approximately NZ$350,000 in 2002 to almost NZ$1.2 million in 2010 and was primarily channelled into grants, scholarships and allowances to early education teachers and students.

6 The growth in participation is reflected in the increase in government spending on the sector, which went from NZ$409 million in 2002 to NZ$771 million in 2007, double the budget of 1999 when Labour took office (p. 263).

7 According to the 2018 census, about 17 per cent of the population self-identify as Māori in New Zealand.

8 In a testimony to the Waitangi Tribunal, Ms Harata Gibson described a number of situations where regulatory requirements had conflicted with marae facilities and Tikanga Māori: the use of change tables, forcing nappy-changing into outside toilets; the fencing of exclusive kōhanga reo outside areas from roads, rivers and other parts of the marae or school; children's sleeping arrangements; and an emphasis on toys and outside play equipment rather than the natural environment (p. 40).

References

Berndt, C. & Boeckler, M. (2010). Geographies of markets: Materials, morals and monsters in motion. *Progress in Human Geography*, 35(4), 559–567.

Birch, K. & Siemiatycki, M. (2016). Neoliberalism and the geographies of marketization: The entangling of state and markets. *Progress in Human Geography*, 40(2), 177–198.

Brennan, D., Cass, B., Himmelweit, S. & Szebehely, M. (2012). The marketisation of care: Rationales and consequences in Nordic and liberal care regimes. *Journal of European Social Policy*, 22(4), 377–391.

Cohen, D. (2018). Between perfection and damnation: The emerging geography of markets. *Progress in Human Geography*, 42(6), 898–915. https://doi.org./10.1177/0309132517729769.

Daly, M. (2002). Care as a good for social policy. *Journal of Social Policy*, 31, 251–270.

England, K., Eakin, J., Gastaldo, D. & McKeever, P. (2007). Neoliberalising home care: Managed competition and restructuring home care in Ontario. In K. England & K. Ward (Eds.), *Neoliberalisation: States, networks, people* (pp. 169–194). Oxford: Blackwell Publishing.

Esping-Andersen, G. (2002). *Why we need a new welfare state*. Oxford: Oxford University Press.

Frankel, C., Ossandón, J. & Pallesen, T. (2019). The organization of markets for collective concerns and their failures. *Economy and Society*, 48(2), 153–174.

Gallagher, A. (2017). Growing pains? Change in the New Zealand childcare market 2006–2016. *New Zealand Geographer*, 73(1), 15–24.

Gordon, L. (1992). The New Zealand state and educational reforms: 'Competing' interests. *Comparative Education*, 28(3), 281–291. https://doi.org/10.1080/0305006920280305.

Harris, N. (2006). *Kaikohe Kohanga Reo cops a blast from ERO*, 2 March 2006, retrieved from www.nzherald.co.nz/northernadvocate/news/article.cfm?c_id=1503450&objectid=10936283.

Jenson, J. (2004). Changing the paradigm: Family responsibility or investing in children. *The Canadian Journal of Sociology/Cahiers canadiens de sociologie*, 29(2), 169–192.

Kelsey, J. (1993). *Rolling back the State: Privatisation of power in Aotearoa/New Zealand*. Wellington: Bridget Williams Books.

Krippner, G.R. (2002). The elusive market: Embeddedness and the paradigm of economic sociology. *Theory and Society*, 30(6), 775–810.

Larner, W. (2006). Brokering citizenship claims: Neo-liberalism, biculturalism and multiculturalism in Aotearoa New Zealand. In A. Dobrowolsky (Ed.), *Women, migration and citizenship: Making local, national and transnational connections* (pp. 154–172). London: Routledge

Laugeson, R. (2007). Childcare centres warned not to profit from subsidy. *Sunday Star Times*, 6 May 2007.

Lewis, N. (2004). Embedding the reforms in New Zealand schooling: After neo-liberalism? *GeoJournal*, 59(2), 149–160.

Mahon, R. (2010). After neo-liberalism? *Global Social Policy*, 10(2), 172–192.

Manning, S.(Ed.) (2016) *Dictionary of Educational History in Australia and New Zealand (DEHANZ)*, retrieved from https://dehanz.net.au/entries/meade-reportbefore-five.

May, H. (2009). *Politics in the playground: The world of early childhood in New Zealand*. Dunedin: Otago University Press.

Milligan, C. & Power, A. (2010). The changing geography of care. In T. Brown, S. McLafferty & G Moon (Eds.), *A companion to health and medical geography* (pp. 567–586). London: Wiley-Blackwell.

Ministry of Education. (1990). *Education (early childhood education) regulations*.

Ministry of Education. (1995). *Report on the direct (bulk funding) of kindergartens to the Education and Sciences Select Committee*.

Ministry of Education. (2002). *Pathways to the future: Ngā Huarahi Arataki. A 10-year strategic plan for early childhood education*.

Mitchell, L. (2003). Views on children and investment in ECE: New Zealand experiences [Paper presentation]. European ECE Research Association Conference, Glasgow, 3–6 September 2003.

OECD. (2001). *Starting strong: Early childhood education and care*. OECD, Directorate for Education, OECD Publishing, Paris. https://doi.org/10.1787/9789264192829-en.

OECD. (2006). *Starting Strong II: Early childhood education and care*. OECD, Directorate for Education, OECD Publishing, Paris. https://doi.org/10.1787/9789264035461-en.

Ouma, S. (2015). *Assembling export markets: The making and unmaking of global food connections in West Africa*. Chichester: Wiley Blackwell.

Peck, J. (2005). Economic sociologies in space. *Economic Geography*, 81(2), 129–175.

Peck, J. & Tickell, A. (2002). Neoliberalizing space. *Antipode*, 34(3), 380–404.

Polanyi, K. (1944). *The great transformation: The political and economic origins of our time*. New York, NY: Farrar & Reinhart.

Pollard, J. & Samers, M. (2007). Islamic banking and finance: Postcolonial political economy and the decentring of economic geography. *Transactions of the Institute of British Geographers*, 32(3), 313–330.

Prentice, S. (2009). High stakes: The "investable" child and the economic reframing of childcare. *Signs*, 34(3), 687–710. https//doi.org/10.1086/593711.

Quirke, M. (2005). Aussie Bank buys Kiwi preschools. *Dominion Post Online*, 30 September 2005.

Rose, N. (1989). *Governing the soul: The shaping of the private self*. London: Routledge.

Schweinhart, L. J., Montie, J., Xiang, Z., Barnett, W.S., Belfield, C.R. & Nores, M. (2005). *Lifetime effects: The HighScope Perry Preschool study through age 40* (Vol. 14). Ypsilanti, MI: HighScope Press.

Schwiter, K., Berndt, C. & Truong, J. (2018). Neoliberal austerity and the marketisation of elderly care. *Social & Cultural Geography*, 19(3), 379–399.

Shields, M. (1989). NZPD 502, p. 264 [New Zealand Parliamentary Debates], 11 October 1989.

Simon-Kumar, R. (2011). The analytics of "gendering" the post-neoliberal state. *Social Politics: International Studies in Gender, State & Society*, 18(3), 441–468. https://doi.org/441-468. 10.1093/sp/jxr018

Te Kōhanga Reo National Trust. (2020), retrieved fromwww.kohanga.ac.nz/en.

Tuiwhai-Smith, L. (2007). The Native and the Neoliberal down: Neoliberalism and 'endangered authenticities'. In M. De La Cadena & O. Starn (Eds.), *Indigenous experience today* (pp. 333–354). Oxford: Berg.

UNICEF. (2017). *Children in developed countries*. Retrieved from www.unicef-irc.org/research/children-in-high-income-countries/.

Waitangi Tribunal. (2012). Matua Rautia: The report on the Kohango Reo claim. Retrieved from www.waitangitribunal.govt.nz/assets/Documents/Publications/WT-Matua-Rautia-Report-on-the-Kohanga-Reo-claim.pdf.

Walker, R. (2016). Reclaiming Māori education. In J. Huthchings & J. Lee-Morgan (Eds.), *Decolonisation in Aotearoa: Education, research and practice* (pp. 19–38). Wellington: NZCER Press.

Walters, W. (2004). Some critical notes on governance. *Studies in Political Economy*, 73 (Spring/Summer), 27–46.

Zelizer, V. (2013). *Economic lives: How culture shapes the economy*. Princeton, NJ: Princeton University Press.

4 Time work

Assembling regularity in lamb's market geographies

Matthew Henry

SCHOOL OF PEOPLE, ENVIRONMENT AND PLANNING, MASSEY UNIVERSITY

Introduction

For well over a century, farmers, meat processors and governments in New Zealand have traded perishable commodities – mutton, lamb, beef and pork – with markets located thousands of kilometres away.[1] Meat industries in New Zealand, Australia and across the Americas were early pioneers in the organisation of volume production across globally stretched supply chains (Cronon, 1991; Perren, 2006). Technologies such as refrigeration provided the means of creating novel market topologies for perishable commodities and, in doing so, opened up different economic futures for sheep farmers and processors in places such as New Zealand. But refrigeration created new temporal problems that needed resolving in order for global meat markets centred on places such as Smithfield in London to work. The problems that refrigeration exposed revolved around synchronising discordant rhythms of seasonal production, shipping, and consumption. By presenting meat's temporalities as contingent socio-technical assemblages created in response to emergent, specific problems rather than the inevitable articulation of a universal temporal experience, the chapter exposes time and expectations about its economic qualities as a matter of concern in commodity market relations. As matters of concern the chapter suggests that temporal expectations can be understood as infrastructural relations that deeply shape the conditions of routine possibility in markets, but which almost inevitably disappear as matters of fact into the fabric of those markets (Carse & Kneas, 2019; Larkin, 2013; Star & Ruhleder, 1996).

Framed by these ideas this chapter asks what forms of time work were undertaken to maintain New Zealand's lamb trade at Smithfield Market in London; how was time work strategically mobilised to create particular temporal expectations in that market; and what were the implications of making temporal relations infrastructural? To explore the assemblage of meat time this chapter focuses on a temporal project orchestrated by the New Zealand Meat Producers Board (NZMPB) to promote sales of lamb in the United Kingdom's markets before World War Two. As the chapter argues the NZMPB engaged in sustained time work with a range of actors – farmers, processors, shippers, butchers and consumers. This work was intended to assemble a specific temporal order in lamb

DOI: 10.4324/9780429296260-4

markets that confronted and governed the issues of irregularity and unevenness generated by raising, trading and consuming a seasonal and perishable commodity across the globe.

Time, temporality and meat

Speed is often generalised as the paradigmatic condition of contemporary temporal experiences. However, Sharma (2014, p. 8) argues for a recognition of the temporal as, 'not a general sense of time particular to an epoch of history, but a specific experience of time that is structured in specific political and economic contexts' in order to produce temporal orders. While speed is undeniably important as a temporal experience it is imagined and made through specific assemblages that integrate multiple, different temporal practices. Consequently, the tendency to transform speed into a universal experience of time renders invisible how it is a specific quality that is only made possible through its relationship to other temporal practices. Temporalities are shaped by the heterogenous materialities, imaginaries and labour that continually (re)produce them in constant recalibration with the demands and possibilities posed by other temporalities. Time, as an assemblage, is subject to a complex governmentality that revolves around the identification of states of desired temporal normality, and the strategic assemblage of actors, devices and materials to achieve that end. It is a resource to be made and strategically used in order to pursue particular projects through various forms of material and imaginative time work. Under these conditions, particular temporal qualities or experiences such as speed or synchronicity are not universal abstractions but are emergent outcomes initiated by temporal projects, and performed through situated and purposeful time work (Gregson, 2017; Sharma, 2014). The idea of time work as constituting the active, strategic making of temporal relationships needs to be seen as a direct counter to assumptions about the independence and immutability of time. Consequently, when we observe changes in temporal qualities or experiences our attention should be drawn to trying to understand the project, and practices through which particular temporal relations have come to be problematised, stabilised and governed.

Time, as something more than a maker of change either disappears from accounts of food or is transformed into something else. Perren (2006) in his book *Taste, Trade and Technology* offers the most comprehensive, recent account of the development of the frozen meat trade (for older accounts of the trade see Armstrong, Dunlop-Young, Hogg, Medcalf & Watson, 1929; Critchell & Raymond, 1912; Grant, David, Ramsey, Rey-Alvarez, Richelet & Watkins-Pitchford, 1929). Here, time is present either as an external, independent flow within which events can be chronologically located, or indirectly as synonymous with refrigeration's defeat of perishability. The perishability-refrigeration nexus is a common touchstone for discussions about meat and its material transformation into a ubiquitous staple (Horowitz, 2006). But as in most accounts of infrastructural technologies just as temporal relations are transformed by refrigeration, refrigeration itself disappears as a matter of concern at the moment of its success (Star, 1999). The effect is to render the sociotechnical relationships, including temporal relations, required for refrigeration's success invisible (Rees, 2013), while simultaneously naturalising its generative role in creating specific food worlds (Freidberg, 2009). Alongside the literal freezing of time through preservation, speed has been another key quality through which time becomes present in discussions about the meat industry. Horowitz (2006), for example, argues that demands from consumers (and governments) for lower cost meat led to ongoing changes in animal rearing and meat processing practices. This took multiple forms ranging from changes in breeding and feed regimes, innovations in preserving technologies through to the mechanisation of the craft work of butchering that collectively had the effect of decreasing the time taken between pasture and plate (Anderson, 2009; Genoways, 2014; Godley & Williams, 2009; Oddy, 2016). Similarly, speed has also been identified as an emergent feature of consumption practices with consumer demands for smaller, faster-to-cook cuts of meat being a backdrop to changes in consumption patterns (Henry, 2017; Henry & Roche, 2018; Oddy, 2016). However, in these treatments of meat, time and its strategic use becomes reduced to the single quality – that of speed. What needs to be recovered is a richer sense of meat's multiple temporalities, the relationality of different temporal experiences, and the forms of time work undertaken to synchronise these experiences in order to better understand the strategic weaving of time into the infrastructural fabric of commodity markets.

To explore these concerns the paper draws on broad ideas of assemblage theory. Imbuing inquiry with a genealogical sensitivity to the conditions of possibility that the past has generated for the present (Baker & McGuirk, 2017) assemblage theory argue Jones *et al.* (2018) provides a means of mapping how diverse production networks form via the relational practices of heterogenous actors, devices and materials. At the heart of these assemblage ideas are the linked notions of territorialisation and deterritorialisation (DeLanda, 2006). While explicitly spatial these ideas can be stretched to encompass those multiple acts of boundary making and purification through which relationships between heterogeneity and homogeneity are negotiated within specific assemblages. Such work takes multiple forms, but a key field of effort revolves around assemblage defining acts of discursive coding and classification through which more or less homogenous market territorialisations can be identified and imbued with particular qualities. Time is one of these territorialised qualities. Territorialisations generate complex topological forms which are also equally complex temporal relationships. They transform the messy heterogeneity of differently lived times into homogenous and collectively held expectations that synchronise the material, political, business, financial and technological translations required to trade at enormous distance.

The work expended to remake deeply disrupted lamb assemblages by the NZMPB after World War One involved embedding and storying lamb with new temporal qualities that reterritorialised the material and seasonal heterogeneity of fragmented lamb relations. This was not the imposition of a singular, universal time ruling all the actors, but rather the fashioning of expectations that translated temporal heterogeneity throughout lamb's assemblage into synchronisable market relations. While lamb remains a powerful material and discursive actor in defining rurality in New Zealand, the remainder of the chapter moves beyond stories of rural locality to focus on the making of a transnational market assemblage and the temporal relations strategically assembled within it. The analysis pays attention to the time work of largely unrecognised actors (meat merchants, advertisers, cool stores and so on) operating in sites (Smithfield, butcher's shops, marketing magazines) that generally fall outside of the conventional analysis of commodity networks that tend to privilege the sites and practices of production and processing. While disparate and largely invisible the actors exposed in this chapter come to be powerful mediators in the hidden infrastructures of commodity assemblages (Pilcher, 2016).

Seasonality and time: Lamb's temporalities

By the end of World War One the United Kingdom had developed as the world's largest market for frozen meat (Perren, 2006). Supplying this market created profound spatial transformations in landscapes across the globe. In New Zealand native forests, swamps and tussock lands were cleared to make way for more productive 'English' grasslands (Pawson & Brooking, 2013). Political projects coalesced around making the family farm the moral and economic engine of development. Sheep and grass were materially reconstituted to make them more efficient generators of profit (Brooking, Pawson & Star, 2010; Woods, 2012, 2015). In the United Kingdom opposing flows of capital and food enabled new forms of urban and industrial development while simultaneously creating novel, distanced dependencies. The often-cited phrase that 'New Zealand was Britain's farm' reflected the deep imaginative, material and economic interconnectedness that evolved from New Zealand's involvement in the British-centred global meat trade. These connections have been widely documented, but a starting point for examining their temporal qualities lies in the recognition that no single market for frozen meat existed connecting together farmers and consumers. Instead the meat trade was a tangled skein of biological, technological, political and economic relations that linked farmers at one end and consumers at the other through chains of market encounters. Each encounter had its own temporal, and potentially fissiparous, rhythms but the expectations of lamb's temporal qualities storied by intermediaries such as the NZMB provided a synchronicity that enabled the fictive solidity of a 'global market' to assemble.

Following the resumption of normal trading after World War One, the United Kingdom's Ministry of Agriculture and Fisheries (UKMAF) (1925) identified a clear rhythm of lamb supply from Australian and New Zealand farms. It was a rhythm that was intimately tied to biological cycles of sheep fertility. In the Southern Hemisphere ewe fertility increased with the decrease in sunlight after the December summer solstice, with peak fertility being reached between February and April. Depending upon the timing of tupping, lambs conceived between February and April started to appear in paddocks in July. While the general rhythm of the season was orchestrated by changes in sunlight, the season's actual start, duration and quality was heavily shaped by climatic variability. Drought and its impact on grass growth loomed large as a crucial influence in shaping the linked timing of farm production and slaughter. A dry spring might delay the killing of lambs as they struggled with a lack of grass to put on weight, while the threat of a summer drought might hasten killings as farmers sought to get rid of sheep they might not be able to feed.

Biology and climate gave lamb-rearing and processing a seasonal temporality that deeply framed the market relationships performed between farmers selling lambs and the stock agents buying them. The biological cycle of lamb growth meant that there was an intense peak of suitable lambs around December and January as they reached prime weight for slaughter. In the bustling spot markets for lambs performed at sale yards across New Zealand pricing was calculated on estimates of weight. The target being the 30lb export lamb. Once lambs came close to this weight, farmers aimed to get them killed as quickly as possible to avoid them losing value by being graded as overweight by processors (Henry, 2017). Consequently, this pressure for swift sale and slaughter produced steep seasonal peaks in demand for killing contacts with processors. Variable weather and grass conditions might change the timing of the peak, but not the peak's existence.

The seasonality of sheep fertility and growth framed two long term dynamics that shaped the industry throughout the 20th century. First, difficulty spreading the temporal supply of lambs alongside a price imperative to get lambs slaughtered as soon as they reached an ideal export weight meant that freezing companies needed to try and kill as close to capacity as possible for as long as possible in order to remain profitable (Curtis, 2018). The realisation that profitability was a function of the relationship between killing capacity and actual killings meant that bitter competition existed between freezing companies for lambs. And farmers were quite willing to play off freezing companies against one another in spot markets to get higher prices for their lambs. Farmers also proved resistant to calls from freezing companies to adapt their stock management practices in order to spread the killing season's peak. Second, profitability was also driven by how fast lambs could be slaughtered. The drive for speed that provoked investments in new killing equipment and methods also produced a deeply uneasy labour relationship between freezing companies and unions. Introduced into New Zealand in 1932 from Victoria, the 'chain' system represented a means of exercising managerial control over artisanal, sole trader butchers, but one that was quickly co-opted by unions to control throughput and resist the casualisation of employment (Curtis, 2018). The need to maximise throughput for profitability, intense seasonal competition for lambs, the pressure from farmers to slaughter at ideal weights, and unionised control over 'chains' meant that lamb assemblages were vulnerable to threats of temporal disruption, especially when disrupted killings reverberated throughout supply chains (Curtis, 2018).

The particular rhythms of breeding, killing and storage that played out across New Zealand, Australia and South America meant that lamb arrived in the United Kingdom in different waves over the year. Before World War Two, Australian and South American lamb tended to dominate imports between

November and January, while the situation was reversed between March and October as New Zealand lamb arrived (see Figure 4.1).

The staggered arrival of frozen meat from the Southern Hemisphere occurred in markets with their own counter-cyclical rhythms of domestic (or 'home') supply. The timing of lamb's arrival in British markets also encountered consumption patterns operating at a range of scales, and with regional differences. Meat consumption tended to follow a regular pattern for many families. Oddy (2016, pp. 236–37) notes that up until World War Two, weekly meals might typically consist of, 'a joint roast of meat on Sunday, roast meat eaten cold on Monday, a meat pie (from the scraps) … on Tuesday, sausages on Wednesday, offal (liver) on Thursday – and fish on Friday. Saturday might be cold meats, pork pies, potted meats or tongue, with corned beef….' Over the course of the year the weekly cycle of demand for lamb was marked by recognisable annual peaks during Christmas and Easter. *Long durée* changes were also occurring that gradually changed weekly and yearly patterns of consumption. After World War Two the increased participation of women in the formal work force further changed patterns of meal production. Meals requiring less preparation and cooking and the greater use of pre-prepared, convenience foods encouraged by the emerging supermarkets became much more prevalent. The roast leg of lamb – the building block in the weekly pattern of pre-war consumption – became smaller and increasingly relegated to holidays. Summer saw demand grow for quickly cooked, smaller cuts like chops, steaks and racks. Conversely the arrival of winter saw demand shift back towards cuts suitable for slow cooking. Consumption, then, just like production, was

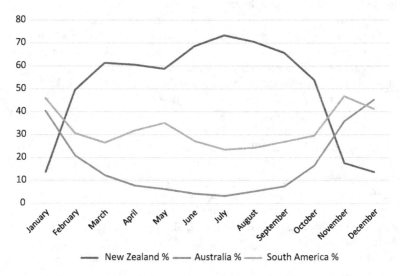

Figure 4.1 Seasonal patterns of lamb imports into the United Kingdom, 1924–31
Source: Adapted from Stephens & Barnicoat (1936)

characterised by deeply embedded temporal practices that encompassed regular weekly, seasonal and celebratory patterns of use. Making lamb a global economic object required finding ways to synchronise these disparate temporalities.

Making and selling the expectation of regularity

Selling New Zealand lamb involved the creation of expectations about the future of lamb. Expectations, as Beckert (2016) shows, are an integral feature of capitalist temporal orders. As such, their management involves sustained work to create imaginaries about what the future will hold as a means of guiding action in the present. In the meat trade, multiple actors engaged in building and maintaining a range of expectations storied at a range of temporal scales. This work represents an intense form of storytelling intended to align the reciprocal expectations of lamb's qualities among different markets actors situated in deeply different circumstances (Bogdanova, 2013). This storytelling revolved around maintaining provenance claims in the context of fierce competition and potential mislabelling (Higgins, 2004), the stabilisation of the material qualities of lamb carcasses (Henry, 2017), and the fashioning of regularity as an economic quality.

At a national scale in New Zealand, farmer-politicians, company directors, trade associations and other bodies regularly talked about the season gone, the season to come and the long-term prognosis for the meat trade. While there might be good or bad seasons the almost inevitable outlook was that the meat trade would continue to have a rosy future if farmers and meat companies worked co-operatively, paid attention to competitors and consumers, and maintained unfettered access to the United Kingdom's market. Binding together the expectation of future wealth was the practical realisation that prosperity required the production of certainty. The end of World War One generated a crisis in the meat trade as certainty evaporated. During World War One the relationship between New Zealand's meat producers and the United Kingdom's consumers had been maintained through a bulk supply agreement ('the commandeer') signed between the New Zealand and United Kingdom governments (Henry, 2017; Watson, 2007). However, disruptions to the supply of food markets in Europe after the end of the war in 1918, together with unemployment and falling wages, caused a significant drop in prices. New Zealand's exporters were also shaken by threats of limits to British markets as British government officials challenged the assumption that they would unquestioningly take the entirety of New Zealand's expanding meat production (Perren, 2006). The certainty of growing demand and with-it prosperity was being challenged.

During the 1920/21 season prices for New Zealand lamb at Smithfield fell dramatically. In that single season almost two seasons worth of carcasses from newly killed lambs and existing frozen stores were pitched onto a market already suffering from declining demand. The disruption caused by the collapse of the normal temporal rhythm of supply meant that by November 1921 significant agitation was growing for the government to bring some order to the supply of lambs (Woods, 1989). A committee of government members of parliament investigating the problem concluded that the situation was the result of the uneven scheduling of meat shipments and the costs of handling fragmented consignments. Despite arguments that the establishment of any organisation to control meat exports represented an unacceptable form of government intervention, the NZMPB was established by the Meat Export Control Act in February 1922, with wide powers to make any arrangements that it saw as necessary to ensure the economic and orderly sale of New Zealand meat.

The first significant act of the NZMPB was the imposition of a uniform grade standard for lamb carcasses upon exporters (Henry, 2017; Henry & Roche, 2018). Embedded in the stabilisation of lamb's physical qualities were stories about two necessary forms of time work. Analysis by the NZMPB had shown that significant numbers of lambs were being slaughtered underweight and fetching lower prices at Smithfield Market. Consequently, farmers were encouraged to hold lambs on farms for longer, so that they could put on enough weight to be graded as 'prime'. More time equated to more weight, and more weight translated into improved prices. The second form of time work revolved around improving the certainty and speed of transactions conducted between Smithfield's buyers and freezing companies. The NZMPB argued that a consistent, commonly understood quality of lamb would enable purchasing in advance without the delays caused by potentially fraught inspections by buyers once landed in the United Kingdom. The NZMPB's chair, David Jones argued that while 'Time may mean nothing to the sheep but it is gold to the owner' and that the future of the meat industry lay in its ability to consistently get lambs to the right weight, to improve the regularity of transportation, and to reduce the conflicts between different parties caused by different expectations about what was being sold (Jones, 1929, p. 155). Future prosperity rested upon weight and conformation being better synchronised by the creation of a set of quality expectations common across the market actors. The ultimate aspiration being the confidence by meat buyers to buy immediately 'off the hook' rather than wait for the physical inspection of lamb on Smithfield's buyers' walk.

Discussions of New Zealand's lamb industry have tended to focus on farms, farmers or geopolitical manoeuvring around trade access such as occurred at Ottawa in 1932. Far less attention has been paid to the organisation of the United Kingdom's meat markets, the multiple actors, imaginaries, devices and practices territorialised in those markets and the stretched topologies of day-to-day time work synchronising them. Consequently, while we have a picture of the temporalities of lamb-raising, processing and ultimately consumption, there is little understanding of the specific temporalities of the myriad butchers, jobbers and merchants that laboured to make lamb markets, and how they were mobilised as matters of concern into projects to fashion regularity.

In 1925 UKMAF reported on the growing refrigerated meat trade and the situation in which 'home' meat producers were facing competition from large, international organisations that brought, 'a more or less standardised, if refrigerated, product from overseas to the very heart of rural Britain' (Markets and Co-operation Branch, Ministry of Agriculture and Fisheries, 1925, p. iii). The report highlighted the crucial role of Smithfield Market in London as the de facto price setter of meat throughout the United Kingdom. Inside Smithfield lay an intricate set of territorialised relationships knitting together retailers, wholesalers and meat importing companies (See Figure 4.2). These relationships, performed through 'goodwill', sociability and speculation, were also intensely topological, connecting together New Zealand farmers and freezing companies with the Port of London's Royal Docks, Smithfield Market itself,

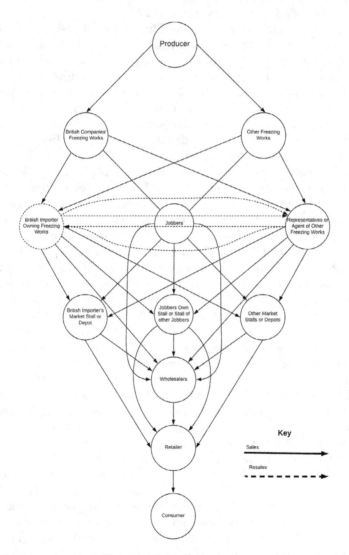

Figure 4.2 Imported meat – Channels of distribution
Source: Adapted from Markets and Co-operation Branch, Ministry of Agriculture and Fisheries (1925)

the cool stores clustered around and under Charterhouse Street, the underground rail sidings connecting Smithfield Market to Farringdon & High Holborn Station and beyond to the United Kingdom. J. Watson, writing in *The Frozen Meat Trade*, captured the intimateness of the global meat trade in Smithfield Market, where he observed the 'conservatism and clannishness' of meat buyers happy to deal with the same firms year after year regardless of price, intersecting with the, 'fact that hundreds of retailers make all their purchases on the Top and Middle sections and never, on any account, enter either the Poultry or Village sections' (Watson, 1929, p. 18).[2]

Just as pressure for killing space provided spot markets in New Zealand's saleyards created a temporal ebb and flow, a temporal rhythm also pushed and pulled at Smithfield's intimate socio-spatial relationships. Each day, beginning at midnight, meat was pitched onto the market from cold stores, where it was purchased by wholesalers before the arrival of retail butchers at 4am. The material properties of the various meats being sold imposed distinctive temporal imperatives on these pitchings. Large sides of chilled beef were particularly risky, because once pitched onto the market they had to be sold that day because of the labour required to return them to cool stores. A miscalculation would mean that sides would be left hanging to compete with fresh, and more desirable, supplies from cold stores the following day. Frozen lamb and mutton were less risky, because carcasses could be more easily retrieved during the day from cold stores if demand had been underestimated or re-deposited without spoilage back into storage at the close of the market. Decisions about the level of pitchings were a complex, situated calculation involving a fine sense of the interplay between the meat being pitched, its condition, and the particular day-to-day dynamics of myriad other factors, ranging from changes in the weather to the arrival of unexpected meat shipments. A sense of the swirl of rumour and opinion that made the market at Smithfield each day can be glimpsed in regular columns such as 'My Walk Through Smithfield' by 'Buyer' carried in the trade journal *Modern Meat Marketing*. 'Buyers' March 1934 column, for example, contained observations about the state of the markets caused inter alia by the forthcoming Fat Stock Commission findings, the psychological state of butchers, the Church Calendar, chilled beef from the new Westfield Works in Auckland, a shift in demand for home-killed lamb, quotes from the Mikado designed to illustrate pork and bacon policy and an exhibition of fat lambs from the Wairarapa described as 'New Zealand's best yet' (Buyer, 1934, p. 103).

A serendipitous discovery had been that lamb's slow physical transformation by enzymes such as pepsin and trypepsin improved its tenderness. This meant that hard frozen New Zealand lamb benefited from the enforced ageing required by being produced months from market. But while taste developed over time, maintaining unsold lambs in cold storage was not an unqualified panacea to an overestimation of demand. Keeping meat in cold storage in perpetuity, either in dedicated cold stores such as operated by the London Central Markets Cold Storage Company or on ships themselves, was theoretically possible, but in practice much more time-sensitive. Frozen meat stored for any significant length of time began to grow moulds on its exterior. Described as 'store staleness', these moulds did not generally affect the eating qualities of the meat, but they affected its visual appeal to buyers (wholesale and retail) and consequently value. Cold storage also generated costs, and indeed by the late 1920s the majority of frozen lamb was being sold ex-ship by Smithfield's buyers without physically passing through Smithfield. Nonetheless, jobbers and other wholesalers could – and did – use cold storage as the opportunity for speculation by buying meat when there were heavy pitchings, storing that meat and then trying to sell it again when supply was shorter. What made this risky was that the market operated in an informational vacuum. There was little knowledge about the amount and types of meat being stored, the amount of meat being processed in either the United Kingdom or the various exporting countries, the amount of meat 'on the water' in ships and the longer-term seasonal fluctuations in supply caused by benign conditions in New Zealand or drought in Australia. Finding out the temporal dynamics of supply – how much, what quality and importantly when – became a matter of deep concern for Smithfield's merchants following the disruption of the early 1920s. The concerns of Smithfield's merchants intersected with producer boards, such as the NZMPB because an irregular market driven by information uncertainties, volatility in meat supplies and the fear of speculation was storied as creating price swings that drove consumers to alternative meats, or worse reduced meat consumption altogether.

One often repeated fear from farmers in New Zealand was that meat prices were being manipulated by 'meat rings' in London, which used the unknowable timing of current and future meat supplies to periodically corner the market (O'Connor, 1973). The *Poverty Bay Herald* editorialised, for example, that meat was being sacrificed to meat combines who having private cold storage, 'hold back, or flood the meat market, at their will'. The required response opined the paper was that the NZMPB needed to begin using its powers to control meat, and it warned that, 'Until trusts and combines in the food of the people are dealt with effectively there can be no assurance of stability of markets for Dominion produce' (Poverty Bay Herald, 1924, p. 4). Conversely, the NZMPB was itself not immune from the suspicion that it was deliberately manipulating the timing of lamb supplies in order to drive prices up. The NZMPB's London manager defended its powers, arguing that unregulated flows of meat, and the resulting gluts and shortages, only benefited speculators. Investigations into these claims concluded that while the role of the Board in regulating the supplies of meat being exported had had no impact on the general increase in lamb and mutton prices, it gently suggested that the Board's actions be subject to ongoing scrutiny (Royal Commission on Food Prices, 1924/25). To make the flow of meat supplies more transparent the NZMPB began publicly advertising the quantities of meat from New Zealand that were either in cold storage in the United Kingdom or on route to the United Kingdom. But the NZMPB argued that without some ordering of lamb exports through the allocation of shipping space the seasonal ebb and flow of lamb killing meant that, 'if supplies were shipped and placed on the market as soon as they were ready there would be periods of gluts followed by periods of shortage' (p. 125). Consistent with a strategy of reducing uncertainty through carcass grading and regular information bulletins the enduring rationale of the NZMPB's shipping policy emerged as being, 'To keep a steady flow of meat going forward to the British market over the twelve months of the year' (Stephens & Barnicoat, 1936, p. 633). In these words we can see the project of temporal regularity coalescing.

It is within this project of creating market regularity that we can understand the specific advertising work done by the NZMPB in wholesale trade magazines such as *Modern Meat Marketing*. Meat marketing has gathered little attention, apart from glancing references to organisations such as the Empire Marketing Board, national histories of advertising, or more contemporary examinations of place-based provenance claims. In her discussion of New Zealand's commodity marketing in the United Kingdom, Barnes (2013, p. 156) describes the post–World War One years as an intensely busy period of image making as commodity advertising, 'refined and redoubled the presentation of New Zealand as a settled, Home-styled farm, not distinctive nation'. By the mid-1930s the NZMPB was regularly spending the majority of its budget undertaking mass advertising campaigns across the United Kingdom (Barnes, 2012, 2013). In 1932 the NZMPB distributed over 3 million postcards of various New Zealand pastoral scenes and 2 million copies of a booklet providing recipes as well as information on the inspection of meat products. In these campaigns consumers were targeted through advertising to butchers in the belief that, 'shops throughout the United Kingdom are the best ground on which to acclaim the merits of our lamb' (New Zealand Meat Producers Board, 1932, p. 8). Pains were taken to ensure that the board's free advertising material only went to suitable retailers. Applicants for material were required to obtain the signature of their wholesaler attesting to the fact that they consistently stocked New Zealand lamb. The desired result was that the Board would have, 'the satisfaction of knowing that only the genuine retailer of New Zealand lamb is displaying the material, and also that wherever the material is displayed New Zealand lamb may be obtained on demand' (New Zealand Meat Producers Board, 1935a, p. 8). The outcome was an intense and sustained effort by the NZMPB to place New Zealand lamb in front of butchers and consumers and to imbue that lamb with hygiene, purity and health qualities that resonated with emerging anxieties about the quality and supply of industrial food.

As the advertising landscape quickly evolved during the 1920s and 1930s, stories of a pastoral New Zealand producing 'The Best Lamb in the World' were increasingly joined by images of consumers delighting in their purchase (Barnes, 2013). However, purity and health were only ever a part of the qualities being touted by the Board. Underpinning the Board's marketing to butchers was the selling of regularity as an integral quality of New Zealand lamb. This relationship was partly articulated through the forms of corporal regularity wanted by butchers, produced by the Board's grading standards for carcasses, and demonstrated in competitions and displays at both rural agriculture and production shows in New Zealand and in Smithfield galleries (Henry & Roche, 2018). It was also performed through work to show buyers how they could identify genuine New Zealand lamb by paying attention to the regularity of the size, placement and wording of marks on carcasses and of the labelling of meat on display, in order to avoid being duped into buying inferior (or at least non-New Zealand) lamb. Irregularity was a marker of danger and the threat of being duped. Regularity was also a temporal relationship that needed careful management, given the distance between meat suppliers in New Zealand and purchasers in the United Kingdom. Consequently, the NZMPB's advertising stressed regularity in terms of a steadiness of supply to wholesalers, and of supply 'on demand' to butchers. Simultaneously, the selling of regularity went beyond high-lighting the supply of lambs and included claims about how New Zealand lamb would drive continuous business to butchers. These multiple layers of storytelling can be seen, for example, in advertisements in Modern Meat Marketing from the New Zealand Meat Board's 1935 campaign. Under the slogan 'Spring Now for Lamb Sales!' new season lamb from New Zealand is extolled for its perfect condition and the crucial quality that new stocks were arriving on the market everyday (New Zealand Meat Producers Board, 1935b, p. 103).

The result, as suggested in another one of the Meat Board's advertisements, was that by stocking and displaying New Zealand lamb, retailers would sell, 'not just spasmodically, but regularly everyday of the year' and that they should 'Try this profitable policy tomorrow and everyday from now on' (New Zealand Meat Producers Board, 1935a, p. 255). This advice was summed up by the call for retailers to follow the 'golden rule' of 'NEW ZEALAND Lamb every day of the Year!' Those retailers who did this, 'find by doing this they can rely on customers returning to them again and again - regular orders the whole year through' (New Zealand Meat Producers Board, 1936, p. 273). These themes were repeated across multiple campaigns. The 1938 campaign talks of the arrival of new season's lamb into the United Kingdom, and encourages retailers to stock them because, 'You'll not only get immediate, profitable results but will create good 'lasting' business too! (New Zealand Meat Producers Board, 1938, p. 149), and well into the 1960s adverts promoted the fact that, 'When you order New Zealand lamb you can be certain that you will always receive the same high quality meat every time' (New Zealand Meat Producers Board, 1963, p. 13). In its 1939 review of its activities, the NZMPB argued that in addition to making New Zealand meat visible in the United Kingdom market, its campaigns showed consumers, and in particular the fabled British 'housewife', how lamb could be 'obtained with certainty' at any time (New Zealand Meat Producers Board, 1939, p. 9). By working in this way, lamb was positioned in a virtuous cycle, whereby retailers could rely on consistent supplies of lamb, thus avoiding the price swings that accompanied gluts and shortages. In turn, this would reliably create new business since consumers could expect butchers to stock lamb and to be able to plan a week's shopping with certainty about price and supply.

The outbreak of World War Two in 1939 profoundly altered the global market for frozen meat well into the 1950s. In the United Kingdom, as in New Zealand, meat became rationed, and its procurement, distribution and sale were removed from the tight networks of importers, wholesalers and jobbers who controlled Smithfield. A feature of the wartime frozen meat trade was the emphasis on expanding production and a shift in the temporal character of supply contracts. Expanding production still occurred within the limits of biological seasonality, a perilous journey to the United Kingdom and finite freezer space. What did change, however, was the chain of spot markets, from farmer to processor, processor to wholesaler, wholesaler to retailer and retailer to consumer, which characterised global trade in meat. From World War Two until the 1950s lamb from New Zealand was sold to the United Kingdom on the basis of long-term supply contracts. These contracts took the work of the Board before the war a step further, insofar as they were devised around maintaining regular shipments: 'Subject to freight, being available, shipments to be made as far as possible in equal monthly quantities' (New Zealand Meat Producers Board, 1940, p. 5). The last of the long-term supply contracts ended in 1955 and with it the Board could note that it had reached the end of an era as the United Kingdom government relinquished control of its meat markets, and Smithfield reopened. As the trade returned to commercial control, the NZMPB quickly and unequivocally restated its policy of regulating shipments to smooth the supply of meat and avoid market fluctuations, as well as restarting extensive advertising extolling the regularity of New Zealand lamb.

Conclusion

Sharma (2014) argues that much of the debate about time and modernity has revolved around a combination of the celebration of speed and anxiety about its effects. The result underplays other experiences of time and crucially how those experiences are assembled into distinctive temporal orders that structure social and economic relationships. This chapter has explored the making and maintenance of regularity as a key temporal quality in the assemblage of meat markets for New Zealand lamb between World War One and World War Two. The meat industry in New Zealand has been built around the assemblage of specific places (farms, freezing works, Smithfield), relationships (the United Kingdom and consumer desires), materialities (sheep and lamb carcasses) and technologies (refrigeration). However, woven through all of this has been the project of making and maintaining a temporal order that transformed the regular consumption of a perishable, seasonable commodity produced weeks of sailing away into what Law (2014) terms a 'daily miracle'.

The enduring significance of the assemblage of this temporal order is that time and its governance became infrastructural. The effect of this, however, is that time work produced conditions of possibility that gradually disappeared into the background as a matter of fact about the operation of meat markets. Yet this poses all manner of future questions. Market assemblages are often understood as fragile achievements, yet the temporal order exposed in this chapter has been practiced for over a century, and despite profound changes in economic relationships wrought by entry of the United Kingdom unto the European Economic Community in 1973, the chill winds of neoliberalism from 1984 onwards or the dissolution of the NZMPB in 1995, its enduring success is such that it is difficult to think of other ways that the market could exist. As this shows, time is neither an accidental nor independent market relationship. It is strategically worked on to produce particular outcomes for particular actors, and it produces effects that can be remarkably durable. Consequently, in thinking about how markets are placed, peopled and materialised, it is crucial to examine how markets rely on the specific storying and practice of time work and the invisible conditions of possibility created by the socio-technical assemblage of temporal orders. Time becomes an economic quality, and we need to ask how, why and for whom does the experience of when become significant.

Notes

1 While New Zealand is the official name for the country, emerging practice is to refer to the country as Aotearoa New Zealand to signal its bicultural origins and future. However, following Campbell's (2020) argument about the ontological politics signified by shifts between Aotearoa, New Zealand and Aotearoa New Zealand, I use New Zealand to overtly situate the chapter within the ontological frame of Pākeha settler society.
2 Smithfield market in the late 1920s had five distinct sections: the Meat Section West (split into Top Market and Middle Market); the Poultry Section; the General Section (known as the Village); and the Annexe which stood outside the main market.

References

Anderson, J. (2009). Lard to lean: Making the meat-type hog in post-World War II America. In W. Belasco & R. Horowitz (Eds), *Food chains: from farmyard to shopping cart* (pp. 29–46). Philadelphia, PA: University of Pennsylvania Press.

Armstrong, A., Dunlop-Young, T., Hogg, J., Medcalf, J. & Watson, J. (Eds). (1929). *The frozen and chilled meat trade: A practical treatise by specialists in the meat trade* (Volume II). London: Gresham Publishing Company.

Baker, T. & McGuirk, P. (2017). Assemblage thinking as methodology: Commitments and practice for critical policy research. *Territory, Politics, Governance,* 5(4), 425–442.

Barnes, F. (2012). *New Zealand's London: A colony and its metropolis.* Auckland, New Zealand: Auckland University Press.

Barnes, F. (2013). Bringing another empire alive? The Empire Marketing Board and the construction of dominion identity, 1926–33. *The Journal of Imperial and Commonwealth History,* 42(1), 61–85. https://doi.org/10.1080/03086534.2013.826456.

Beckert, J. (2016). *Imagined futures: Fictional expectations and capitalist dynamics.* Cambridge, MA: Harvard University Press.

Bogdanova, E. (2013). Account of the past: Mechanisms of quality construction in the market for antiques. In J. Beckert & C. Musselin (Eds), *Constructing quality. The Classification of goods in markets* (pp. 153–173). Oxford: Oxford University Press.

Brooking, T., Pawson, E. & Star, P. (2010). *Seeds of Empire: The environmental transformation of New Zealand.* London: I.B. Taurus.

Buyer. (1934). My walk through Smithfield. *Modern Meat Marketing,* VII, No. 3, 103.

Campbell, H. (2020). Farming inside invisible worlds: Modernist agriculture and its consequences. London: Bloomsbury Academic.

Carse, A. & Kneas, D. (2019). Unbuilt and unfinished: The temporalities of infrastructure. *Environment and Society: Advances in Research,* 10, 9–28. https://doi.org/10.3167/ares.2019.100102.

Critchell, J.T. & Raymond, J. (1912). *A History of the frozen meat trade.* London: Constable & Company.

Cronon, W. (1991). *Nature's metropolis: Chicago and the Great West.* New York, NY: W. W. Norton.

Curtis, B. (2018). New Zealand's meat board, markets and the killing season: A Twentieth-Century labour history of unintended consequences. *Labour History*, 114 (May), 93–112.

DeLanda, M. (2006). *A new philosophy of society: Assemblage theory and social complexity*. London: Continuum.

Freidberg, S. (2009). *Fresh: A perishable history*. Cambridge, MA: The Belknap Press of Harvard University Press.

Genoways, T. (2014). *The chain: Farm factory and the fate of our food*. New York, NY: Harper Collins.

Godley, A. & Williams, B. (2009). Democratizing luxury and the contentious "Invention of the technological chicken" in Britain. *Business History Review*, 83(2), 267–290.

Grant, R., David, J., Ramsey, R., Rey-Alvarez, G., Richelet, J. & Watkins-Pitchford, H. (Eds). (1929). *The frozen and chilled meat trade: A practical treatise by specialists in the meat trade*, Volume I. London: Gresham Publishing Company.

Gregson, N. (2017). Logistics at work: Trucks, containers and the friction of circulation in the UK. *Mobilities*, 12(3), 343–364. https://doi.org/10.1080/17450101.2015.1087680.

Henry, M. (2017). Meat, metrics and market devices: Commensuration infrastructures and the assemblage of 'the schedule' in New Zealand's red meat sector. *Journal of Rural Studies*, 52, 100–109. https://doi.org/10.1016/j.jrurstud.2017.03.001.

Henry, M. & Roche, M. (2018). Making lamb futures. In E. Pawson & Biological Economies Team (Eds), *The new biological economy: How New Zealanders are creating value from the Land* (pp. 41–60). Auckland: Auckland University Press.

Higgins, D. (2004). 'Mutton dressed as lamb?' The Misrepresentation of Australian and New Zealand meat in the British market, c.1890–1914. *Australian Economic History Review*, 44(2), 161–184.

Horowitz, R. (2006). *Putting meat on the American table: Taste, technology, transformation*. Baltimore, MD: The Johns Hopkins University Press.

Jones, D. (1929). New Zealand trade. In *The frozen and chilled meat trade: A practical treatise by specialists in the meat trade*, Volume I (pp. 101–158). London: Gresham Publishing Company.

Jones, L., Heley, J. & Woods, M. (2018). Unravelling the global wool assemblage: Researching place and production networks in the global countryside. *Sociologia Ruralis*, 59(1), 137–158.

Larkin, B. (2013). The politics and poetics of infrastructure. *Annual Review of Anthropology*, 42, 327–343.

Law, J. (2014). *Working well with wickedness*. (CRESC Working Paper 135). Milton Keynes: Centre for Research on Socio-Cultural Change.

Markets and Co-operation Branch, Ministry of Agriculture and Fisheries. (1925). *Report on the trade in refrigerated beef, mutton and lamb*. London: His Majesty's Stationary Office.

New Zealand Meat Producers Board. (1932). *Tenth annual report and statement of accounts for the year ending 30th June 1932*. Wellington.

New Zealand Meat Producers Board. (1935a). A good tonic! *Modern Meat Marketing*, June, 255.

New Zealand Meat Producers Board. (1935b). Spring! Now for lamb sales. *Modern Meat Marketing*, March, 103.

New Zealand Meat Producers Board. (1936). Follow the golden rule. *Modern Meat Marketing*, June, 273.

New Zealand Meat Producers Board. (1938). New season's milk-fed New Zealand lamb. *Modern Meat Marketing*, April, 149.

New Zealand Meat Producers Board. (1939). *Nineteenth annual report and statement of accounts for the year ended 30 June 1939.* Wellington.

New Zealand Meat Producers Board. (1940). *Eighteenth annual report and statement of accounts for the year ended 30 June 1940.* Wellington.

New Zealand Meat Producers Board. (1963). What does New Zealand lamb mean to you? *Meat Marketing*, November, 13.

O'Connor, P.S. (1973). Mr Massey and the American Meat Trust: Some sidelights on the origins of the meat board. Massey Memorial Lecture, Massey University.

Oddy, D.J. (2016). From roast beef to chicken nuggets: How technology changed meat consumption in Britain in the Twentieth Century. In A. Drouard & D. Oddy (Eds), *The food industries of Europe in the Nineteenth and Twentieth Centuries* (pp. 231–245). Aldershot: Ashgate Publishing.

Pawson, E. & Brooking, T. (Eds). (2013). *Making a new land: Environmental histories of New Zealand.* Dunedin: Otago University Press.

Perren, R. (2006). *Taste, trade and technology: The development of the international meat industry since 1840.* Aldershot: Ashgate Publishing.

Pilcher, J.M. (2016). Culinary infrastructure: How facilities and technologies create value and meaning around food. *Global Food History*, 1–27. https:doi.org/10.1080/20549547.2016.1214896.

Poverty Bay Herald. (1924). The Meat Producers' Board., p. 4, 2 September.

Rees, J. (2013). *Refrigeration nation: A history of ice, appliances, and enterprise in America.* Baltimore, MD: Johns Hopkins University Press.

Royal Commission on Food Prices. (1924/25). *First report of the royal commission on food prices.* London: His Majesty's Stationary Office.

Sharma, S. (2014). *In the meantime: Temporality and cultural politics.* Durham, NC: Duke University Press.

Star, S. (1999). The Ethnography of infrastructure. *American Behavioral Scientist*, 43(3), 377–391.

Star, S.L. & Ruhleder, K. (1996). Steps toward an ecology of infrastructure: Design and access for large information spaces. *Information Systems Research*, 7(1), 111–134. https://doi.org/10.2307/23010792.

Stephens, F.B. & Barnicoat, C.R. (1936). Marketing of meat. In H. Belshaw (Ed.), *Agricultural organisation in New Zealand: a survey of land utilization, farm organisation, finance and marketing* (pp. 623–647). Melbourne: Melbourne University Press.

Watson, J. (1929). Wholesale Meat Markets. In A. Armstrong, T. Dunlop Young, J. Hogg, J. Medcalf & J. Watson (Eds), *The frozen and chilled meat trade: A practical treatise by specialists in the meat trade* (Volume II, pp. 3–21). London, UK: Gresham Publishing Company.

Watson, J. (2007). Patriotism, profits and problems: New Zealand farming during the Great War. In J. Crawford & I. McGibbon (Eds), *New Zealand's Great War: New Zealand, the allies and the First World War* (pp. 534–549). Auckland: Exisle Publishing.

Woods, R. (1989). *The history and role of producer marketing boards in New Zealand.* Wellington: Economic Development Commission.

Woods, R. (2012). Breed, culture, and economy: The New Zealand frozen meat trade, 1880–1914. *Agricultural History Review*, 60(2), 288–308. Retrieved from www.ingentaconnect.com/content/bahs/agrev/2012/00000060/00000002/art00009.

Woods, R. (2015). From colonial animal to imperial edible: Building an empire of sheep in New Zealand, ca. 1880–1900. *Comparative Studies of South Asia, Africa and the Middle East*, 35(1), 117–136.

5 Pre-conditions for making (desired) markets in the spirit of Ki Uta Ki Tai – Mountains to the Sea

Re-commoning and economic-environment transitionings

Dan Hikuroa†*, Richard Le Heron†** and Erena Le Heron*** and the Participatory Processes Research Team

†CO-LEAD AUTHORS
*TE WĀNANGA O WAIPAPA, UNIVERSITY OF AUCKLAND
**SCHOOL OF ENVIRONMENT, UNIVERSITY OF AUCKLAND
***LE HERON LEIGH CONSULTANCY

Whakataukī[1]

Toitū te whenua	If the land is well
Toitū te moana	If the sea is well
Toitū te tangata	The people will thrive

Introduction

Aotearoa New Zealand (Aotearoa NZ) is arguably in an unprecedented moment of disconnecting and reconnecting economic and environment relations. The moment springs from multi-faceted engagement of investors and institutions with a remarkable connecting metaphor – Ki Uta Ki Tai/Mountains to the Sea[2] (KUKT/MS) (Tipa, Harmsworth, Williams & Kitson, 2016; Winder & Le Heron, 2016). This conception in Aotearoa NZ is the idea of creating a holistic framework drawing on Māori and European knowledge systems has often been vigorously resisted in the face of increasing championing. We contend the moment has major implications for making and remaking desired markets.

Empire and colonial relations continue to constrain the imagination of Aotearoa NZ research into economy. Export earnings, quantity and metropolitan destinations drove national development investment. In the international division of labour the country was a bulk supplier of undifferentiated commodity products processed in large-scale overseas owned processing plants, with much output channelled through single desk Producer Marketing Boards. This enclosure of commercial thinking and practices gave restricted meaning to marketing. A perennial concern has been that local value adding is stifled by supply and sales arrangements dictated from offshore or

DOI: 10.4324/9780429296260-5

enforced by legacy capital. State-led or state-induced restructuring opened the economy in the 1980s and 1990s. This saw the collapse of many historical at-a-distance arrangements and in the 2000s energised the exploration of alternative ways of connecting into overseas markets — at the same time as striving to meet the demands of externally imposed audit, benchmarking, certification and standards systems in global markets. As KUKT/MS conceptions in the 2000s gathered momentum, the implications of different knowledge foundations of science and Māori understandings became increasingly obvious. Holistic science ideas mostly ignored institutional politics and power arrangements and actor motives, while Māori world views that brought collective competencies and holistic practice to discussions were often disregarded in a compartmentalised mainstream institutional landscape. The gradual rise of new market-making imagination and ambition was embroiled in the tensions and contradictions of an unknown knowledge space demarcated by differing world and organisational views. The chapter engages with and within these dynamics, exploring preconditions for value adding, in order to link it back to market-making that is emerging from historically and place conscious relational agency, deeply cognisant of KUKT/MS relations.

The chapter is an outgrowth of co-development of KUKT/MS ideas among geographers and social scientists in Aotearoa NZ aimed at extending understandings of collective efforts to re-common economic-ecological relations. The findings of the Marsden Funded land-based Biological Economies project (R. Le Heron et al., 2016; Pawson *et al.* 2018), the MIBE supported marine focused Marine Futures project (R. Le Heron *et al.*, 2016) and Phase 1 of the Sustainable Seas National Science Challenge over the past decade have concluded that transformative knowledge gains would accrue from adopting holistic conceptions of ecology and economy relations. The span of this research meant that the historical dilemmas of utilising the country's land, coast and sea ecosystems and territorial positioning in empire and globalising processes centred on largely property-based societal organisation, could be re-interpreted because of the conceptual reach of the KUKT/MS knowledge systems.

The chapter responds to three main concerns. First, we hold that while a 'moment of connecting' is upon us, we fear that any potentially transformative holistic re-conception will be overwhelmed by description of connections and new relationships that omit networks of power, politics and social co-learning within which the concepts and the connecting are appearing (Greenaway *et al.*, 2020). This has major implications for how Aotearoa NZ presents itself into world commerce. Second, it stimulates identification and lines of interrogation of new and adaptive connections through the use of a thought experiment (TE) that deliberately 'collides' two extreme sites of radical relational agency, one involving investment (Wakatū) and the other regulation (HBRC). The TE provides a glimpse of who we posit to be leaders at the frontiers of KUKT/MS framings, philosophy, knowledge and practice. Third, by forcing co-habitation of two exemplars through a TE it confronts unstable complexities of real political economy in different settings. Through the TE methodology we investigate attempts to *create collectively owned and administered relational assets*, a phenomenon we name as *'re-commoning'*.

The chapter opens with an Aotearoa NZ genealogy of the Thought Experiment idea and a collation of defining features of the idea as practiced in geographical research. This is followed by an internationally pioneering co-framing of KUKT/MS as an intellectual land-coast-sea framework for re-focusing collective efforts to re-common. The TE as a knowledge intervention is then positioned in the evolving dynamics of economic activities and environmental management, including why particular exemplars were chosen. The interrogation of the exemplars has two phases. First, situated empirical evidence is assembled around four key indicators of connecting associated with commoning-like intentions. Second, discussion moves to consideration of the emergent trajectories of each exemplar with a view to establishing potentialities and constraints that presently define the exemplar organising principles and practices and attendant strategies. This is achieved by asking two questions: 'If every enterprise in Aotearoa NZ was like Wakatū, what does this mean for Regional Councils?' and 'If every Regional Council was like Hawke's Bay, what new relationships with enterprise could be forged and what could enterprise look like?'

Why a thought experiment?

Thought experiments are increasingly being used to develop enactive geographies (R. Le Heron *et al.*, 2016; E. Le Heron, Lewis & R. Le Heron, 2016; Carolan, 2019; Lewis & Le Heron, 2019). They are bold departures from standard knowledge approaches that describe and explain. TEs are interventions in politics and power relations of existing knowledge, while having the aspiration to sketch disruptive and seemingly impossible directions and dynamics. They are predicated on bringing to the table (virtual or real) a diversity of interests in 'let's take a look' framings that are outside the usual boxing of knowledge. Crucial to this co-learning and co-production strategy are participatory processes that typically diversify views (E. Le Heron *et al.*, 2019a; E. Le Heron *et al.*, 2019b). A distinguishing feature is attention to boundary conditions and associations among multiple world views in order to release new kinds of knowing, make new knowns and evaluate extant knowledge.

The Aotearoa NZ scene is replete with the use of TEs especially in socioscientific research as well as pioneering legislation.[3] This has been unwittingly nurtured by government funded research in the form of a National Science Challenge (NSC) process commenced in 2014, which has put a premium on impactful conscious engagement (Blackett *et al.*, 2020). Despite a NSC structure that administratively and intellectually separates and isolates each Challenge (mirroring legislative compartmentalisation), the mood and action of many researchers has been to explore the new knowledge generated in prescribed orbits **and** undertake cross-boundary inquiry when evidence and opportunity overwhelmed the artificial dictates of the Challenge structure.

The New Zealand Geographical Society/Institute of Australian Geographers (NZGS/IAG) joint conference held in Auckland 2018 gave an opportunity to rehearse new intellectual directions about politics, economy and environment.

A special session on KUKT/MS was convened. The invitation stressed the unique opportunity presented to develop place-based, interconnected, and equitable environmental policy and management, with an emphasis on the role of indigenous rights and knowledge, and in particular the interconnectedness of ecosystems inclusive of people. The aspiration was to further develop a community of participatory practice working from KUKT/MS. This explicit holistic framing shifted the ground upon which those at the conference might participate, especially giving some prominence to ideas emanating from Post Structural Political Economy (PSPE) (Campbell, 2020; Larner & Le Heron, 2002; Lewis & Le Heron, 2019).

The idea of a TE as a contribution to the special session drew inspiration from projects with which members of the team were associated. First, the project 'Navigating marine social-ecological systems' (Davies *et al.*, 2018) and 'Enabling inter-agency collaboration on cumulative effects' (Davies *et al.*, 2017) were creating new knowledge in this vein. This turned out to be a call to social scientists and ecologists to cement their collaborations around what it meant to focus on generating a new ordering of holistic and situated knowledge. Second, a systematic exploration began of the emergence of independent participatory processes in the country's marine spaces, as seen through the multiple lens of social, political, economic, administrative, cultural and ecological processes and intersections (E. Le Heron *et al.*, 2019a). This project, 'Testing participatory processes for marine management' (E. Le Heron, 2019b), has led to new relational research capacities and capabilities aimed at exploring and forging alternative futures. Third, a blue economy project centred on melding principles and practices from kaitiakitanga[4] and the Māori economy[5] with those of science informed Ecosystem Based Management in the mainstream economy (Lewis, 2018). The project 'Creating value from a blue economy' was an experimental frontier itself, increasingly focusing on a green-wave investment experiment. The primary implicit interest of these projects is that of arriving at interventions on behalf of collective commons-making.

Co-framing KUKT/MS

The intellectual fusing of KUKT/MS is in the spirit of collective commons building. It has had many immediate and interdependent outcomes on knowledge priorities. Perhaps foremost, it engendered a growing sensitivity to look both upstream to originating processes and downstream to noticeably impacted ecologies, in multi-level framings. This quickly morphed in two directions, into an explicit recognition of both more-than-human and human agency in the complex movement of water or pollutants from innumerable sources and realisation that new meanings and mappings of territory and scales of spatial relations were needed. A new level of appreciation grew of the centrality of relational agency in re-shaping the economic investment and regulation. The choices being made by individuals somewhere could be seen to be traceable and their consequences known and better understood. Imagining habitation in every respect resonated with Māori perspectives. But accepting that having to acquire and use societal and ecological knowledge in equal, respectful and generative measure seemed for many insurmountable. Positively, asking historically new questions of the complexities being exposed gave new impetus to research, especially on the frontiers of contrasts between rates/ duration/intensity of ecological and social flows, feedbacks and tipping points has allowed individual enterprises and institutions to be re-comprehended.

Aotearoa NZ has been the setting of an extraordinary effort to cross-fertilise Māori and iwi[6] conceptions of KUKT with science based ones focusing on Ecosystem Based Management (EBM) (Hewitt, Faulkner, Greenaway & Lundquist, 2018). In spite of a widespread commitment to exploring the knowledge systems, differences in starting positions in this conversation are often overlooked. KUKT is an expression of a diversity of collective social organisation oriented to intergenerational resourcefulness. EBM is a science-colonising philosophy that regards resources as endlessly available for extraction or appropriation. This basic difference needs to be kept in mind when engaging with the exemplars.

Collective re-commoning

The special session carried an implied provocation, to address understandings of commons lost and efforts to re-common. The collective but distinctive imaginaries invoked by KUKT/MS were accepted as requiring conscious critical and reflective interrogation in terms of their placement of commons ideas. There are, however, risks in introducing the European word commons and accordingly its conceptual basis. It has limited currency in contemporary socio-scientific framings in Aotearoa NZ, but has traction among some Māori researchers who also speak of natural resource capture as evidenced in the Sustainable Seas Phase 2 workshop series held February 2019 in Wellington. The category springs from political economy and has received attention through the work of economists Ostrom (1990) and Poteete, Janssen & Ostrom (2010) who have internationally surveyed localised initiatives using principles for resolving demands for existing finite common pool resources and sought to extend their use more widely. As a concept it presents itself as an object of collectively assembled understandings and rejects the knowledge blanket of so called market solutions to societal organisation. But it is also a concept removed from the actual realities of commoning, which carries with it knowledge and practice risks when applied in contemporary settings. In Aotearoa NZ we regard commoning as encompassing active processes of reinstatement, restoration, regeneration and new directions. We posit the notion that Aotearoa NZ has its own situated experiences with the erosion and re-making of commons relations, which are visible in the TE. Crucially, commons platforms are fundamentally as much distributive and redistributive processes as they are collectively owned and governed resource spaces. These pressing governance issues are integral to the TE framing.

The TE was an outgrowth of dialogue in the participatory processes work stream that has been progressing understandings of how to negotiate conversations in and among multi-verse cross cultural spaces. The researchers felt they had the requisite skills to put under the spotlight one of the most vexing social challenges laid bare by the co-framings of KUKT/MS, that of re-commoning against the backdrop of property rights distributional arrangements

Thought experiment methodology

A selection process was devised to identify possible exemplars that were living out the issues of re-commoning and resisting resource exploitation, from the perspectives of Māori enterprise and a natural resource management regulator. To give credibility to the TE it was felt necessary to identify and select publicly recognised examples of alternative inspiration, practice and different economic-environment outcomes; examples where the potentiality of changes and new connecting was both visible and on the public record through research documentation and media coverage.

We wished to highlight expansionary enterprise that through its connections was undertaking collective assembling that enriched value creating relations beyond the enterprise, but that were intimately tied into stabilising regulatory pressures and requirements, so the enterprise could achieve its goals which included governing market opportunities. In a similar vein we sought an exemplar regulatory agency that was seeking to shift its performance from regulatory box ticking to adding value to economy through regulatory support. Such a disposition re-shapes regulatory interpretations and investor behaviours to create and extend collective benefits through collaboration and participation. We quickly realised that two contrasting exemplars fulfilled our criteria.

Given the Aotearoa NZ context where the Māori or 'taniwha' economy (Le Heron & Roche, 2018) is growing, the Sustainable Seas deep commitment to Vision Mātauranga and the research team's research protocol of co-journeying with iwi and hapū[7] in marine spaces, kaitiaki-centred Māori enterprise (Rout *et al.*, 2019), then Wakatū Incorporation formed the most demonstrative trajectory of holistic business organisation and performance consistent with intersecting with KUKT/MS. It has interests on land and in the sea. HBRC's case rests on it being one of the country's largest regional councils, European settlement was early, its regional catchment spans mountains to the sea, and its land-based economic activities are major contributors to ecological degradation. The HBRC's CEO declared at the New Zealand Marine Society's 2018 conference held in Napier in the HBRC area that the Council must 'understand the realities of the ecosystem' and rule through its regulatory processes because 'marine and land (are) connect (ed)' (Palmer, 2018). While the TE elided the developmental trajectories of enterprise and institution to answer the questions that we posed at the beginning of the chapter, it proved to be very productive of what we consider to be commoning preconditions for making markets.

Exemplars in context

This section introduces prevailing investment-institution conditions and relations, highlighting the visibility of Māori enterprise as a now discernible component of the economy (e.g. Te Puni Kōkiri, 2015; Chapman Tripp, 2017) and the centrality of the Resource Management Act 1991, in Aotearoa NZ over the past quarter century. The Resource Management Act (the RMA) explicitly provided for tangata whenua[8] to participate in RMA processes. The RMA specifically recognised *Te Tiriti o Waitangi* [9] and kaitiakitanga, defining the latter as '…the exercise of guardianship by the tangata whenua of an area in accordance with tikanga Māori in relation to natural and physical resources, and includes the ethic of stewardship'[10] (Section 2). It also identified, as matters of national importance, the relationship of Māori, with their ancestral lands, water, sites, wāhi tapu[11] and other taonga, and the protection of customary rights. Although these aspects of the RMA were bold and innovative, those implementing the RMA have not always met those commitments, which has caused significant issues for tangata whenua, and impacted their ability to act as kaitiaki[12], in part because of the restriction of kaitiakitanga to 'natural and physical resources', reflecting the inability of the law makers to incorporate holistic framings (Williams, 2016).

This contextually situates the exemplars. Attention is drawn to how the relative autonomy and collectivist aspirations are both enabled and constrained. The twinning of enterprise and institution is more than a simple juxtaposition. By probing the manner by which Wakatū extends its collective-inspired presence in relational spaces beyond its immediate whenua forms one lens. In a like fashion, the characterisation of the HBRC as a malleable opportunity space opens up avenues for economy supportive top down environmental management.

The confidence to identify the exemplars stemmed from two crucial knowledge gains made by geographers as part of the Sustainable Seas research. The first was a categorisation of enterprises (Lewis, 2018) using criteria compiled from international writings. This gave visibility to Māori/iwi/hapū enterprises as a distinctive group emerging in a Treaty of Waitangi context. The classification disrupts simplistic ideas about the homogeneity of the country's business, by stressing differences in business practices and performance measures that are decidedly social, an enterprise culture of prioritising how profits should be achieved over profits per se. Importantly the triple bottom line of scientific management of resources has been resisted, as usually not transferring well in a cultural sense (Spiller and Nicholson, 2017).The second crucial knowledge gain was the place of kaitiaki-centred business models as the hallmark of Māori enterprise (Hikuroa, Morgan, Henare & Gravley, 2010; Rout et al., 2019). Arguably 21st-century Māori enterprises are collective expansionary projects that are seeking restoration of lost customary commons and collaborations to expand commons making activity (Lewis et al., 2020).

Research (Taylor, 2013; Severinsen, 2020) that has unveiled the powerful and restrictive societal effects of the Resource Management Act (1991) had brought about a fresh and critical look at Regional Councils and other environmental management institutions. The RMA is a property-privileging system. It imposed on an existing mosaic of land uses a linear and singular process of appraisal and consenting of investment proposals using the catch all idea of 'effects'. In catering for discrete investments only, the process is systematically biased against commons-like arrangements, downplays or ignores cumulative and cumulating effects and the reach of their spatialities and temporalities. The result has been hotspots of controversy which have been difficult to resolve because of the lack of holistic framings to give wider guidance.

Wakatū – a Māori enterprise

Wakatū are very clear in their vision, in their mission and their purpose. The first thing one sees when encountering the website is "A Business of the Land and Sea, He Taonga Tuku iho". A taonga tuku iho is a valued treasure handed down through the generations. They further state:

> Actively involved in the lives of whānau whānui, the wider community, and business development, Wakatū has a big agenda. Based in Nelson, New Zealand, Wakatū has approximately 4,000 shareholders who descend from the original Māori land owners of the Nelson, Tasman and Golden Bay Regions – Te Tau Ihu.
>
> Whenua is the foundation of our business with 70% of assets held in land and water-space. We manage a diverse portfolio from vineyards, orchards to residential properties, large retail developments, office buildings, marine farms and waterspace.
>
> Kono is our food and beverage business focused on high quality beverages, fruit bars, seafood products, pipfruit and hops. We understand that innovation and adaptability is the key to our success. We are an efficient organisation and adapt to our customer needs quickly.
>
> Our purpose is to preserve and enhance our taonga for the benefit of current and future generations.

Wakatū put gravity to their vision and mission when they launched their 500-year plan – *Te Pae Tawhiti*. To enable whānau[13] to achieve and maintain spiritual, environmental, social and cultural well-being they manage commercial operations in a way that meets kaitiakitanga obligations. Kaitiakitanga is constantly re-evaluated to ensure the highest quality and ethic of care. It becomes a strategy when it is woven into the fabric of the entire organisational planning and management process. Economic well-being is not valuable if it is detrimental to the well-being of the landscapes and its people.

Hawke's Bay Regional Council

Behind recent initiatives begun by the Council is the realisation that on the East Coast of the North Island of the country there is a need to find land uses in keeping with water realities. Decades of land use expansion and intensification drawing on multiple catchment waters reached limits in late 2000s when the Ruataniwha Water Scheme was proposed for Central Hawke's Bay. The dam was the latest in a long lineage of both water and irrigation schemes for agriculture that had propelled land use intensification around the country. It was rural Aotearoa NZ's entitlement to have a dam; dams had been endorsed for decades. Looking back we can see the proposal strained the tunnel vision of RMA procedures. The proposal was a classic instance of a property driven enclosure acquisition of public land. The special significance of the Ruataniwha, however, was the extended political furore in which it was immersed and which exposed environmental concerns that many would prefer to ignore. The proposal stepped too far in its presumptions, leading to a Supreme Court ruling in 2017 that prevented the Minister of Conservation selling Crown land to the HBRC to facilitate flooding of land for the dam.

Our research interest was crystallising at the time of the Supreme Court ruling, and just as the HBRC appointed a new CEO James Palmer. In a perceptive review a local journalist wrote:

> The last twelve months have been turbulent for the Hawke's Bay Regional Council. The Havelock North water crisis and its political, social and financial fallout; … controversial reappointments and resignations; an election that transformed the leadership make-up; a multi-million dollar project struggling to see a single foundation laid after seven years (Ruataniwha dam); … an oil and gas moratorium putting the local body at odds with government policy; consenting controversies; storm water and feedlot issues; and numerous fresh water challenges, to name but a few.
>
> (Price, 2017, p. 1)

Palmer's expertise in transformational leadership has been subsequently directed to what can be called re-commoning at new geographic scales.

Re-connecting new economic-ecological relations

We heighten a focus on grounded re-commoning action by the exemplars through Table 5.1 that consists of four variables that are integral to knowing aspects of commons-like connecting. The table is a synopsis of tangible developments over the period 2018–20. It is illustrative, neither comprehensive nor complete, but being sufficient we suggest, to give glimpses of what is possible under different guiding metaphors as shown in the table. It is important that we acknowledge that at the time of the NZGS/IAG (July 2018) we really had no grasp of the pending transformative collectivist pushes that would be associated with the exemplars. By 2020 some hugely ambitious initiatives had become visible. The table thus encapsulates important in-the-making steps and indications of possibilities that were being followed.

What does Table 5.1 bring into focus? Foremost are signs of adopting a resourcefulness mind set. Resourcefulness is outward looking, a window which starts to lay the foundations of possibilities packages, unlike a resource inventory which is a static compilation devoid of agency, but available to agency (Murray-Li, 2019). We give importance to re-territorialisation traces. These are connections transcending current boundaries and measurement systems and putting in place alternative ways of knowing, measuring and assessing performance. We see glimpses of often sophisticated political alignments that give momentum in the dimensions. They are like doors configuring choices.

Its format consists of four dimensions that are illustrative of the workings connecting for re-commoning. The table is energised by the demands of existing in the emergent worlds of KUKT/MS. The emphasis on dimensions is a break from the descriptive posture that we have brought up so far for the exemplars. The connections are place-grounded but potentially space-seeking and space-transformative. They signal accomplishments of iwi/hapū and community access to resources, organisational arrangements to secure their retention and distributional solutions. When we complied the tangible expressions of connecting we found ourselves reflecting on the intensities of purposeful assembling that underlie connecting. The connecting can hardly be described as random. Rather they are better seen as pre-conditions for possibilities of economy and environmental organisation. The impulses of connection in the table are deliberate examinations of extant relationalities within holistic framings which are being critiqued and often extended. The table can also be read as the interpenetration of empowering dimensions transforming relations encountered, introducing mutualities to the new vectors of change, altering the map of possibilities perceivable, and encouraging renewed emphasis on cultivating collectivist cultures. Importantly Table 5.1 then is a tentative sketching of actual principles and practices that give content to commoning ideas.

In the discussion below we explore the anatomy of two starkly different directions and content of collective organisation, strategy and articulation of principles and practice that have come to characterise the exemplars. We are especially cognisant of the formative entangling of efforts dedicated to re-commoning and the potentialities that accompany this activity.

As we embarked upon this project we engaged in ways consistent with the very essence of the conference theme, Creative Conversations, Constructive Connections and as a result through rich, intense, meaningful dialogue, we have discovered a great deal as a research team, trying to tease out the story lines, exploring the metaphors of KUKT/MS. The TE meant that we could bring into sharp relief the exemplars as *enactive relational agency*.

Our thesis is that both Wakatū and the HBRC should be regarded as contributing to the political project of KUKT/MS, with expanding reach and influence in the strategic planning, expertise and practices of collectivist initiatives directed to re-commoning. Following Lewis and Le Heron (2019) the term political project is used as it is in PSPE to describe strategic narratives that align a set of interests and material resources to achieve some sort of social transformation. Initiatives such as Wakatū and HBRC both undertake the assembling of intellectual resources, methodologies and claims about what is or

Table 5.1 Key Dimensions of Re-commoning

Key dimensions	Wakatu	Hawke's Bay Regional Council
Guiding metaphor/focus	Holistic, kaitiakitanga, multiple pillars of guardianship Region as commons Commons for present and future generations	Embed EBM for economy Spatial management of region Regulate for land and marine connect
Contextual pressures	Growing an autonomous Māori enterprise for whānau and community etc	Responding to pollution from farming, forestry and urban storm water and calls for new kinds of farming futures
Valuing for resourcefulness	Landscape scale conservation Collaboration working on collective action with communities, industry and variety of organisations Identifying intervention points Research on Māori enterprises Being associated with high tech enterprises (AgriSea, Sanfords) Intervention with green tech in terms of four 'capitals'	Education-led stance Focus on wetlands – common enemy of sediment (high value spawning environment sediment laden) Identifying potentialities of Aquarium and Aquaculture Ruataniwha Water Storage Scheme a contentious irrigation project that was fought in Regional Council elections Public and Regional Council reaction to plantation forestry harvesting and subsequent massive sedimentation runoff Hawke's Bay heartland of Biological Agriculture and Regenerative Agriculture movements
Reterritorialisation	Developing production networks centred on whānau economic activity Conceptual mapping to create new future resilient commons	Wide realisation that forestry harvesting has externalities in rivers and at coast Biological Agriculture consultancy Integrity Soils expanded into Canada, USA, Australia, South Africa Systematic diversification of high quality flat land in every property
Generative governing	Innovative intergenerational regional strategy advanced for Te Tauihi Proactive stance for extending connections with existing industries, regions and government agencies	Aiming in long term planning collaborations to be 'good and trusted partner' HBRC undergoing internal changes as new environmental officers hired Cape Sanctuary at Cape Kidnappers, predator fence erected by landowners Shift from outputs to outcomes focus, services to impacts Regulation function is part of economic proposition

(*Continued*)

Table 5.1 (Cont.)

Key dimensions	Wakatu	Hawke's Bay Regional Council
Political alignments	Targeting political connections/laws Top of the South Forum Māori Leadership Forum Wakatu Inc in partnership with Nelson City Council, Tasman District Council, Marlborough District Council and Nelson-Tasman Regional Development Agency Pan-Māori institution building	Gradual shift towards the political project of changing environmental management practices to support wider regional economy –exemplified in new resources for Integrated Catchment Management Angry rural public treated to a science-based visualisation of how upper catchment erosion flows downstream to degrade habitat which carried the 'room'

ought to be, into knowledge formations that configure power and knowledge capabilities to make the world in particular ways.

This requires methodological adeptness in inquiry, at least in the sense of recognising the expansionary networking that underpins creating commons platforms and to imagine from the evidence at hand what might arise. For Wakatū, re-commoning was a historical urgency and a comprehensively internalised priority. Table 5.1 is a snapshot of 30 and more years of fulfilling their whānau aspirations by building unique capacities centred on taking the idea into other contexts. This re-territorialising implies an agenda that is greater in scope and ambition than mere business success. The content of its agenda was unveiled and executed during 2019 and early 2020.

Early in 2018 the 'Board of Wakatū decided it was time to have a conversation … to look at a new approach to regional development that was business-convened to ask 'How can we work together to address some of the key challenges facing the region?' (Morgan, 2019) To the outsider, this is an extraordinary development – a Māori enterprise taking collective co-leadership at a regional level. Yet it makes complete sense to Wakatū. The region will always be home, a place inexorably linked to their identity, so it was both politic and pragmatic for them to take these steps. Their planning has a 500-year horizon. These views are embraced in the Innovative Intergenerational Regional Strategy for Te Tauihu 2077. The year 2077 is the 100th year of Wakatū, chosen as a horizon to reflect the importance of long term thinking and commitment to deliver to intergenerational benefits across the region. Significantly the Strategy was submitted to and funded by the Coalition government's Provincial Growth Fund (PGF). To mainstream Aotearoa the content is revolutionary, though not to pan-Māori advocates.

The detail of the operational processes and elements of the strategy are noteworthy and in keeping with the precursors identified in Table 5.1. First Wakatū proposed a collaborative and co-ordinated approach. The Steering Committee comprised three Mayors, iwi, education and business leaders across Te Tauihu. The core to the Kaitiakitanga Strategy is combining science with mātauranga Māori –

Māori knowledge, culture, worldview, values and theory, and the interconnected relation between the spiritual, the natural world and people. This is more expansive than the usual focus of Crown Entities which limit their interpretation of kaitiakitanga to environment, being concerned with care and guardianship for humanity, both because humans are viewed as part of the environment and because the concept of mauri and the centrality of relationships means interactions between humans and environment must aim to be optimally mutually beneficial.

What the novel boundary crossing behaviour of Wakatū gives us is a basis for claiming that Aotearoa NZ is nurturing generative governing. Wakatū is salutary for the manner in which it has legitimately appropriated a governmental stance for *iwi* and by extension communities, which is customarily seen as the prerogative of the central State. Wakatū has occupied the high ground by enacting collective recommoning on a regional scale, running intensive collaborative processes among hitherto un-partnered parties, around an open ended intergenerational agenda. The PGF facilitated the process (so the central State as we know it remains influential) but the transformational leadership resided with the Strategy, under Wakatū's watchful eye. Wakatū's emblematic efforts are a confirmation that re-commonings-led transitioning steps are doable.

The top-down HBRC scene is less clear cut on accomplishments but insightful on the value of participatory disciplines. The historically new ground evident for the HBRC has been its multi-faceted shift towards regional overviews and multi-level political mobilising to advance collaborative frameworks (Newman, 2020). The stage was set for this direction with the formulation of the three area Integrated Catchment Management strategy in 2017 spanning the whole of the region and its resourcing and the Future Farming Initiative embedded in the Long Term Plan. The ultimate question the Future Farming Initiative aims to answer is 'What do we want Hawke's Bay's 'best performance' to look like in the future with respect to soil health, clean waters, food quality, animal welfare, biosecurity and profitability?' (Bedford, 2019). These moves have fed into the TANK plan that embraces the Tutaekuri, Ahuriri, Ngaruroro and Karamu (TANK) rivers, which feed into the Heretaunga Plains. TANK is explicitly a top-down management framework, also funded by the PGF that purports to contribute to the region's economic growth and environmental integrity, while providing for the values identified by the community. More relational leadership very recently has helped build a culture of collaboration among the disparate bureaucracies in the region (Bedford, 2019). This has taken the form of policy managers from Hawke's Bay councils' at large exploring ways to prevent restrictive local and central government rules, regulations and procedures getting in the way of regional progress.

A change in interpretive perspective is demanded by the nature of the HBRC initiatives, from a focus on individual council efforts to the regroupings around collective arrangements. The region's efforts illustrate the political challenges of stitching 'social' commons of various kinds at any scale amid property owner assumptions and expectations. Is this what all regional councils might be able to do, is it the beginning of regrouping towards collective arrangements for collective outcomes, guided by the local State, and is it specific to the moment or more long term? There are, however, two significant omissions to the HBRC organisation and experiences. First, Ngāti Kahungungu's reaction to the TANK draft indicates disconnect with local iwi. Bradley (2019) writes that they allege they were tricked into supporting a water project they vehemently opposed, saying TANK favours irrigators over the environment. In particular they assert there was no indication that the proposal submitted to the PGF spoke of taking water from underground aquifers into streams to boost flows. Relevant correspondence (2019) shows the perils of parties signing off in good faith about proposal content when submitting to the PGF. Regional Economic Development Minister Shane Jones summed up the political dilemma facing all – 'the process has to involve all stakeholders … the outcomes I am pursuing through science and technology … is to resolve the paucity of water in Hawke's Bay' (cited in Bradley, 2019). Once again, the manipulation of 'resources', rather than the limits to or suitability of land uses, and the power relations supporting them is centre stage.

Market-making possibilities from pre-conditions

The TE has been a productive framework to consider the emergence of pre-conditions for making markets that are beginning to eventuate as different agencies engage with the conceptual and practical necessities of KUKT/MS. The choice of exemplars was doubly generative: it brought together the relational agency of 'new generation' Māori enterprise with that of a multi-catchment regional council, and, it morphed into contrasting choice architectures about pivoting environmental relations into supporting and re-imagining the possibilities of economy that deeply entrain KUKT/MS dynamics. The insights from the situated place-rich relational agency of Wakatū and HBRC enable a discussion of what pre-conditions might mean.

The TE temporalities and spatialities coincide with a 'once in the era of European settlement' present moment. This coincidence was not foreseen. The *reviving of commoning through strategic and tactical connecting is informed by and generative of holistic approaches by relational agency.* The TE raises new interpretive angles. Prevailing marketing ideas and market solutions are politicised by the detectable disturbances of relational agency. The politicising performs the double act of showing tendencies to adopt norms from pre-the- KUKT/MS era while raising sensitivities to different possibilities that come from re-organising to cope with holistic imperatives. What we have to appreciate is that Wakatū is an emergent enterprise responsible for shaping its own agenda and using collectivities it deems strategic. HBRC is equally emergent, shifting into broad spectrum developments involving both re-territorialisations and process changes that aid re-commoning. Our contention is that these are antecedents of new forms of governing to provide stabilities to make future markets.

The quite unexpected finding from the TE is evidence of the blurring of the categories of business enterprise and regulatory institution. This may be an uncomfortable finding for many as it flies against the notions that categories and classifications once created are fixities. It certainly surprised us. We had not imagined the turning towards the other that is empirically detectable. Upon reflection it is foreshadowed in the detail of Table 5.1's dimensions but the subsequent internal and external political alignments by the exemplars allow significance to be attached to this behavioural and definitional feature. The blurring comes from a number of pressures. Accommodating multiple interests is a discernible feature of the exemplar worlds, it means a single story line is on anything is unlikely. Seeing natural resource exploitation for what it is − finite, destructive, linked to ideological and colonial legacies − has (at least as we perceive it as researchers) encouraged efforts to articulate and collaboratively develop novel and imaginative value propositions. The move from collating value positions to engaging in collective scrutiny and formulation of practices consistent with KUKT/MS values as a basis for choices, decisions and investor-regulatory relations epitomises new sorts of ethical thinking. The source of the re-mixing and boundary crossing of enterprise into regulatory dispositions and regulatory institutions attempting to collectivise environmental platforms for improved agency performance at different scales, if the preliminary evidence is being appropriately interpreted, is a wave of re-thinking that emanates from living by the KUKT/MS metaphor. It is as if KUKT/MS is an authorising metaphor, releasing relational agency to explore new bases for production-consumption relations (see E. Le Heron *et al.*, 2020, for an outline of the power of metaphors in Aotearoa New Zealand's contemporary marine spaces).

The TE was originally intended to look at relational changes of agency in holistic worlds of KUKT/MS, with an emphasis on transformative co-leader-ship, rather than making markets. As the TE methodology was applied we detected the ingredients of assembling and re-setting by each exemplar. Ori-ginally our research had the emphasis on transformative co-leadership, rather than making markets. But it became increasingly obvious that re-making mar-kets was exactly what the re-making of relations was producing. For the exemplars, the holistic KUKT/MS metaphor with its push for new social resolutions around re-commoning has become increasingly important.

And now we cast our gaze back to the whakataukī:

> Toitū te whenua/If the land is well
> Toitū te moana/If the sea is well
> Toitū te tangata/The people will thrive

and use it as a lens to view and reflect on the questions posed – 'If every enterprise in Aotearoa NZ was like Wakatū, what could this mean for Regional Councils?' and 'If every Regional Council was like Hawke's Bay, what new relationships with enterprise could be forged and what would enterprise look like?

Conclusion

The chapter has sought to enliven understandings of Aotearoa NZ's contemporary moment of connecting by centring two 'living and situated' questions that epitomise the present moment: The questions guided the TE. We dared to imagine different possibilities for economic and environmental relations in the context of KUKT/MS. The counterpoising of the questions was intended to make visible both the demands of trying to live holistically in Aotearoa NZ from different positionings and perspectives, and, to direct inquiry into the *actual relational agency of re-commoning that is being attempted in the new material and discursive contexts of KUKT/MS.* What we have demonstrated in the TE microcosm is that if we acknowledge that everywhere, everything is always in- the-making, we don't limit the future possibilities we can create.

In the Aotearoa NZ context, KUKT/MS conceptions demand answering why holistic thinking was ignored under European settlement and how re-commoning has a rightful place as a strategy to re-organise into new kinds of economy-environment relations. Although KUKT/MS is controversial to some interests, it is the new *leading or authorising metaphor* in the contemporary moment. It provides comprehensive mapping directions and scope to analyse wider dynamics that have been masked by past and present property oriented ideologies. *KUKT/MS is a monumental shift in the politics of knowledge.* This comes from the fact that the framing opens the horizons on what can be known, especially through connecting what has previously been unconnected.

The aspiration of re-commoning is not an unreasonable goal as it breeches the possessive borders of property, replacing them instead with common ownership and distributional aspirations arrangements. It is happening in places, through the creation of new kinds of connections, territorial links and unexpected political alignments to gain collective footings and protect collective gains. The biggest contribution of re-commoning is how collective ownership both supports and backstops the development of resourcefulness platforms. The ever present spectre of sudden property sales, or the property churn of the growth ethos, is diffused by the stabilising properties of collective ownership, particularly when the aim is intergenerational retention and enhancement of collective environmental and economic assets.

We speak of pre-conditions for (*desired*) market-making because it accents the presence and formative role of relational agency. Pre-conditions place to place will differ. The exemplars suggest this should not be concerning, since their trajectories are predicated on continuing evolution of enterprise and regulatory expertise *developed in context.* Our exemplar focused TE offers glimpses of trajectories of emergence but it stops short of predictive claims about market-making solutions. Instead the emphasis is on examining how the exemplars have succeeded in converting possibilities into opportunities. Herein lies the capacity/capability challenge that springs from committing to opportunity based environmental management centred on re-commoning.

Notes

1 Whakataukī are proverbs comprising wisdom guiding Māori culture, often with multiple, nuanced meanings. As a statement this whakataukī is self-evident, in addition it serves as a call to action for people. If we look after the land and the ocean - we will

thrive. The whakataukī served to guide us as we undertook the Thought Experiment – how are 'people' looking after the land and sea – ki uta ki tai?

2 Ki Uta Ki Tai is a Māori holistic philosophy that considers the environment in its entirety (Tipa *et al.*, 2016), inclusive of people, and the interconnections among ecology and economy.

3 See Te Urewera and Te Awa Tupua (Whanganui River) Acts.

4 Kaitiakitanga is adaptive and collective-decision making and action that is tailored to local conditions to realise the principles of reciprocity and intergenerational sustainability via the practices undertaken, drawing from mātauranga Māori, within a Māori worldview.

5 The Māori economy includes a range of authorities, businesses, and employers who self-identify as Māori. With key assets in the primary sectors e.g. 50 per cent of the fishing quota, 40 per cent of forestry, 10 per cent in dairy production and 10 per cent in kiwifruit production, the Māori economy is also diversifying, with new investment areas including geothermal, digital, services, education, tourism and housing. The value of Māori asset base is estimated be over NZ$50 billion (Chapman Tripp, 2017).

6 Often translated as tribe, means 'people' or 'nation'.

7 Sub-iwi, the basic political unit of Māori society

8 The people of the land, Māori.

9 The Treaty of Waitangi.

10 Stewardship is not an appropriate definition, because as well as having overtones of a master-servant relationship, the original English meaning of stewardship is 'to guard someone else's property' (Marsden, 2003).

11 Sacred place.

12 Guardian, guardianship.

13 Family.

Acknowledgements

Arguments relating to the chapter were first introduced at the NZGS/IAG conference, 2018, Auckland, in a presentation by Hikuroa and Le Heron on behalf of the Participatory Processes Research Team, entitled 'Transformative co-leadership through participatory processes using Ki Uta Ki Tai Mountains to the Seas' framing. The chapter was written in 2020 by Hikuroa, R. Le Heron and E. Le Heron. The change in emphasis from the conference presentation resulted from intensive discussions around re-commoning as a progressive collective knowledge intervention strategy which they were engaging in.

Participatory Processes Research Team for the initiative: K. Davies, A. Greenaway, P. Blackett, W. Allen, J. Logie, B. Glavovic and C. Lundquist.

This research was funded by the New Zealand Ministry for Business Innovation and Employment (C01X1515) through the Sustainable Seas National Science Challenge. The authors wish to acknowledge the constructive conversations centred on KUKT/MS in multiple sessions at the NZGS/IAG conference, continuing dialogue in Aotearoa NZ among geographers, social scientists and ecologists on emerging topics and developments with relevance to re-commoning, complementary and supportive land-based research into biological economies (Pawson *et al.*, 2019), narratives for EBM (E. Le Heron *et al.*, 2020), and blue economy and value propositions (Lewis, 2019).

References

References

Blackett, P.*et al.* (2020). Participation, power and politics in multi-use® marine spaces: The importance of conscious engagement, *Environmental Science and Policy*, submitted for publication.

Bedford, T. (2019). Being economically and environmentally successful is where the future of food production lies in Hawke's Bay. Do both or fail. *Bay Buzz*, 1 June.

Bradley, A. (2019). Hawke's Bay TANK fresh water plan has 'fatal flaws' – Ngati Kahungunu. Retrieved from www.rnz.co.nz/news/national/403720/hawke-s-bay-ta nk-freshwater-plan-has-fatal-flaws-ngati-kahungunu.

Campbell, H. (2020). *Farming inside invisible worlds. Modernist agriculture and its consequences*. London: Bloomsbury Academic.

Carolan, M. (2013). The wild side of agro-food studies: On co-experimentation, politics, change and hope. *Sociologia Ruralis*, 53, 413–431.

Chapman Tripp. (2017). *Te Ao Māori: Trends and insights*. Retrieved from www.chapma ntripp.com/Publication%20PDFs/2017%20Chapman%20Tripp%20Te%20Ao%20Ma ori%20-%20trends%20and%20insights%20E-VERSION.pdf.

Davies, K.*et al.* (2017). From mountains to the seas: Developing a shared vision for addressing cumulative effects in Aotearoa New Zealand. *Regions Magazine*, 308(4), 15–18.

Davies, K.*et al.* (2018). Navigating collaborative networks and cumulative effects for Sustainable Seas. *Environmental Science and Policy*, 83, 22–32.

Greenaway, A., Taylor, L., Le Heron, E., Le Heron, R. & Manaakiwhenua Landcare. (2020). *Holistic governance from mountains to the seas*. *LINKOnline Webinar* [Video]. Retrieved from www.youtube.com/watch?v=6zFyWoEWOto.

Hewitt, J., Faulkner, L., Greenaway, A. & Lundquist, C. (2018). Proposed ecosystem-based management principles for New Zealand. *Resource Management Journal*, , November, 10–13.

Hikuroa, D.C. H., Morgan, T.K.K.B., Henare, M. & Gravley, D.(2010). Integrating indigenous values into geothermal development. *Geothermal Research Council Transactions*, 54, 51–54.

Larner, W. & Le Heron, R. (2002). From economic globalisation to globalising economic processes: Towards post-structural political economies. *Geoforum*, 33(4), 415–419.

Le Heron, E., Lewis, N. & Le Heron, R. (2016). Geographers at work in disruptive human-biophysical projects: Methodology as ontology in reconstituting nature-society knowledge. In R. Le Heron, H. Campbell, N. Lewis & M. Carolan (Eds), *Biological economies: Experimentation and the politics of agri-food frontiers* (pp. 196–211). Oxford: Routledge.

Le Heron*et al.* (2019a). Diversity, contestation, participation in Aotearoa New Zealand's multi-use/user marine spaces. *Marine Policy*, 106. https://doi.org/10.1016/j.marpol. 2019.103536.

Le Heron*et al.* (2019b). It's not a recipe… but there are ingredients: Navigating negotiated change through participatory processes in multi-use/r marine spaces. *Planning Quarterly*, 213, 32–37.

Le Heron*et al.* (2020). Participatory processes as 21st century social knowledge technology: Metaphors and narratives at work. In E. Probyn, K. Johnston & N. Lee (Eds), *Sustaining the seas. Oceanic space and the politics of care* (pp. 155–172). London: Rowman & Littlefield.

Le Heron, R.*et al.* (2016). Non-sectarian scenario experiments in socio-ecological knowledge building for multi-use marine environments: Insights from New Zealand's Marine Futures project. *Marine Policy*, 67, 10–21. https://doi.org/10.1016/j.marpol. 2016.01.022.

Le Heron, R. & Roche, M. (2018). The Taniwha economy. In E. Pawson (Ed.), *New Biological Economies* (pp. 157–176). Auckland: Auckland University Press.

Lewis, N. (2019). Cultivating diverse values by rethinking blue economy in New Zealand. In J. Morrissey & P. Heidkamp (Eds), *Coastal transitions: Towards sustainability and resilience in the coastal zone*. Abingdon: Routledge.

Lewis, N. & Le Heron, R. (2019). Poststructural political economy. In A. Kobayashi (Ed.), *International Encyclopedia of human geography* (pp. 365–373). Amsterdam: Elsevier.

Lewis, N. & Le Heron, R. (2020). Re-imagining economy-environment relations for a regenerative marine environmental management: Lessons from New Zealand. In Heidcamp, P (ed), *Blue economy: People and regions in transition*. Abingdon: Routledge.

Lewis, N., Le Heron, R., Hikuroa & D. & Le Heron, E. (2020) Remaking regional development. Blue economy rent platform in Kaikoura, Aotearoa New Zealand, *Regional Studies*, submitted for publication.

Marsden, M. (2003). Kaitiakitanga: a definitive introduction to the holistic worldview of the Māori. In C. Royal (Ed.). *The Woven Universe* (pp. 54–72). Ōtaki: Te Wānanga o Raukawa.

Morgan, P. (2019). Chair's remarks in Kotahitanga mo te taino strategy. Retrieved from https://drive.google.com/file/d/1eW5NssWnXC5COZ6xNIV3VORCfpD_2HNY/view.

Murray-Li, T. (2019). Politics, interrupted. *Anthropological Theory*, 19(1), 29–53https://doi.org/10.1177/1463499618785330.

Newman, K. (2020). Cross-council cohesion matures. *Bay Buzz*, June.

Ostrom, E. (1990). *Governing the commons: The evolution of institutions for collective action.* Cambridge: Cambridge University Press.

Palmer, J. (2018). *Keynote address.* New Zealand Marine Society Annual conference, Napier.

Pawson, E. and Biological Economies team (R. Le Heron, H. Campbell, M. Henry, E. Le Heron, K. Legun, N. Lewis, H. Perkins, M. Roche & C. Rosin) (2018) *The New Biological Economy. How New Zealanders are creating value from the land.* Auckland: Auckland University Press.

Poteete, A., Janssen, M. & Ostrom, E. (2010). *Working together: Collective action, the commons and multiple methods in practice.* Princeton, NJ: Princeton University Press.

Price, S. (2017). The man with a plan. *Bay Buzz.* www.baybuzz.co.nz/2017/07/31/the-man-with-a-plan.

Rout, M.*et al.* (2019). *Maori marine-based enterprises and kiatiaki-centred business models.* Wellington: Sustainable Seas.

Severinsen, G. (2019). *Reform of the Resource Management System: A model for the future.* (Synthesis Report). Auckland: Environmental Defence Society.

Spiller, C. & Nicholson, A. (2017). Wakatu Incorporation. Balancing Kaitiaki stewardship and commerce. Sage Business Cases. http://dx.doi.org/10.4135/9781473999039.

Taylor, G. (2013). Environmental policy-making in New Zealand, 1978–2013. *Policy Quarterly*, 9(3). https://doi.org/10.26686/pq.v9i3.4453.

Te Puni Kōkiri. (2015). Te Ōhanga Māori 2013 – Māori Economy Report 2013. (Report prepared by BERL). Retrieved from www.tpk.govt.nz/en/a-matou-mohiotanga/business-and-economics/maori-economy-report-2013.

Tipa, G., Harmsworth, G.R., Williams, E. & Kitson, J.C. (2016). Integrating mātauranga Māori into freshwater management, planning and decision making. In P.G. Jellyman, T.J.A. Davie, C.P. Pearson & J.S. Harding (Eds), *Advances in New Zealand Freshwater Science*. Christchurch: New Zealand Freshwater Sciences Society & New Zealand Hydrological Society.

Williams, J. (2016). *Te Reo me Tikanga Thriving indigenous languages.* [Keynote address]. International Indigenous Research Conference2016, Nga Pae O Te Maramatanga, Tamaki Makaurau Auckland.

Winder, G.M. & Le Heron, R.B. (2017). Further assembly work. *Dialogues in Human Geography*, 7(1), 50–55. https://doi.org/10.1177/2043820617691663.

6 On the non-assemblage of a local producer/resort hotel market in Fiji

Gabriel C.M. Laeis* and Carolyn Morris**

*IUBH INTERNATIONAL UNIVERSITY
**SCHOOL OF PEOPLE, ENVIRONMENT AND PLANNING, MASSEY UNIVERSITY

Introduction

While much has been written about how markets that have assembled, and some work has been done on markets under construction and the human and non-human actants critical to such assembling, much less has been written about non-assemblage.[1] While it is possible (with work) to trace the contingencies of the histories of already assembled markets and to explore the processes and practices of markets as they assemble, it is more difficult to examine non-assemblage. The reasons for this are obvious and are both empirical and theoretical. Empirically, of course, because no market was assembled, there is no market to trace and describe, although there may be traces of the labour of the attempt. Theoretically, the problem is to divine the significance of the non-assemblage. Did a possible network simply not assemble because there was no interest (in a Latourian sense), or, were there actants whose active work (intentional or not) thwarted the goals of others working to assemble? Practically, it is more possible to explore the second kind of non-assemblage than the first, and theoretically, we will argue, such incidences of non-assemblage have something to tell about processes of assemblage more generally. Instances of non-assemblage and non-stabilisation of networks into assemblages draw attention to the constant labour of assembling and reassembling that makes it possible to take social orders somewhat for granted and to the critical actants that might be critical for the building of a market (in this case) in a particular place at a particular time.

The non-assembled that we explore here is a market by which local food producers can supply large scale resort hotels in Fiji. As an 'underdeveloped' country, Fiji has been the subject of much development over several decades, with the aim of improving local incomes and making those incomes sustainable. In recent decades, since the advent of the mode of capitalism known as neoliberalism, markets have become *the* development solution. With tourism as the most important economic sector in Fiji and agriculture as the biggest employer, projects that will hopefully become enduring supply chains connecting large resort hotels with local horticultural and agricultural producers appeal, as the materials (human and non-human) necessary for the assembling of such markets, and strong interest in assembling them, are there. Despite repeated attempts to assemble and embed such a market, it has not really

DOI: 10.4324/9780429296260-6

eventuated. We do find Fijian producers who supply resort hotels, but these are most often relationships between two particular people (commonly a chef and an individual farmer) that are actively sustained through the concerted efforts of a chef animated by a belief in the importance of ensuring that some of the economic benefits of tourism flow to the community in which the hotel is located.

In any given locality there are multiple markets and multiple market relations. As a result, we distinguish between what we will call individual supply relationships and market relationships, or markets. Individual supply relationships are arrangements between particular individuals (chefs and either farmers or traders) to buy and sell goods; market relationships, by comparison, are 'between autonomous and independent agents' (Çalışkan & Callon, 2010, p. 3) and so the collapse of a relationship between two particular individuals does not mean the collapse of the market – individuals can then sell to or buy from someone else. The aim of this chapter is to explore why individual supply relationships rather than market relations dominate hotel/local producer supply chains.

There are numerous reasons in the literature identified as to why hotel/local producer supply chains have been so difficult to assemble: in this paper we focus on one reason identified by hotels and mobilised as an explanation of the lack of emergence of a market, namely specific local cultural and political histories and the kind of strategic subjects such culture-histories have produced. What this points to is the critical importance of the particularities of people and place in the formation (or not) of markets.

Theorising non-assemblage

Describing and accounting for a non-assembling market means paying attention to many of the same things and process that analysing an assembled market does – materialities, technical devices and 'the affective, cognitive and social qualities of human beings' (Webb & Hawkey, 2017, p. 9) with the intention of divining which of these actants was the obligatory *blockage* point rather than the obligatory *passage* point (to play with Latour). In our case, consider the non-formation of market subjects as the obligatory blockage point, which meant that a resort hotel/local producer market has failed to form.

Subjects, of course, are never purely market subjects, and it is those other subjectivities, formed and practised in other arenas of social life (and other economies) that allow, but in this case impede, the kinds and levels of participation in exchanges with resort hotels that might have led to the emergence of a market. Our analytic orientation to this question is strongly informed by the work of Gulledge, Roscoe and Townley (2015), and we draw heavily on their framing of the issue of culture and marketisation. The question as raised by Gulledge *et al.* is 'How do individuals navigate the intersections and contradictions between the economy and elsewhere?' (2015, p. 638). They thus open up the matter of 'the tacit judgements and cultural constructions that give rise to modes of calculation beyond the economic' (p. 638), or the modes of calculation formed in other economies, for there is rarely, perhaps never, just one economy in any given place (see also Frankel, 2015). Referring to Entwistle and Slater (2014), they argue that much of the Callon-influenced marketisation literature has focused too much on technologies and materialities, and as a result 'has been too hasty to dismiss culture, together with its values, norms, fashions and aesthetic conceptions, as an inadequate, fuzzy explanation' (Gulledge *et al.*, 2015, p. 638). Consequently, they argue for more research into how culture shapes calculative practices and what happens when actors constituted by and deploying different calculative rationalities engage.

An assembled market necessarily implies market subjects, i.e. people with the capacities and desire to act in that market, people who have what Bourdieu would call the appropriate habitus, people who have a 'feel for the game'. The failure of a resort hotel/local producer market to stabilise in Fiji, despite the constant work by seemingly powerful actors (chefs and managers from hotels, staff in government agencies and development specialists and analysts) can basically be explained by the inability of those actors to enrol farmers in this project, that is, by the failure of such projects to cultivate farmers with the appropriate subjectivity.

Investigating non–assemblage in Fiji

The account of the assemblage work and its disappointments described in this chapter is based on the PhD fieldwork of Gabriel Laeis, the aim of which was to investigate why the kinds of local producer/hotel linkages constantly promoted as development solutions so often failed to emerge. Having trained as a chef, his hunch was that there might be something going on in hotel kitchens (which is the point at which local produce is turned into food for hotel guests to eat), that meant that kitchens were a site of previously unexplored blockages that thwarted attempts at creating desired and worked-for linkages. As a result, he undertook a four-month long ethnography, involving participant observation in the kitchen of a large-scale resort, interviews with management, chefs and kitchen staff at the hotel and at similar resorts, and interviews and observations with actors along actual and potential linkages between the hotel and local horticultural producers. He chose the hotel (which we will call The Palm Breeze) for a number of reasons. First, it is a classic example of a large-scale, internationally owned resort, comprising around 250 rooms under an American resort brand that operates 28 such properties globally. The resort provides nine food outlets, from coffee shops and poolside snack bars, to a large restaurant seating 250 people, and a fine-dining restaurant seating 30, so they provide and therefore need a lot of food. Second, it is located close to the Sigatoka valley, a fertile agricultural area known as 'the salad bowl of Fiji', so there is potentially a convenient source of local food. Moreover, and very unusually, the Executive Chef at The Palm Breeze is Fijian, meaning that he has the kinds of local connections, knowledge and interests that made him well-placed to source produce from local farmers – something that he was interested in doing and actively pursued. As a result, if, despite the chef's efforts, The Palm Breeze had not been able to access or assemble a stable supply of local produce, the reasons why would be visible. The Palm Breeze actually does source some of its produce from three local suppliers, but as we will see, this represents a tiny fraction of its expenditure on food and does not exhaust local potential. And these three supply linkages shine further light on why a perduring hotel/local producer market has not emerged. What follows is an account of one of the local explanations proffered for the failure of supply relationships between local producers and The Palm Breeze to develop into a market. The account we relate draws attention to local understandings of what shapes the actions and strategies of both The Palm Breeze and local producers – an account that is framed in terms of local culture. Theoretically this account points to the way in which not only particular histories and geographies but local understandings of those histories and geographies are critical to instances of market making.

The dynamics of non-assemblage

There are several sites of knowledge that can usefully be drawn on to untangle the seemingly persistent non-assemblage of resort hotel/local producer markets. This includes development literature (as there is a considerable amount known generally about what might thwart the emergence of such markets, and this body of knowledge continues to motivate attempts to discover the 'Rosetta Stone' of non-emergence in order to overcome it) and social science and historical writing on the already assembled cultural, social and economic order in Fiji.

Tourism and development

Since the 1950s tourism has been advocated as a development solution for many countries, particularly for small island states like Fiji, which have few other resources with which to grow their economy (e.g. Asiedu & Gbedema, 2011). Despite debate in academic literature about the efficacy of such development, with some authors arguing for its utility (e.g. Sharpley, 2015; Simons-Kaufmann, Kaufmann, Sloan & Legrand, 2012; Torres & Momsen, 2004) and others raising doubts about tourism's ability to provide value for the poor (e.g. Medina-Muñoz, Medina-Muñoz & Gutiérrez-Pérez, 2016; Oviedo-Garcia, González-Rodríguez & Vega-Vázquez, 2018), development projects focused on advancing tourism remain popular as solutions to local economic problems. The problem faced is leakage – that is, how to keep more of the tourism-generated money locally, as research shows that on average about 50 per cent of such income is lost to non-local actors (Worldwatch Institute, 2003).

One key strategy for dealing with the problem of leakage is the construction of linkages between the tourist industry and other economies along what is conceptualised as the tourism value chain (Sharpley, 2015; Telfer & Sharpley, 2008; Torres & Momsen, 2005). Tourism's *direct* economic impact on local communities primarily materialises as wages, but the creation of links between tourism enterprises and local food producers has the potential to channel more tourism-derived income into local communities (e.g. Hunt & Rogerson, 2013; Lejarraja & Walkehorst, 2007; Pillay & Rogerson, 2013; Saarinen & Rogerson, 2014; Scheyvens, 2011; Torres & Momsen, 2004, 2005). This solution is based on the fact that some 70 per cent of the world's rural poor depend on growing food to make their living (World Bank, 2016) and as such there are local reservoirs of skills, knowledge and resources available to be mobilised (Torres & Momsen, 2004) in the assembling of such linkages.

Though there are good theoretical reasons for assembling tourism /local producer networks, and much advocacy in development circles, in reality the hoped-for benefits from such synergies have rarely come to fruition (Timms & Neill, 2011; Torres & Momsen, 2011). There are a number of reasons for this, as identified by seminal writers in this field, Rogerson (2012) and Torres and Momsen (2004). In terms of production and supply, problems identified include the lack of sufficient quantity and quality of locally produced food because of the seasonality of production and low adoption of formal quality assurance systems by producers; the high prices of locally produced food; the nature of local farming systems which are often plantation based rather than horticultural and geared towards export markets; lack of access of producers to capital, credit and technology; labour availability; and poor infrastructure (roads, electricity, irrigation, processing, storage). In terms of demand, tourist preference for home-country foods which are not grown locally; tourist demand for organic/fair trade certified foods which cannot be readily supplied locally; hotel chef familiarity with and preference for imported foods; chef concern about the health and safety of local food; existing connections between international hotel chains and international suppliers which exclude local producers; hotel aversion to dealing with multiple small growers for logistical reasons; and difficulties in communication and mistrust between producers and hotel purchasers (Rogerson, 2012; Torres & Momsen, 2004) have been identified as things which work against market assemblage. In general, what we see is a context in which a Western-style tourist industry (dominated by ideas of efficiency and standardisation) meets a farming sector not geared to such production, either economically or culturally.

Moreover, there is concern about the potential dependence of agricultural producers on tourism, if supplying the tourist trade becomes their main source of income. Tourism is notorious for its susceptibility to external factors over which destinations have no control (Harrison, 2003; Mowforth & Munt, 2016). Visitor numbers can be dramatically impacted by political instability or environmental disasters, as seen in the aftermath of the 2008–09 global financial crisis, the 2004 Indian Ocean tsunami and the 2005 terrorist attacks on Bali. Of these last, Tarplee (2008) notes that the most vulnerable people were not those employed directly in tourism, but those on the fringes of the industry, such as suppliers and farmers. This suggests that there could be significant risks for agricultural producers if they come to rely on tourism to make a living. Thus, there are a number of circumstances, dynamics and actors identified which have the potential to thwart the assembling of a tourist hotel/local producer market.

Food and tourism in Fiji

Tourism in Fiji has a leakage rate of 40–60 per cent (Berno, 2011, pp. 91–92; Berno, 2006; South Pacific Tourism Organisation, 2005, cited in Robertson, 2006, p. 24), with a major source of this leakage being imported food: in 2004 the Ministry of

Tourism suggested that some 80 per cent of food sold to tourists was imported (Berno, 2011, p. 92). However, Fiji's horticultural sector does have the potential to substitute food imports, especially with respect to fruit and vegetables (Veit, 2007, 2009), as a number of local products are already used by hotels — fruit in breakfast buffets, as salads and vegetable accompaniments to Western-style meals and in traditional Fijian lovo (earth oven) nights (Berno, 2011, p. 92). As a result, growing food to supply the tourist industry seems to present a good opportunity for local producers.

But, this potential has not been realised, largely for the general supply and demand reasons outlined above (see Young & Vinning, 2006, for a Fijian example) with the addition of more local dynamics. Berno (2015) identifies factors inhibiting the formation of local agriculture/tourism linkages in Samoa: namely the poor perception of local cuisine by locals themselves, as well as by international tourists and the subsequent lack of willingness of chefs to serve local food; the incompatibility of some local recipes with the tourist palate; the absence of a recognisable Samoan cuisine beyond lovo; the lack of chef knowledge about local food and the absence of training in local food preparation; the failure of previous initiatives; and questions of land tenure. Laeis found the situation in Fiji to be the same.

A range of projects to overcome these problems and assemble agriculture-tourism networks have been tried. The Oloolo Farm Project was initiated by a member of a mataqali[2], who was also a resort manager at the Palm Breeze (Juanahali Holdings Ltd, 2005). The Palm Breeze signed a Memorandum of Understanding with a producer company and with a development non-governmental organisation which was to provide training and guidance to the farmers. After a successful start, however, the project was discontinued owing to internal problems (Berno, *pers comm*, in Laeis, 2019, p. 54). Another project produced a cookbook titled *Cooking the South Pacific Way* (Parkinson, 1989), which aimed to assist chefs in 'knowing when and what to look for in local markets' and assist with 'produce choice and tips on quality to correct storage, preparation and cooking methods' with the hope that the book would become the 'basis for further imaginative development by the chefs of Fiji and the South Pacific' (Parkinson, 1989, p. viii). Despite interest, the project did not result in longer-term changes in food procurement by the tourism industry. Apparently, chefs were dissatisfied with the quality and reliability of local produce and the programme lacked co-ordination among farmers, chefs, purchasing managers and Government departments (Berno, 2006, p. 217). Currently the Government's 'Fijian Tourism 2021' plan dedicates one of its 29 strategies to the support of such linkages (Ministry of Industry, Trade and Tourism, 2017). The Strategy proposes to develop a rewards system for tourism providers who make an effort to promote local food, the provision of grants and capacity building programmes for farmers, and the fostering of synergies between Government, farmers and tourism businesses through stakeholder forums and workshops; and the introduction of 'Fijian Grown' and 'Fijian Organic' brands to market Fijian produce and encourage consumption.

Overall, it seems that in Fiji there is potential for the development of agriculture-tourism linkages and active work by some to assemble such a market. There is a well-established and flourishing tourism industry, fertile agricultural areas that could supply that industry with desirable produce and, because Fiji retains a sizeable subsistence economy, a significant number of people experienced in horticultural and agricultural work. However, there are a number of local factors beyond those generally identified in the development literature that work to inhibit the assemblage of such a network, namely elements of the already-assembled cultural, social and political order.

The Fijian context

The specificities of the local socio-cultural order have powerful shaping effects on the Fijian economy. Fiji has a population of about 885,000, made up of two main ethnic groups. Indigenous Fijians, iTaukei, account for about 57 per cent of the population, with Indo-Fijians making up about 37 per cent. The category of Indo-Fijians includes descendants of Indian labourers who were brought to Fiji as indentured labourers during in the late 1800s to work on sugar cane plantations, as well as more recent migrants from India (Fiji Bureau of Statistics, 2018). In the past few decades Fiji has experienced political tension and social unrest along this ethnic divide. Conflicts between iTaukei and Indo-Fijians as well as inter-iTaukei rivalries contributed to four coups d'état – in 1987 (twice), 2000 and 2006 (Naidu, 2013), the first three of which aimed at safeguarding indigenous Fijian interests against rising Indo-Fijian political presence. This history is, as it will emerge, an important one for understanding non-assemblage.

Agriculture remains an important part of Fiji's economy, employing about two-thirds of the workforce (Ministry of Agriculture, 2014, pp. 10–11). However, between 1991 and 2009 the number of farms reduced by 32 per cent to about 65,000 mostly small-scale farms, according to the most recent agricultural census. The average farm size was 3.9 ha in 2009, a reduction of more than a third (2.3 ha) since 1991. Just under one-half of all farms (44 per cent) were subsistence farms of less than one hectare, and another 39 per cent were between one and five hectares (Department of Agriculture, 2009, p. 33; Ministry of Agriculture, 2016a, p. 5, 2016b, p. 20). Meanwhile, the contribution of the agricultural sector to Fiji's gross domestic product declined from about 16 per cent in 1995 to 7.6 per cent in 2014 (Ministry of Agriculture, 2016a, p. 5, 2016b, p. 19). The ration of food sourced domestically compared with total food available was 32 per cent in 2015, and this was expected to increase to 42 per cent by 2021 (Ministry of Economy, 2017, p. 10). Overall, while small-scale agriculture puts the food on the tables of many families in Fiji, and the sale of surplus produce is an important source of income for some, the agriculture sector is in decline, and there are few large-scale, commercial farms. Duncan and Sing describe Fiji's agriculture as divided between a commercial sector and a 'village sector' (2009, p. 169). Major products produced for commercial sale are fruit and vegetables such as papaya, eggplant, chilli, okra and curry leaves for export (Laeis, 2019, p. 73) and pineapple, mango and traditional crops like yaqona, ginger, taro and cassava for the local market. (Duncan & Sing, 2009, p. 168; Ministry of Agriculture, 2014, p. 19). Much production is not commercial. Instead, fruit is often causally harvested 'from scattered and poorly maintained plantings' (Ministry of Primary Industries, 2012, p. 21).

Scholars have identified a range of factors inhibiting the development of the agricultural sector in Fiji, including insecure land tenure and a lack of access to formal land titles (particularly an issue for Indo-Fijian farmers) and socio-cultural obligations to share (particularly an issue for iTaukei). Duncan and Sing note that 'the absence of secure individualised tenure to land and the resulting difficulty in accessing credit without such secure collateral' (2009, p. 168) are key challenges. The iTaukei collectively own about 88 per cent of Fiji's land (iTaukeu Land Trust Board, 2018), mostly as shared property of a mataqali. In this context, land is allocated to community members according to custom and not through formalised land titles. However, without such titles, farmers cannot apply for Government grants. Moreover, the strong cultural obligation to share what one has with one's kin (kerekere), which is underpinned by collective ownership of land, is understood to make farmers wary of establishing businesses. Such cultural values are often seen as impediments to development by Westerners; from a local point of view, however, they represent a preference for participation in a different economic network, one infused with and animated by values of reciprocity rather than market exchange. The situation for Indo-Fijian farmers is different but has similar outcomes in terms of supplying hotels. Indo-Fijian farmers lease land from the iTaukei for the most part, but since the time of the coups many indigenous landowners have not renewed those leases (McCarthy, 2007). Loss of access to land obviously makes it impossible to farm, and insecure access to land shapes economic strategies and which markets they are able and willing to engage in assembling. This brief narrative illuminates some of the dynamics which both make assemblage possible, and thwart it. What follows is a tracing of what Laeis discovered as he sought to find out why the Palm Breeze was not supplied by local producers.

Provisioning the Palm Breeze

There are a number of circumstances that make it difficult for local producers to supply the Palm Breeze. Non-human as well as human actants shape market emergence, and while their agency is not the focus of this chapter, here we draw attention to them. The nature of particular products (meat, fish, dairy, fruit, vegetable) make them more or less able to be enrolled in market assemblage.

In a representative month in 2017 the Palm Breeze procured food costing around FJ$500,000 (US$236,000), and 65 per cent of that budget was spent on imported food. This means that 35 per cent of food is sourced locally. At first glance this seems to point to significant linkages between local producers and the hotel, but a closer examination suggests that some of those local actors are not in fact very local and that other connections are singular supply relationships rather than elements in a stabilised market.

The greatest share of the food bill is spent on meat products, more than half of which is imported. Prime cuts of beef, lamb and bacon are generally imported, while chicken, pork and minced beef are procured locally. One of the prime restaurants at the Palm Breeze is a steak restaurant, and in the past chefs have reported that guests found that local beef had an unpleasant taste, so prime cuts of beef are imported from Australia. The Palm Breeze uses about 900 kg of bacon a month, and it is imported, because local supply does not suffice. Some lamb is grown locally, but not in the quantity or quality demanded by the resort. These factors stymie the emergence of a local market. Chicken is sourced locally, from one company, Crest Chicken, as is non-bacon pork. This means that around 15 per cent of the Palm Breeze's expenditure on food is channelled into the local meat economy, although Crest Chicken is in fact a subsidiary of a Australasian food company, Goodman Fielder, which is in turn owned by Wilmar International and First Pacific, meaning that it is unlikely that significant money (aside from wages) goes back into the local economy. Crest Chicken is certainly not the kind of small-scale local producer targeted by development projects.

Fish and seafood are important items on Palm Breeze's menus, and account for 13 per cent of the food bill, half of which (e.g. green-lipped mussels, prawns, oysters, salmon) is imported. Most of the other fish (mahi-mahi, wahoo and tuna, as well as lobster) is caught locally and varies seasonally. Locally sourced items depend on season and availability. For example, according to a manager at the hotel, local fishermen will not dive for lobster in the cooler months between May and October, as they find the water too cold. So the share of the fish budget that is sourced locally varies throughout the year, but significant percentage of imported food in this category is the result of two factors. First, the local fishing economy does not seem to be able to satisfy the resort's requirements for consistent variety and quality of local fish, and second, guests at the hotel demand familiar non-local seafood like mussels, salmon and oysters.

While there are significant limitations to increasing local supply for meat and fish, sourcing more fruit and vegetables locally seems to have greater potential. The category of fruit and vegetables accounts for just over 12 per cent of the resort's food costs, about 55 per cent of which is sourced locally, the highest share of local procurement in any category. This seems at first glance to suggest that a resort/local producer market is well established, but closer investigation shows that this is not the case. What we see is that local procurement focuses on a comparatively limited range of produce, and a very small number of suppliers.

Traditional local foods (banana, bele,[3] breadfruit, cassava, coconut, dalo,[4] ota,[5] heart of palm, jackfruit, rourou,[6] sweet potato and vudi[7]) make up about 23 per cent of locally sourced produce, amounting to only 1.5 per cent of the budget spent on local food. More than half of this expense is for cassava for staff meals rather than for food for resort guests. Many of the other local vegetables are used only in Island-themed buffet nights and are not integrated into the everyday hotel menu, limiting the amount of such produce required. As with fish and seafood, seasonality determines what the resort buys locally. Some fruit, such as papaya and pineapple, are available year round. By comparison, tomatoes, avocado, lettuce, cabbage and mango are seasonal and are imported during the off-season. Other fruits and vegetables are imported – potatoes, onions, carrots, mushrooms, leek, asparagus, parsley, rosemary, thyme, kiwifruit, nashi pears, oranges, apples, pears, strawberries and grapes.

Whether particular fruits or vegetables are imported or not generally depends on availability, quality, reliability of supply and price, but there are a number of cases where produce is imported because of guest preferences. A case in point is the importation of orange-skinned oranges, even during the period when local green-skinned oranges are available. Green-skinned oranges are tasty and juicy, but have a green skin and yellow flesh. They can be used in place of orange-skinned oranges, but according to one of the chefs, 'Our guests don't' like this', and so orange-skinned orange-fleshed oranges are for desserts such as fruit platters. And despite the abundance of locally grown tropical fruits, the Palm Breeze imports temperate-climate fruits such as apples, pears and kiwifruit – with most of the apples being used in bircher muesli for breakfasts.

The kitchen at the Palm Breeze used local food in a number of ways. First, they substituted an otherwise imported item with a similar local product (e.g using roro or dalo leaves in place of spinach), they created a dish that was similar in concept to a Western-style dish but used local products (e.g. using local fruits to make a salsa to serve with fish) or offered local-style dishes made from local produce. Generally the latter took the form of kokoda (a salad of raw fish marinated in coconut milk and lemon with tomatoes, capsicum and cucumber) or the weekly 'Island Night' themed buffet. Here (though we do not delve into this in this chapter) we see the guest palate shaping market potential.

Procuring fruit and vegetables

The Executive Chef at the Palm Breeze expressed a desire to source locally: 'when we have a local supply we use it, otherwise we import', he stated. As noted above, the Executive Chef is Fijian, and he believes that it is because of him that the Palm Breeze sources a higher percentage of local products than many other resorts in Fiji: 'It is because of my decisions. It is because of the produce I use'. Palm Breeze has a list of suppliers who they invite to tender to supply produce on a weekly basis. As well as established suppliers, theoretically any farmer can seek to supply the resort, as long as they are able to deliver the produce and can do so in a closed vehicle. However, while Laeis was working in the resort kitchen only three traders/farmers tended for and delivered fruit and vegetables consistently during that period. Whoever offers the best price or best quality will receive the business on a per-item basis. For example, one supplier might provide papaya and pineapple and another might just be chosen for herbs and root crops. The aim of the tender system is to inhibit monopolies, to 'keep things fair, to keep things above water', in the words of the Executive Chef, and to drive competitive pressure on price and quality. The Palm Breeze acts as if there is an established, competitive market, but acting in this way may in fact work to inhibit the development of the very market they claim they want, as it makes it difficult for small-scale farmers to engage.

The Palm Breeze, then, imports most of the food it feeds to its guests, but sources more local food than other large resorts. The Executive Chef, who ultimately makes the decisions about what is on the hotel menus and therefore decides what food is needed and where to source it, would like to use more local food, but finds this difficult. What follows is his explanation of why he has been unable to establish and stabilise a local market to supply the resort.

The view of the Palm Breeze on non-assemblage

The Palm Breeze needs reliable sources of fruit and vegetables of consistent variety, quantity and quality, and achieving this requires the establishment of relationships with growers or traders. The Executive Chef (and chefs from other resorts) explained why. The Chef has tried to establish direct relationships with local farmers in the past: 'We want more of this... I'd love to have them here', he said. But he also said, 'we have tried, but it didn't work'. The Chef had tried to explain to farmers the varieties of produce he wanted and the kind of quality required. If they could produce it, he told them, they could sell directly to the resort. That way, they could evade intermediary traders and obtain a higher price. He found, however, that even though he is a local and comes from a farming background, he could not manage to convince the farmers to produce for him because, he intimated, they did not have the capacities necessary for dealing with a hotel:

> I was so much trying to entice the farmers, talking to them – I know most of them – encourage them, ' come, come come!'. I talk to them in their own language, but no [it did not work]. ... I'm talking about your original Fiji people. We go to Valley Road, these guys are typical farmers. You see them any time of the day: their shirts are a little torn and dirty. For them, to come to a hotel to talk to a purchasing manager – *a manager!* – you need to be properly dressed. These farmers, they don't have the time to dress up and present them[selves]. They know their stuff, they are proud of what they do. But they are not sales people.
>
> (Executive Chef)

Although the Chef noted that lack of education was an important reason for farmer unwillingness or inability to supply the hotel, the key problem that he identified was to do with local culture. 'It's the mind-set!', he often claimed. This was the dominant explanation for why efforts to co-operate with local farmers constantly failed. The General Manager of the Palm Breeze also supplied a cultural explanation. Under his predecessor's management the Palm Breeze had attempted to set up its own beef production on part of the resort's 350 acres of freehold land. The local mataqali participated in the venture, with the aim of creating a local food supply as well as creating jobs for local people. However, this venture failed: 'They gave it a go, but unfortunately, once again with Fijian custom, when their Paramount Chief passed away, it was requested that they slaughter half of the herd to give for the feast that was associated with that particular celebration', the General Manager explained. Despite these setbacks, the Chef was hopeful about the future, as 'farmers are getting educated, facilities are coming in, so maybe down the road you will get more of them', meaning educated farmers who are willing and able to supply hotels.

Chefs and managers from other hotels had had similar experiences and reiterated the view of the Palm Breeze Executive Chef. Several had made attempts to establish direct links with farmers and to support the development of a hotel-focused market. As one chef said, 'I think as a big company it's our duty to support the community …', and as such, another stated, he aims 'to support the locals to get their product right', to grow what the hotels need, not what the farmers want to grow or are used to growing. One had established a small horticultural farm at the resort he worked at to grow herbs and salad vegetables for the kitchen, and another had established a farm nearby to produce similar kinds of highly perishable produce.

One chef seemed to have a lot of local connections and claimed that he could source almost anything locally:

> I think it is how you make friends with everybody and how your reputation is with them. You can pretty much get anything at a decent price. Also, you can get decent quality, but then they look after you only. So that's how I made friends, especially down Sigatoka way. Beautiful farms over there. So I look after them quite a bit…. Strawberries are no problem. One guy is growing them for me, no issues.
>
> (Chef)

The localness of local supply could be very local indeed. One chef mentioned that he acquired all of his prawns, in fact 90 per cent of his seafood, locally, while another was adamant that 'there are no local prawns!'. Another chef had a local farmer who supplied him with cherry tomatoes 'in beautiful little punnets, fresh, fresh, fresh!', while another was not able to source cherry tomatoes locally at all.

What this points to is the importance of relationships between individuals in establishing and sustaining supply, with some chefs finding particular suppliers reliable and other chefs finding the same supplier unreliable. 'Looking after', for the chef quoted above, meant buying from his suppliers even if the quality, quantity or price was not ideal. They reported that there is a lot of local food available, but it tended to be in small quantities, which meant that to supply the hotel a chef had to establish relationships with a number of farmers, which was not always possible given the constraints of organising a large resort kitchen.

Even though many chefs had established successful relationships with individual local farmers, they were critical of farmers more generally, and blamed farmers and a set of practices and values they understood as local culture, for their inability to source the local food they desired. The Executive Chef of the Palm Breeze identified this problem as one of 'mind-set', implying that farmers lacked the attitudes and aptitudes necessary to transforming their farming systems and orienting them to resort-focused production. They mobilised a kind of cultural-deficit explanation, in which local culture inhibited the development of the kind of entrepreneurial subjectivities necessary for market-making.

Two chefs simply stated that lots of farmers were lazy. One thought this 'laziness' was the result of established agricultural systems: 'dalo, cassava – you just stick it in the ground and it grows!' and 'no-one has taught them to grow something else, they need to learn'. With regards to iTaukei one chef said that they only grow a very specific set of crops: dalo, yam, cassava, vudi, banana and bele – 'everything else that is sold by iTaukei is what you gather. They are not the best gardeners'. He suggested that it was not part of their culture to seriously engage in horticulture as their lands provided food like coconuts, breadfruit, moca, water cress and ota which could simply be gathered. By comparison, Indo-Fijian farmers were reported to be only used to growing sugar cane: 'they think nothing else is possible'. Many local farmers, whether iTaukei or Indo-Fijian, were said to be only willing to grow culturally and historically embedded crops, anything else, 'they don't trust'.

The 'mind-set' problem applied to selling as much as it did to growing. iTaukei were said to only sell when they needed to. One chef recalled how the community in which his hotel was located regularly supplied him with about 20 kg of lobster. But as soon as the mataqali needed money for an event, things changed:

> Then all the village men got together and decided to go diving and then they come up with 400 or 500 kg worth of lobster [laughs]. And they want to sell it *now!*. That's the thing with consistency: they will only get [the product to sell] when they need the money.

A Fijian himself, he understood the situation and bought the entire catch, on-selling what was surplus to his requirements. Another chef had been regularly supplied with fish and as such had put the fish onto his menu. But the supply suddenly stopped:

> So I called the guy and asked 'what's going on? I ordered 40 kg of fish for Wednesday and 40 kg for Saturday'. And he said, 'oh no, I didn't go fishing!'. And I went, 'why didn't you go fishing?' He said, 'oh, you paid me enough on Wednesday!'.
>
> (Chef)

He explained this behaviour as an outcome of many iTaukei owning land and therefore not needing to earn a lot of money. Another stated, 'In Fiji, you might have realised, people don't think in the long-term', why sell more tomorrow if I have enough money today? Others were confronted with the fact that the supplier had sold his produce elsewhere or supplied less than ordered: farmers frequently 'over-commit[ted] and under-deliver[ed]', in the words of one chef. 'You can't do business with people like that, as much as they are lovely and you want to be as patient as you can', said one chef. Local farming, Laeis was told by a chef, '[has] to do with their kind of social needs, which doesn't necessarily mix with business, tourism, peak seasons and all that'.

Chefs also complained that high quality produce was grown in Fiji, but it was not available locally. Instead, it was exported. This pertained to fruit and vegetables, as well as fish and seafood. One chef said that he had received second-grade eggplants, and had only later realised that A-grade eggplants actually existed. The

A-grade eggplants were not available on the local market because exporting them was more lucrative for growers. It was the same for fish: 'the people overseas are willing to pay big dollars for quality fish. Here? No!', said a chef.

So, it appears that there is local produce available of the quality and quantity desired by resort hotels, but it is not available on the local market for hotels to purchase (in part because the hotels are unwilling to pay for it). The account of the resort chefs suggests that local produce it is not regularly or reliably provided for sale because of the mind-set (read culture) of farmers. However, this explanation is not borne out when farmers are asked why they do not produce for hotels.

The view of the farmers on non-assemblage

Farmers who direct their operations towards the hotel market are unusual, and the Palm Breeze suppliers noted a number of reasons why many farmers do not engage in making such a market. Laeis talked to the three suppliers who regularly provided the Palm Breeze with fruit and vegetables, to find out why they had established supply relationships with the hotel, and why other farmers do not. The suppliers in question were not small-scale farmers, but traders. One supplied several resorts as well as supermarket chains, and the second sold to airport/airline caterers, as well as resorts. Both were among the biggest and most important traders in the Sigatoka Valley, sourcing produce from a large number of small scale farmers. The third had a 20-ha farm, but also acted as a trader and bought from other farmers if he could not provide an entire order from his own farm.

The traders faced some of the same challenges as chefs who source directly, namely inconsistency of supply in terms of quality and quantity. Likewise, they need to work hard to get growers to grow for hotels. One had convinced a farmer to grow lemongrass, basil and mint, only for him: 'It took me a good couple of months to get it through his head, but now he is laughing', meaning he is making good money. To persuade the farmer to grow what he wants, the trader supplied the farmer with inputs (seeds, fertiliser, pesticides) and bought all of his harvest at an agreed price. In order to sustain such supply chains, traders needed to pay farmers a 'fair share' of what the hotel pays. If farmers thought they were being exploited, they would no longer supply.

Traders also faced challenges from the hotel side. One said that resorts will suddenly change their order: 'they are using 300 kg of vudi a week, but before it used to be 3 kg a week!'. This is not only a challenge for him as a trader, but also produces uncertainty for farmers, who might suddenly find themselves without a market for what they have grown.

The farmer/trader said that he has a long list of fruits and vegetables that he could easily sell to hotels for a good price, but he has not been able to find farmers to grow for him. Most farmers, he said, echoing the words of the chefs, only plant what they are used to. Another stated: 'It's the mind-set, which I think the old generation had, and it is really hard right now to change the system in [the farmers'] heads'.

So we have a situation where it seems that all of the conditions for the assembling of a market are in place, but yet it has not assembled. Why? The answer is actually quite simple and has little to do with the kind of cultural mind-set identified by chefs and traders. The answer does have to do with a mind-set, but the mind-set in question is more that of a rational economic and social actor than it is of a cultural deficiency and lack of education. Farmers choose not to supply hotels for reasons largely to do with reducing and mitigating economic risk — a decision that seems a perfectly rational choice.

First, farmers find that supplying a hotel is a lot of extra work, and choose not to undertake work they find a hassle. Supplying a hotel means careful sorting and cleaning produce and packing into crates that then need to be transported to the hotel in a closed vehicle. It means regular, reliable and punctual delivery of specified quantities. Hotels also have demanding standards, and may reject produce. By contrast, to supply the local markets 'they just load in big trucks, 100 bags [of] eggplant, 100 bags of cabbage [laughs], just load it and ship it', said one trader. Moreover, as the traders experienced, hotels can be fickle in their demands in terms of variety, quantity and quality, creating uncertainty and insecurity.

Furthermore, and in line with their preference for hassle-free production, farmers prefer to grow for export. Exporters pay the most. Exporters, however, require only a few items — eggplant, okra, papaya, curry leaves and a certain kind of chilli. For a farmer, putting all of their eggs in the export market is risky, as they are at the mercy of the importing country.[8] Supplying a wide variety of items to hotels potentially mitigates this risk. However, concentrating on growing a few key products is easier and more efficient, and perhaps it is more likely that the experienced grower will produce export quality produce more easily than they could a wide variety of things that the hotel might want. In weighing up the risks and rewards, exporting is seen as a better bet.

Not farming to supply hotels is a different kind of better-bet for iTaukei and Indo-Fijian farmers, and there were differences underpinning the decision to not supply. Historically, Indo-Fijian farmers grew sugar cane. Sugar cane, farmers agreed, is a 'lazy man's crop'. It is a perennial, drought-resistant plant that flourishes in a wide variety of soils and does not need irrigation, and only requires weeding and fertilising in the initial growth stages. The only 'hard work' required is harvesting the cane once a year. Moreover, sugar cane production has traditionally taken place under the authority of the Fiji Sugar Corporation, which set prices and supported farmers, providing certainty and security for growers. Successful production of the market-garden kind needed to supply hotels demands a diverse range of horticultural skills, planning capacity and ability to assemble a set of market relations, given the absence of an already-established set of supply conduits. Continuing to grow sugar (if possible) or growing one of the major export crops fits better with Indo-Fijian farming experience.

For Indo-Fijian farmers, many of who live precarious economic lives, reliable short-term economic return was paramount. Many do not own the land they farm and were understandably hesitant to invest in any long-term or expensive ventures involving things like irrigation, permanent crops such as fruit trees, or in new crops that they do not have expertise in growing and selling and where there is, therefore, a higher risk of failure. Moreover, the history of coups, noted above, led to the displacement of Indo-Fijian farmers from their lands as iTaukei owners declined to renew leases. This insecurity of tenure has had two consequences. First, Indo-Fijian farmers have (sensibly) shied away from long-term capital investment into farming ventures (World Bank 2017), and second, they had not been interested or able to pass their farms on to the next generation (Crocombe, 2013, p. 199). As such, the kinds of long-term investments needed to forge and participate in a market supplying hotels are simply too risky.

iTaukei farmers, by comparison, as owners of land, do not need to take the risks associated with growing new crops, and to the frustration of some development professionals, seem to continue to prefer to invest in a traditional exchange economy rather than in a market economy. As a development practitioner engaged in promoting a tomato growing venture stated:

> The iTaukei have an extremely strong culture. It is a strength, but like all strengths it is also a weakness. And so the obligation is very strong within the culture to be a groupist and not future oriented culture, the tendency is that it doesn't necessarily fit with the business concept. That's what we've got to change. Well, we don't have to change the people, we have to get them to culture-shift, to accept that business is a new way of life, and we will change and adapt. As long as they agree to the work ethic, we are in business.

Many farmers from both groups, if they do choose to grow for the market, appear to prefer the comparative simplicity and security of growing for export. It is not that they cannot (because of culture) grow for resort hotels, it is because they do not want to.

Conclusion

There are a number of reasons for the failure of a market for the supply of produce to resort hotels in Fiji to emerge and these general reasons are widely known. From a hotel point of view, there is a lack of produce of the variety, quality and quantity they need. But they consider that there is potential for these problems to be overcome, and as a result, there are continuing efforts by hotel management and development agencies to create a market by encouraging farmers to produce for hotels. This, it is argued, will improve the incomes of local people and contribute to strengthening the Fijian economy. Despite persistent work, the desired market has failed to emerge and stabilise. Instead, we see the development of individual supply relationships between particular chefs and hotel managers and traders and growers. These relationships are inevitably fragile and contingent. The hotel-side explanation for the frustration of their repeated attempts at creating a market is the 'mind-set' of farmers, by which they mean a culture which inhibits the development of market-focused entrepreneurialism. The farmer-side explanation for the failure of the market to assemble is that fundamentally, also for cultural reasons, farmers are just not that interested in assembling it, because they have better options.

In making sense of market non-assemblage in Fiji, our strategy has been to locate the obligatory blockage point (OBP), and what (or more precisely who) we found that OBP to be were human subjects. Fijian farmers were not the kind of market subjects imagined and desired by the hotels, but what made them non-compliant and non-enrolled subjects was not the cultural-deficit-mind-set that hotel chefs and managers advanced in explanation. Instead, they were calculating subjects, deploying locally formed strategic rationalities to decide not to supply resort hotels. The calculations that they made were formed in arenas of cultural and economic life outside of the tourist industry, and it was the calculations that they made in those arenas that shaped their lack of engagement with the hotels. For iTaukei, it was embeddedness in a 'traditional' economy, animated by rationalities of reciprocity and kinship that shaped their decisions; for Indo-Fijians it was the experience of the uncertainty and insecurity generated by the history of the coups that shaped their assessment of risk. Culture as a concept might well be fuzzy and irritatingly difficult to define, but whatever it is, it is almost always one of the things that shapes the assemblage and non-assemblage of markets in particular places.

Notes

1 Notable exceptions include Latour (1996) and Webb & Hawkey (2017).
2 A mataqali is a clan or landowning unit.
3 *Hibiscus manihot*, also known as slippery cabbage.
4 *Colocasia esculenta*, more widely known as taro. The leaves are used as a spinach substitute.
5 A local tree fern.
6 Taro leaves.
7 Plantain.
8 For example, between April and June 2017 New Zealand banned the import of Fijian produce due to bio-security concerns, resulting in significant losses for Fijian exporters and farmers (Fiji Broadcasting Corporation, 7 June 2017).

References

Asiedu, A.B. & Gbedema, T.K. (2011). The nexus between agriculture and tourism in Ghana: A case of unexploited development potential. In R.M. Torres & J.H. Momsen (Eds), *Tourism and agriculture: New geographies of consumption, production and rural restructuring* (pp. 28–46). London: Routledge.

Banks, G., Scheyvens, R., McLennan, S. & Bebbington, A. (2016). Conceptualising corporate community development. *Third World Quarterly*, 37(2), 245–263. https://doi.org/10.1080/01436597.2015.1111135.

Beaglehole, A. (2013). *Refuge New Zealand: A nation's response to refugees and asylum seekers*. Otago: Otago University Press.

Berno, T. (2006). Bridging sustainable agriculture and sustainable tourism to enhance sustainability. In G. Mudacumura, M.S. Haque & D. Mebratu (Eds), *Sustainable development policy and administration* (pp. 207–223). New York, NY: Taylor & Francis.

Berno, T. (2011). Sustainability on a plate: Linking agriculture and food in the Fiji Islands tourism industry. In R.M. Torres & J.H. Momsen (Eds), *Tourism and agriculture: New geographies of consumption, production and rural restructuring* (pp. 87–103). London: Routledge.

Berno, T. (2015). Tourism, food traditions and supporting communities in Samoa: The mea'ai project. In P. Sloan, W. Legrand & C. Hindley (Eds), *The Routledge handbook of sustainable food and gastronomy* (pp. 338–347). London: Routledge.

Çalışkan, K. & Callon, M. (2010). Economization, Part 2: A research programme for the study of markets. *Economy and Society*, 39(1), 1–32. https://doi.org/10.1080/03085140903424519.

Crocombe, R. (2013). Tenure. In M. Rapaport (Ed.), *The Pacific islands: Environment and society* (2nd ed., pp. 192–201). Honolulu, HI: University of Hawai'I Press.

Department of Agriculture. (2009). *Fiji national agricultural census 2009*. Suva: Department of Agriculture, Economic Planning and Statistics Division. Retrieved from www.fao.org/fileadmin/templates/ess/ess_test_folder/World_Census_Agriculture/Country_info_2010/Reports/Reports_3/FJI_ENG_REP_2009.pdf.

Duncan, R. & Sing, Y.W. (2009). The failure of agricultural policy making in Fiji. *Pacific Economic Bulletin*, 24(2): 168–184.

Fiji Broadcasting Corporation. (2017). Ban on Fiji eggplants lifted. 7 June 2017. Retrieved from www.fbc.com.fj/fiji/51484/ban-on-fiji-eggplants-lifted.

Fiji Bureau of Statistics. (2018). *Population and demography: 2007 population census*. Retrieved from www.statsfiji.gov.fj/statistics/social-statistics/population-and-demographic-indicators.

Frankel, C. (2015). The multiple-markets problem. *Journal of Cultural Economy*, 8(4): 538–546.

Gulledge, E., Roscoe, P. & Townley, B. (2015). Economizing habitus. *Journal of Cultural Economy*, 8(6), 637–654. https://doi.org/10.1080/17530350.2015.1047785.

Harrison, D. (2003). Themes in Pacific island tourism. In D. Harrison (Ed.), *Pacific island tourism* (pp. 1–23). New York, NY: Cognizant Communication Corporation.

Hunt, H. & Rogerson C.M. (2013). Tourism-led development and backward linkages: Evidence from the agriculture-tourism nexus in southern Africa. In G. Visser & S. Ferreira (Eds), *Tourism and crisis* (pp. 159–179). London: Routledge.

International Finance Corporation. (2018). From the farm to the tourist's table: A study of fresh produce demand from Fiji's hotels and resorts. Retrieved from www.ifc.org.

iTaukei Land Trust Board. (2018). Land statistics. Retrieved from www.tltb.com.fj/LandStatistics.htm.

Juanahali Holdings Ltd. (2005). *Farming project work plan*. Sigatoka.

Laeis, G.C.M. (2019). *What's on the menu?: How the cuisine of large-scale, up-market tourist resorts shapes agricultural development in Fiji*. [Unpublished doctoral dissertation], Massey University.

Latour, B. (1996). *Aramis, Or, The Love of Technology*. London: Harvard University Press.

Lejarraja, I. & Walkenhorst, P. (2007). *Diversification by deepening linkages with tourism*. Washington, DC: International Trade Department, The World Bank.

McCarthy, S., (2007). Political instability in the Asia-Pacific: Lessons from the 2006 coups in Thailand and Fiji. *Griffith Asia Institute regional outlook*. Brisbane, QLD: Griffith University.

Medina-Muñoz, D.R., Medina-Muñoz, R.D. & Gutiérrez-Pérez, F.J. (2016). The impacts of tourism on poverty alleviation: An integrated research framework. *Journal of Sustainable Tourism*, 24(2), 270–298.

Ministry of Agriculture. (2014). *Fiji 2020 – Agriculture sector policy agenda*. Suva.

Ministry of Agriculture. (2016a). *Fiji livestock sector strategy*. Suva.

Ministry of Agriculture. (2016b). *In-depth country assessment of the national system of agricultural and rural statistics in Fiji*. Suva. Retrieved from http://pafpnet.spc.int/attachments/article/744/Fiji%20IDCA%20Report%202016.pdf.

Ministry of Economy. (2017). 5-year and 20-year national development plan. Suva. Retrieved from http://www.fiji.gov.fj/getattachment/15b0ba03-825e- 47f7-bf69–94ad33004dd/5-Year20-Year-NATIONAL-DEVELOPMENT-PLAN.aspx.

Ministry of Industry, Trade and Tourism. (2017). Fijian tourism 2021, draft document for the 1st consultation. Suva. Retrieved from https://fhta.com.fj/wp-content/uploads/2017/02/Fijian-Tourism-2021.pdf.

Ministry of Primary Industries. (2012). *Agriculture investment guide: Discovering opportunities, harvesting potentials.* Suva.

Mowforth, M. & Munt, I. (2016). *Tourism and sustainability: Development, globalisation and new tourism in the Third World* (4th ed.). London: Routledge.

Naidu, V. (2013). *Fiji: The challenges and opportunities of diversity.* London: Minority Rights Group International.

Oviedo-García, M.Á., González-Rodríguez, M.R. & Vega-Vázquez, M. (2018). Does sun-and-sea all-inclusive tourism contribute to poverty alleviation and/or income inequality reduction? The case of the Dominican Republic. *Journal of Travel Research*, 58(6), 995–1013.

Parkinson, S. (1989). *Cooking the South Pacific way! A professional guide to Fiji produce.* Suva: Tourism Council of the South Pacific.

Pillay, M. & Rogerson, C.M. (2013). Agriculture-tourism linkages and pro-poor impacts: The accommodation sector of urban coastal KwaZulu-Natal, South Africa. *Applied Geography*, 36, 49–58.

Pretty, J.N. (2001). Some benefits and drawbacks of local food systems. (Briefing Note for TVU/Sustain Agrifood Network). Retrieved from www.sustainweb.org/pdf/afn_m1_p2.pdf.

Robertson, R. (2006). Fiji futuring: Connectivity and development. *Pacific Economic Bulletin*, 21(2), 22–35.

Rogerson, C.M. (2012). Strengthening agriculture-tourism linkages in the developing World: Opportunities, barriers and current initiatives. *African Journal of Agricultural Research*, 7(4), 616–623.

Saarinen, J. & Rogerson, C.M. (2014). Tourism and the millennium development goals: Perspectives beyond 2015. *Tourism Geographies*, 16(1), 23–30.

Scheyvens, R. (2011). *Tourism and poverty.* New York, NY: Routledge.

Sharpley, R. (2015). Tourism: A vehicle for development? In R. Sharpley & D.J. Telfer (Eds), *Tourism and development: Concepts and issues* (pp. 11–34). Clevedon: Channel View Publications.

Simons-Kaufmann, C., Kaufmann, F., Sloan, P. & Legrand, W. (2012). Introduction: Scarcity of natural resources or 'Cockaigne'? In P. Sloan, C. Simons-Kaufmann & W. Legrand (Eds), *Sustainable hospitality and tourism as motors for development* (pp. 1–23). London: Routledge.

Sustainable Tourism Development Consortium. (2007). *Fiji tourism development plan, 2007–2016.* Suva.

Tarplee, S. (2008). After the bomb in a Balinese village. In J. Connell & B. Rugendyke (Eds), *Tourism at the grassroots: Concepts and issues* (pp. 35–78). Clevedon: Channel View Publications.

Telfer, D.J. & Sharpley, R. (2008). *Tourism and development in the developing world.* London: Routledge.

Timms. B.F. & Neill, S. (2011). Cracks in the pavement: Conventional constraints and contemporary solutions for linking agriculture and tourism in the Caribbean. In R. Torres & J.H. Momsen (Eds), *Tourism and agriculture: New geographies of production and rural restructuring* (pp. 104–116). London: Routledge.

Torres, R.M. & Momsen, J.H. (2004). Challenges and potential for linking tourism and agriculture to achieve pro-poor tourism objectives. *Progress in Development Studies*, 4 (4), 294–318.

Torres, R.M. & Momsen, J.H. (2005). Planned tourism development in Quintana Roo, Mexico: Engine for regional development or prescription for inequitable growth? *Current Issues in Tourism*, 8(4), 259–285.

Torres, R.M. & Momsen, J.H. (2011). Introduction. In R. Torres & J.H. Momsen (Eds), *Tourism and agriculture: New geographies of production and rural restructuring* (pp. 1–10). London: Routledge.

Veit, R. (2007). *Tourism, food imports, and the potential for import-substitution policies in Fiji.* Suva: Fiji AgTrade – Ministry of Agriculture, Fisheries and Forests.

Veit, R. (2009). *A feasibility study of collection centres in Fiji* (AAACP Paper Series – No. 7). Rome: Food and Agricultural Organization of the United Nations.

Webb, J. & Hawkey, D. (2017). On (not) assembling a market for sustainable energy: heat network infrastructure and British cities. *Journal of Cultural Economy*, 10(1), 8–20.

World Bank. (2016). Agriculture and rural development. Retrieved from http://data.worldbank.org/topic/agriculture-and-rural-development.

World Bank. (2017). Republic of Fiji: Systematic country diagnostic. Retrieved from http://documents.worldbank.org/curated/en/668391506585108864/pdf/120106-SCD-P160757-PUBLIC-FijiSCDpostDecisionclean.pdf.

Worldwatch Institute. (2003). *Vital Signs 2003: The trends that are shaping our future.* New York, NY: W.W. Norton.

Young, J. & Vinning, G. (2006). *Fiji: Commodity chain study.* Suva: Food and Agricultural Organization of the United Nations Fiat Panis and Cooperazione Italiana.

7 'I want to sleep at night as well'

Guilt and care in the making of agricultural credit markets

Alexandra Langford, Alana Brekelmans and Geoffrey Lawrence

UNIVERSITY OF QUEENSLAND

Introduction

Financialisation has been described as the growing influence of financial actors, values, and processes on contemporary economic and social life (Epstein, 2005). Since the 1970s there has been an emerging presence of financial entities (merchant and commercial banks, investment finance houses, superannuation funds, sovereign wealth funds, state owned enterprises, private equity firms and hedge funds) employing a variety of financial products and instruments (including credit default swaps, derivatives, commodity index funds, leveraged buy outs, junk bonds and so forth – see Konzelmann, Fovargue & Wilkinson, 2013). These actors, products and instruments have helped to shift capitalism from a production-based system to one dominated by the finance sector (Lapavitsas, 2012). In agri-food studies, increasing investments in land and agribusiness have raised concerns about the potential implications of the financialisation of agri-food industries (Clapp & Isakson 2018a, 2018b), such as growing monopoly control in industries and supply chains (McMichael, 2012; Burch & Lawrence, 2013), increasing cost and volatility of farmland (Gunnoe, 2014; Magnan & Sunley, 2017), food market volatility (Ghosh, Heintz & Pollin, 2012; Clapp, 2014), increasing pressure on family farmers (Magnan, 2012), a shift away from bank mediated financing towards the use of financial equity markets (Webb, 2019), and the increasing use of shareholder value as a measure of success (Williams, 2014).

However, this literature says little about how financialisation occurs in practice, and how it might be identified in ongoing *work* (Williams, 2014). Financialisation has often been applied *post-hoc* as an explanatory concept for broader global patterns that are only identifiable, by their *effects*, as financialising, or de-financialising, in nature (see Christophers, 2015; Ouma, 2015, 2020). There is growing recognition of the need to understand the geographically situated movements of financialisation, and the ways that a range of actors (both human and non-human) assemble broader global patterns. An assemblage approach usefully addresses this challenge by viewing 'financialised' patterns of investments as assembled by a diverse range of often contradictory work by a range of actors. This work is not inherently financialising or otherwise in nature, but becomes so through its interactions within a broader

DOI: 10.4324/9780429296260-7

assemblage. The open potentiality of assemblages alerts us to the work of a much wider range of actors in financialisation processes, highlighting investments as uncertain and messy work (Ducastel & Anseeuw, 2017, 2018; Langford, 2020, 2021) which draws on a range of non-human tools (Higgins 2006; Henry, 2017), and discursive projects (Visser, 2017) and dissolves scalar distinctions between the local and the global (Tsing, 2004; Henry & Prince, 2018). This approach creates space to both recognise the patterns of financialisation occurring over large areas and long timeframes, and to avoid subscribing to a view that these changes are generated by a coherent agenda or occur in predictable ways. Broader ideas structuring economic activity – such as neoliberalism or financialisation – are seen not as structural drivers with pre-determined outcomes, but as parts of assemblages with open potentiality to create different outcomes in different places.

Studying the financialisation of agriculture in this way requires making 'cuts' to the assemblage – isolating key sites of study – to identify and explore crucial moments of negotiation (see Anderson, Kearns, McFarlane & Swanton, 2012, pp. 182–183). One important component of financialisation is the changing role of bank debt in farm financing. Studies of the financialisation of agriculture often describe it as a shift away from bank mediated financing towards the use of financial equity markets (Webb, 2019). However, banks themselves undergo financialised restructuring to different extents, and although there is considerable variation between farmers (Pritchard, Burch & Lawrence, 2007; Cheshire & Woods, 2013; Langford 2019), bank debt is still the primary source of capital for most Australian farmers (Larder, Sippel & Argent, 2018; Meat and Livestock Australia, 2020). Banks mediate connections between global capital markets and farmers and, as such, can introduce global capital market volatility into remote regions. In studying financialisation there is therefore a need to study not only emerging financial tools such as equity and derivatives markets, but also to explore how older institutions, such as banks, shift in response to changing financial circumstances. Rural agri-finance specialists are key mediators between global capital markets and local farmers. They visit farms and make decisions about what to lend, how much to lend and to whom. The role of these rural bankers is often underemphasised, as it is easy to assume that they simply facilitate transactions between remote farmers and their bank. However, these bankers exercise considerable agency in the work of operationalising bank lending policies. In the current global context of increasing financialisation of agriculture (Larder *et al.*, 2015), bank debt facilitates the operation and growth of both family farms and financial investments in land. Understanding the financialisation of agriculture on a global scale therefore requires an examination of the spaces in which land and lending markets are made, as well as the ways connections between global capital markets and remote farms are developed.

In rural agricultural debt markets, relationship lending is common. Finance studies have emphasised the importance of 'relationship lending' for reducing the problem of 'asymmetric information' in debt markets (Beck, Degryse, De Haas & Van Horen, 2018). Here, it is economically rational for banks to develop close relationships with their clients in order to better assess their capacity for loan repayment (Fiordelisi, Monferrà & Sampagnaro, 2014; Moss, Kropp &

Bampasidou, 2018), particularly over the long term (López-Espinosa, Mayordomo & Moreno 2017). In agricultural lending, banks consider it profitable to develop close relationship lending with some borrowers, depending on loan size (Akhavein, Goldberg & White 2004; Hilkens, Reid, Klerk & Gray, 2018). This can provide some benefits to borrowers; relationship lending, while not increasing access to credit in a credit boom, can reduce credit constraints during a downturn (Bolton, Freixas, Gambacorta & Mistrulli, 2016; Beck *et al.*, 2018). In addition, there is some evidence that close bank-borrower relationships can increase lending after environmental disasters (Berg & Schrader, 2012), which could have implications for lending during drought.

Texts about the economics of rural debt market formation emphasise it as a contracting process between the farmer and the banker, in which the banker seeks to assess the likelihood of loan repayment (Moss *et al.*, 2018). However, there are grounds for viewing relationship lending as both part of, and generative of, a moral economy. The concept of moral economy is often used to invoke a range of 'transcendent value[s]' (Carrier, 2017, p. 22) that shape ideas about what and how economic activity should be undertaken (for example, Ho (2009) describes the morality of investment bankers in pursuit of economic efficiency). As Wolford (2005, p. 245) writes, 'moral economies are both the expression of and production of a social group's explicitly normative frameworks outlining the 'proper' organisation of society … They contain ideological elements and are spatially situated in concrete material contexts'. This approach upholds that behaviours are the result of differing moral belief systems (Ho, 2009) which could enable or prevent the extension of financialising logics into rural debt markets. As Sippel (2018, p. 553) writes, '[p]eople do not 'strip off' their social and cultural baggage when they engage in economic activities. They fluidly move within different spheres of value and make use of various and potentially diverging or incompatible justificatory principles for determining worth'.

In this sense, all economies are moral economies, since the separation of society and economy is artificial (Hann, 2016). Carrier (2017) argues that rather than focussing on these broader values and the way they structure economic transactions, moral economy can be usefully employed to explore *how* moral economic activity arises from economic transactions themselves – that is, how a relationship between, for example, a shopkeeper and customer, employer and employee, or banker and client – can create mutual obligations and lead to care for the other. This is a focus on *process* – how certain temporal and spatial patterns of economic transactions generate mutual obligations which underpin moral economic activity. Relationships between bankers and clients are often viewed in 'pure' economic terms – as a way of reducing asymmetric information for the bank. However, seeing these relationships *themselves* as generating new forms of moral economic interaction between banker and client suggests the need to study these spatially grounded interactions and explore how they assemble rural credit markets. Rather than focussing on the way that particular morals or economic drivers structure economies, we see economic morality itself as assembled by a range of interpersonal relations. Broader ideas and structures – such as values about how the world should be – shape and constrain such assemblages, but do not define it in any predictable way. Rather, the morality of lending is negotiated in interpersonal relationships between bankers and clients, and are shaped by the unique geographies over which these relationships form. We take as our focus these banker –client relationships and explore how morality is both enacted, and generated, in their interactions.

This research forms part of a larger project investigating the financialisation of land and agriculture in Australia, for which over 100 interviews were undertaken between 2016 and 2019. This paper draws on a subset of 40 interviews focussing particularly on northern Australia. We also bring to this analysis insights from ethnographic work by the second author who, in 2017, undertook research into pastoralist responses to environmental phenomena and uncertain futures in North West Queensland. We combine these empirical studies with information from Round 4, Part 1 of the Royal Commission into Misconduct in the Banking, Superannuation and Financial Services Industry ('Financial Services Royal Commission'), which investigated the provision of bank finance to farming. These combined research agendas offer insights into the relationships between bankers and pastoralists and highlight the importance of these relationships in making lending markets. The next section introduces the context of financialisation in the unique region of pastoral northern Australia.

Rural lending and financialisation in Northern Australian pastoralism

The state has historically played a key role in mediating connections between agriculture and finance by providing farm credit and financial support and moderating commodity markets (McMichael, 1984; Martin & Clapp, 2015; Larder et al., 2018). Farms are risky enterprises that have typically been unattractive to private investors, leading the state to play a key role in supporting investment propositions through enforcing contracts and bankruptcy laws, providing collateral, undertaking credit provision, supporting marketing boards and intervening in financial markets (Martin & Clapp, 2015; Larder et al., 2018). This involvement of the state has long moderated connections between finance and agriculture. Since the 1980s, however, a withdrawal of state support for agriculture associated with neoliberalisation has seen Australian agricultural markets restructured in pursuit of market efficiency, forcing farmers to rely on increasingly unfavourable debt markets (Larder et al., 2018) or seek equity partnerships with private sector investors (Langford, 2019). In northern Australia, a federal government initiative to 'Develop the North' has made explicit its approach of attracting financial investors to guide development efforts (Australian Government, 2015; Langford, Smith & Lawrence, 2020).

In northern Australia, pastoral properties are typically very large and remote, and it is common for bankers to service large regions and travel for many hours to visit their clients. These pastoral properties often sell for millions of dollars, and over the past two decades or so property prices have become increasingly high and volatile, raising concerns about the effects of speculative investments in land (see Figure 7.1). However, it is not only private sector investors who introduce volatility into land

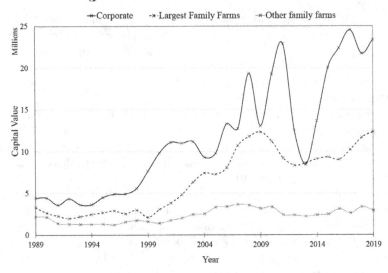

Figure 7.1 Land value of Australian pastoral zone beef farms by ownership type, 1989–
2019
Source: Data from Meat and Livestock Australia (2020). Expressed in A$ 2019–2020

markets; bank lending behaviour can introduce and exacerbate price volatility in
rural pastoral debt markets in three important ways.

First, bank lending is often pro-cyclical (Athanasoglou, Daniilidis & Delis,
2014). This means that banks lend more during times of capital surplus (economic
booms). Banks that previously avoided farm investment can expand into agricultural lending in new regions and offer low cost loans, while existing banks can
reduce their rates or lending requirements. This makes access to loans easier during
global economic expansions. However, banks can reduce access to credit during
slowdowns, declining additional loans to their customers, which might be needed
for property purchases, or for operating costs, or for infrastructure. In addition,
bank loans might contain 'non-financial default clauses', which entitles the bank to
reassess existing loans owing to external factors such as disasters or changed market
conditions. This can, again, substantially reduce the standing of the pastoralist.

Second, pastoralists will experience fluctuations in the value of their property as
a result of changes in investment demand. As a result, during good seasons property values can be high, and they will cyclically reduce during recessions, and this
affects lending ratios and the risks of the loan as assessed by the bank. For example,
a pastoralist whose property is valued at A$1,000,000 during a property price
boom might be offered a 60 per cent lending ratio and borrow A$600,000. The
same property might be revalued a few years later, during a property price collapse,
at just $800,000 – with a 60 per cent lending ratio, the bank would now be
comfortable with lending the pastoralist only $480,000 and might seek repayments
or decline additional lending needed to meet operating costs.

Finally, property values also shift in response to local circumstances such as drought. A drought in a region could result in reduced demand for properties and depressed land prices, again reducing the pastoralist's lending position. This can cause hardship because it is often during drought that pastoralists require additional capital, for example, to purchase supplementary feed. Unwillingness to lend during these times can undermine a pastoral operation with long-term implications. In addition, banks might seek to foreclose upon unprofitable pastoralists during drought, if they cannot meet their repayment obligations. This can further worsen property price depressions if stressed farms are foreclosed upon during drought and forced to sell at short notice, as they will be unable to realise a reasonable property price, further reducing market prices.

As a result, there is substantial scope for banks and pastoralists to have competing needs. A bank responding to opportunities and challenges in global markets might behave with adversarial lending behaviour which undermines the long-term viability of farming operations. The lending is somewhat speculative here; riskier loans are made during booms and these are foreclosed upon during busts. In this way, 'procyclicality has transformed banks from mitigation mechanisms to amplifiers of changes in economic activity' (Athanasoglou et al., 2014, p. 58). However, it is overly simplistic to assume that rural bankers implement financialising bank policy, according to market logics in a neutral and consistent way. Closer attention to the actual mediators of bank–farmer connections reveals these mediators to be important shapers of rural lending decisions.

Relationship lending in pastoral Australia

Relationships are essential to rural lending in northern Australian pastoralism. Rural bankers serving pastoral Australia often live remotely alongside their clients, and so they are embedded in places and communities, as well as in a virtual network of professionals with its own customs, standards and values. It is common for pastoral bankers to drive long distances to visit their clients on farm, and to form professional judgements about the performance and value of the property, and about the farmer's capacity to handle risk. Pastoralism is an unreliable industry which is subject to severe weather fluctuations (especially drought), and these environmental factors create an uncertain environment in which the rural banker's own expertise – drawing on a range of qualitative and quantitative judgements – becomes key to the lending decision.

Pastoralists typically respond to drought through one or a combination of two methods. The first involves selling the majority of one's livestock during a failed wet season to reduce outgoing costs associated with keeping livestock alive in a time of pasture scarcity. This often necessitates selling livestock into a depreciated market and re-investing in livestock at a higher price when the drought has ended. The second method is to retain livestock, either keeping them on the drought-affected property and feeding costly supplements or moving them to another region where the drought has not affected pastures as badly. It is not uncommon for pastoralists or pastoral companies to own or lease land in differing bioregions for this purpose, with some pastoralists we interviewed citing recent droughts as their primary driver for acquisitions of additional properties. Rural bankers work closely with pastoralists to access the costs and benefits of each approach, drawing on knowledge of the particular pastoral property's business plan and long-term goals before making their recommendations.

In climates such as northern Australia that are characterised by high variability, land value is mediated by its ability to carry livestock and support the production of high quality commodities (beef) in a range of environmental scenarios. Soil type, weather, access to watering points, infrastructure and whether the property is sold with livestock on site all influence the value of land. As a result, non-human actors such as particular grass species, livestock and the landscape intersect with calculative tools, such as beast area value and bank documents, in the production of a property as a commoditised space. Non-human actors and their affordances might therefore play a role in business plans and lending practices.

Rural bankers often travel to remote properties and survey it with farmers, and they are tasked with making difficult judgements around the farmer's plans, risks, and likelihood of success. They visit clients on farm, as one banker described, 'to see the operations, to get a better handle on the operation and on the family dynamics'. As one banker explained, 'our job is to try and pick out the better farmers' such that 'we wouldn't do a deal without going and meeting a farmer on farm'. They need to decide whether to extend further capital, deny this lending, or in extreme cases, to foreclose on the loan. These decisions require an in-depth knowledge of rural businesses. Many rural bankers are from pastoral backgrounds themselves, and this is widely considered essential experience to lend to the pastoral industry. As one cattle industry representative described:

> In rural lending, you need to have an understanding and an empathy of what's happening on that property. You really do need to understand the cycles, there's wet years and there's dry years, there's good cattle prices and there's bad cattle prices ... there does need to be a bit of leeway because people might need to borrow money to build the capacity of that asset.

Bankers are 'embedded' rather than 'specialist' advisors (Klerkz & Jansen, 2010), because they provide farm management advice in addition to other services (selling loans). Hilkens *et al.* (2018, p. 87) explore the role of rural bank bankers as providers of farm management advice in New Zealand dairying. They observed that banks appointed relationship managers to develop strong affiliations with larger borrowers as 'an important client-retention strategy [which] allowed them to compete successfully with other banks, and retain customers in situations where other banks may offer cheaper loans' (Hilkens *et al.*, 2018, p. 87). Northern Australian pastoralists are typically larger borrowers than the average Australian farmer, and this trend was also observed in our study. As one rural banker observed, 'money is money, your money is the same as my money, so the difference I suppose with us is the value we can bring to the client - the customer experience they get'.

Specialist agricultural banks emphasise the importance of this knowledge. For example, specialist rural lending bank Rabobank claims to be 'By farmers, for farmers' (Rabobank, 2020, n.p.), emphasising that 'Our rural managers take a hands-on approach, working alongside you to grow your business' (2020, n.p.). Meanwhile, Elders Rural Services underscore that they have 'experts to assist you with all aspects of your farm business' (Elders, 2020). The Financial Services Royal Commission similarly highlighted the important role of bank knowledge of agriculture, with the Commissioner enquiring at several points whether banks had adequately provided agricultural knowledge to their clients (see Transcript of Proceedings, *Royal Commission into Misconduct in the Banking, Superannuation and Financial Services Industry* [2018, June 28]). Clearly, it is important that rural bankers 'know' their clients – including their property, their management skills, as well as wider information about the industry. There is an assumption here that forming relationships are a requirement of behaving 'morally' in this industry. Beyond this, however, relationships were also spaces in which mutual obligations were formed, such that relationship lending was not only symptomatic, but also generative, of moral economic activity.

Loyalty, trust and being local

Northern Australian pastoralism is a unique industry with limited external farm management expertise and highly uncertain and risky parameters. These features valorise local expertise and long tenure and provide a competitive advantage to bankers who can provide it, as one rural banker suggested:

> You tend to develop with your client a trust … you may not be the cheapest in the market but you understand their business better. I've been up here doing this type of work for more than ten years. Most of my counterparts from other firms and banks, they churn over every two or three years. I'm still here doing it. That *means something*. It may be worth it for the client to have a point two or point five of a percent differential just to have me there because I've been there for so long and I've always been able to deliver.

These bankers saw the development of personal relationships as a core part of their role, often going above and beyond expectations to develop these relationships. As one rural banker noted:

> We spend a lot of time with our clients, really understand their business, and we get around the kitchen table with them and become part of the family, and become part of their business I suppose. I like to think we are a pretty crucial partner to them. And to be a successful partner in any business, you need to be open and transparent with them. So we are that way with our clients, and hopefully they are with us as well. They should feel comfortable picking the phone up and talking to me on Sunday night, or whenever it might be. If they've got concerns, get it out and talk about it with us. We don't want to have surprises. I generally think that is the case, that clients will

call me and say 'Oh, I'm really worried about such and such', but if you leave it till the problem has happened, that's no good for anybody.

Importantly, this was not a one-way relationship, as rural bankers expected reciprocity from their clients. One banker emphasised mutual obligation, noting that 'very few clients leave us, so *they're very loyal, as we are to them*'. Bankers felt that they put something of themselves into the relationship, and expected to be valued and appreciated. As one banker explained:

> If all you want is a cheap rate, go somewhere else. If you don't want any service, if you don't value what I bring to your business, I don't want to deal with you. It's not a true partnership, you're just looking for a funding source. If all you want is a funding source get on the internet. The big four banks will bloody fund you, not a problem. But they'll also not take any time to *understand* you.

The bank representative demonstrates that they offer and expect a personal relationship with their clients. They evoke a mantra of trust and reciprocity as guiding features of the financier–debtor relationship. Evidence from the Financial Services Royal Commission suggested that pastoralists similarly expected close relationships with their rural bankers. Early discussion in the Round 4 hearings of the Financial Services Royal Commission ('Experiences with financial services entities in regional and remote communities') discussed the assumption that these relationships were important and the failure of banks to provide this. Pastoralist Melville Ruddy gave evidence to the commission, describing his dissatisfaction with the lack of a personal relationship offered by a new manager at Bankwest:

> I was looking for a long-term relationship with [him] … It was confusing. Like, you – you know, when you're sort of in the drought and cattle prices are totally depressed and you can't sort of go and talk to anyone, they're in Brisbane … I'm used to having a bank manager ring up, he comes out and sees me, we have a cup of tea, we have a drive around and we come to a decision about things, you know. That's how it's been all my life, since I was 23.
> (Transcript of Proceedings, *Royal Commission into Misconduct in the Banking, Superannuation and Financial Services Industry* [28 June 2018, pp. 3443–44]).

Ruddy's experience was instructive on a number of levels where the banker –client relationship failed. Ruddy chose to transition to a different business model on the advice of his banker, a move which would reduce his cash flow for several years and would require the support of the bank during this time – support that was not forthcoming. In assessing his business options, he required the *approval* of the banker – what Hilkens *et al.* (2018, p. 94) refer to as 'binding advice' – which constrained what was possible for him. This illustrates that relationship lending is not merely about increasing the bank's understanding of the business, but that the bank – and the behaviour of the banker – actually plays a key role in shaping the business development trajectory. For Ruddy, the practical and relational aspects of the banker–client relationship were inseparable, and his interactions with the bank were underpinned by an expectation of care on the part of the banker.

Other pastoralists similarly emphasised the importance of their relationship with bankers, particularly during times of drought. One pastoral family spoke about the importance of accessibility – being able to 'just pick up the phone' to bankers to discuss the ways in which the business intended on responding to drought conditions. Another pastoralist described her experience of changing to a specialist rural lending bank as being key for the family business's ability to navigate the period of financial uncertainty. She highlighted her personal connection to her bank manager, describing the manager as a 'god-send'. When the author later met with the banker in question, the banker was already aware of the ethnographer's visit to the property and the various matters the pastoralist had discussed in interviews about drought. By demonstrating such seemingly mundane knowledge about the everyday lives of the pastoralists this banker asserted not only their social connectedness to the community, but also their embeddedness in the particular lives of pastoralists. As another banker explained, 'I get out and about and be interested, which I genuinely am' and 'aim to have meaningful conversations with the client throughout the journey, throughout the year'. In the banker–pastoralist relationship, conversation extended beyond that which was strictly necessary for conducting business to include other events or issues pertaining to the property during drought situations.

Literature on relationship lending has focussed on the benefits it provides to banks in reducing costs of lending (Moss *et al.*, 2018). However, relationship lending might also benefit clients because banks might be more likely to lend during difficult times to clients they know well and have faith in their management ability (Bolton *et al.*, 2016; Beck *et al.*, 2018). In a farming context, this observation was made by Hilkens *et al.* (2018, p. 88), who reported that farmers 'perceived that building personal relationships with their banker would increase the banker's trust in their capability and therefore the bank would more likely provide them financial support when they needed it'. This was also noted in our interviews. One farmer thought that bankers 'know amongst their book of clients who's being doing well even when times have been tough'. Another suggested that because a rural banker was familiar with his business they were able to discuss plans to invest in a new property informally, by having 'a yarn over a beer'. Similarly, one rural banker said that the 'benefit of being in the same place for a length of time is you get to know the people in the region. I have a fair idea of who the better operators are [and] who has what property'. This suggests that bankers are able to understand when circumstances beyond the farmer's control, such as drought, have created farm problems, rather than these being blamed on the pastoralist themselves. This is important for facilitating increased lending to overcome short-term cash flow problems. As one banker indicated:

> for those guys that communicate, are free and open with their business planning with us, [my bank] will bend over backwards for them. If they

need an extra half a million dollars until they get the next big cattle sale away in three or four months' time, not a problem! That's a bloody two hour decision process.

In addition, it speaks to a need to identify as a 'good' farmer (Aitkin, 1985), although what it means to be a 'good farmer' changes with global circumstances (Hunt *et al.*, 2013), and in Australia many family farmers have developed hybrid business models (Pritchard *et al.*, 2007; Langford, 2019). Melville Ruddy's experience described in the Financial Services Royal Commission spoke to this issue, and in his statement he expresses concern that 'We were made to feel guilty, that our farms were u[n]viable' (Ruddy, 2018, p. 3). This connects to ideas of 'countrymindedness' and the 'good farmer' (Aitkin, 1985) and is paralleled in the approach of rural bankers, who seek to develop strong relationships based on loyalty and trust, and some of whom come to identify as a 'good banker' by making strong moral judgements about what lending behaviour is 'right'.

Close farmer–banker relationships are therefore important for practical and relational reasons, and the unique features of northern Australian pastoralism, such as remoteness, low populations, unique environments and frequent drought, create a situation in which close banker–client relationships are important to the functioning of the industry. These relationships exceed those that might be predicted by bank and client self-interest, however, because in their enactment over many years, farmers and bankers developed those 'mutual obligations' that underpin moral economic activity (Carrier, 2017). These mutual obligations shaped the responses of bankers to financialising bank policy, as the next section discusses.

Enacting morality: Guilt and care in financialised markets

Financialisation has been associated with changing global economic circumstances, which can increase the pro-cyclicality of bank lending behaviour. Our interviewees suggested that it was common practice for banks to send additional people into a region in order to grow their client book during economic expansions and to remove these people and exit industries during downturns, often by increasing interest rates to unsustainable levels. This can introduce the volatility of global capital markets to northern Australian rural pastoral markets – a pattern of expanding influence of financial logics into new geographies that some would associate with financialisation (eg. Pike & Pollard, 2010). The expansion of new banks into remote northern Australia creates additional competition in the lending market. This makes it easier for pastoralists to access capital and puts pressure on conservative existing bankers to increase their lending. One banker commented on what they perceived as the divergence of bank and farmer interests in such cases:

Banks obviously look at risk differently than some of our clients do. If the bank says yes, that's a good deal, we'll lend you the money, doesn't mean it's a good business decision for the customer. The bank looks at risks that are appropriate for the bank, and not necessarily from the client's perspective.

Bankers in our study were often aware of lending pro-cyclicality, and some felt under increased pressure to lend money on risky ventures during growth business cycles. As one long-term resident agricultural banker noted:

> When the market's hot, back in that boom time down in five, six, seven [2005-2007] when things were going really good, property and cattle were both strong prices and there was a bit of activity happening. There were banks in the region trying to drum up business everywhere. But as soon as things got a bit wobbly, they're gone. They're offering really cheap rates to people, it's not sustainable and you just know at some point they will start ratchetting up fees and margins. That's probably the hardest time I found in this area, was that period, and it's happening again now where we're seeing them come up and they're writing deals and they're pushing the boundaries. And you come to me and say you want to borrow money and I say 'I don't really feel comfortable with that!' and if I dare show any resistance or any lack of enthusiasm towards you borrowing the money the guy says 'Oh, well if it's going to be too hard doing this deal with you guys, I'll go to another bank, and they'll do it, and they'll do it at a cheaper rate, and they'll probably do it no questions asked!

Such bankers experienced their role as mediators of these competing bank and farmer interests and imposed moral judgements onto lending behaviour. Some reported feeling committed to their clients and refusing to engage in risky lending. Rose (2011) explores how moral behaviours can enhance economic performance by reducing transaction costs and centres guilt as a key factor in deterring negative behaviours. For these bankers, a sense of loyalty to clients and an avoidance of guilt were important to their decision to remain conservative in their lending behaviour, sometimes despite pressure both from farmers and banks to offer loans that the banker considered to be high-risk. One banker described increased pressure that they faced when pastoralists had received offers from competing banks during credit surpluses, noting that 'no one's holding a gun to their head … but sometimes they've been strongly encouraged to borrow the extra money'. This banker described discouraging some of his clients from borrowing extra money, despite approval from the bank they represented, observing that 'I want the best for the customer, whether it's buying this property or getting this deal done for them, or maybe it's not. Maybe the customer doesn't know it yet and you've got to help them with the decision, maybe it's a bit too risky for them'. In this way, the banker aimed to discourage borrowing behaviour that he considered overly risky, and if his advice was not acted upon, to distance himself from the borrowing decision.

These kinds of judgements were often directly linked to bank policies, with bankers making normative statements about the incentives offered by banks. As one long-term resident agricultural banker said:

> I've seen it happen years ago with a manager out pumping money to the community like you wouldn't believe, as in lending to farmers, he wins all these awards and he moves off to wherever he goes, and the next guy

comes in and has got to come and clean up all the mess. I don't think that's *right* ... I personally avoid that situation ... I want to sleep at night as well.

This care for clients appeared to be important across many rural bankers, who often reside in the region long term and developed long-term relationships in farming communities. Conservative lending was associated with an ethos of care for clients, as one banker acknowledged:

We understand that even in good times, yes it might look good, but there's going to be bad times around the corner. We hope that there's not, but there always will be something happen. So some people will say we are very conservative, [but] I like to think that we understand the business better, we're not just here for the good times, we're here for the long time. We want to be able to look after [our clients] through the good and the bad. So when there's a hiccup like the GFC or a drought, we can still support our clients to get through that.

Some bankers associated conservative lending behaviour with agricultural banks, while other interviews both from bankers and pastoralists suggested that clients were loyal to bankers personally rather than the bank itself. This highlights the importance of individuals in mediating connections between banks and rural spaces, as well as of bank policy in creating space for bankers to develop these connections and implement moral responses. One rural banker felt strongly that his association with a specialist agricultural bank enabled him to build connections with clients and undertake his work in a way that he felt to be morally sound. He noted that 'they want me to get growth, and want me to meet certain targets, but I've never felt too threatened if I didn't meet those targets ... they realise I'm still putting the effort in'. This flexibility, to develop relationships with clients and use his own moral judgements in his work was important to his enjoyment of his role, as he described 'that's what appeals to me, why I still work here, what gets me out of bed in the morning. I don't know if I could have that same passion if I was working in another organisation'.

However, the Financial Services Royal Commission highlighted a number of instances in bank lending to rural Australia in which this care for clients did not eventuate. In a series of cases, rural bankers exploited their position to increase their client book by selling high-risk loans, in some cases substantially overvaluing properties, to access incentives offered by the banks. The Financial Services Royal Commission highlighted this potential for exploitation as a serious issue, referring to an earlier report which noted that rural bankers have 'an uncomfortably high level of formal authority in the qualitative aspects of loan approval and management' which 'puts a significant degree of risk into the loan portfolio' (McGrath-Nicol, 2009, p. 40). Policy responses recommend reducing the authority of rural bankers in land valuation and a national scheme for farm debt mediation and recommended that the 2019 Banking Code be amended to prevent charging of default interest on loans in drought declared areas (Commonwealth of Australia, 2019). However, it also recognised the importance of individual banker experience, emphasising that distressed agricultural loans are best managed by 'experienced agricultural bankers' and urging banks dealing with distressed loans to 'recognise and apply their own hardship policies' (Commonwealth of Australia, 2019, p. 102).

The balance between increasing oversight of rural bankers and creating space for the implementation of their expertise contains assumptions about how such bankers relate to their clients and the extent to which they exhibit care for their client in their implementation of bank policy. There is certainly a role for oversight within the bank, as the instances of misconduct in the Royal Commission showed. Indeed, in our research, bankers themselves acknowledged the risk of getting 'too close to a client' and appreciated having oversight from others in the bank who sometimes 'see it a bit differently to what you do on the ground'. However, it is important to resist an overly simplistic policy response that sees a reduced role for the personal judgement of rural bankers as necessarily creating improved outcomes for pastoralists, and to instead recognise the range of ways that bankers relate to their clients, and the role of the remote geographies of northern Australia in shaping these.

Discussion

This study explored the work of rural bankers who lived and worked for many years in close proximity to the clients they served. The remoteness and unique environments of Northern Australia were conducive to the formation of long and close banker–client relationships which many saw as essential to the moral execution of agricultural lending relationships. Cups of tea and Sunday night phone calls are not – and cannot be – contractually obligated, yet they are widely assumed on the part of both borrowers and rural bankers, and are necessary to the functioning of rural lending markets. Trust and care are core parts of this moral economy, and guilt is an important moderator where banker and client interests diverge. However, from our research it was clear that these relationships were not formed merely in response to such moral judgments about how markets should operate, but in themselves were generative of this morality. Many bankers developed a sense of care for their clients and their willingness to engage in high-risk lending was moderated by guilt.

This study contributes to finance literature on relationship lending, which has recognised the effect of relationships on increasing access to credit during a downtown, by also noting the potential of relationships to decrease access to credit in a boom where such an increase is perceived to entail a high degree of risk for the client. Close, long-term banker–client relationships led to conservative lending behaviour during expansions, sometimes despite pressure from both bank and client to increase lending. This behaviour could dampen the effects of pro-cyclical bank lending, reducing the influence of global markets on local debt markets. In this scenario, bankers exerted their agency to moderate the effects of financialisation, yet did so not out of a political response to this phenomenon nor out of allegiance to moral beliefs about the way that markets should function. They did so out of a sense of interpersonal obligation to clients that developed through mutual interaction. In this way, relationship lending did not only indicate, but also generated, moral economic activity. As Carrier (2017) suggested, this approach to studying moral economies as *processes* can offer new insights into the ways that different moral activities arise and are negotiated in local spaces.

This has useful parallels to an assemblage approach to the study of financialisation, which similarly requires a focus on the process and the work involved in executing and mediating financial transactions. Rather than viewing financialisation as a homogenous force restructuring economies in predictable patterns, it alerts us to the individual agencies of human and non-human actors (including livestock and calculative tools) who work in diverse geographies and in pursuit of a range of goals to assemble markets. Financialisation in agriculture has often been viewed as a shift away from bank lending to the use of other financial tools such as equity and derivatives markets (Breger Bush, 2012; Schmidt, 2016). However, we note that it is also evident in a shift in the way that banks lend, and that different banks respond to, perpetuate, and reduce, financialisation in different ways. In our study, bankers developed close relationships with their clients in response to the unique needs of rural northern Australian pastoralists; these relationships themselves generated new ways of interacting with the banks and, in turn, global capital markets, which were not motivated by any political goal associated with financialisation, but in turn affected the extent to which global financialising patterns influenced local credit markets.

This speaks to the indeterminacy of assemblages and the importance of avoiding assumption that policy directives that decrease banker discretion will have predictable and consistent effects in all markets. Rather, we highlight the ways that rural agricultural credit markets are locally constituted and stress the importance of attention to these local nuances for more informed policy. For example, it warns against assumptions that banker discretion is necessarily positive or negative for pastoralists, but highlights the way that bank policy is only one component of a broader assemblage. Some banks appear to find ways to encourage and embed caring lending behaviour in bank culture more effectively than others. Several bankers noted the importance of long-term relationships, rather than three-year postings, in building care into borrower–banker relationships. In addition, oversight of bank decisions can be undertaken to moderate the risks of both exploitative behaviour (in which bankers in pursuit of financial incentives fail to act in clients best interests) and overly sympathetic behaviour (in which bankers, in sympathy with clients, fail to act in the bank's best interests). These measures embed relationships in agricultural lending practice, rather than seek to remove them, but make allowances to avoid negative outcomes.

Conclusion

In this chapter, we used the concept of moral economy to explore the way that rural agricultural credit markets are assembled in northern Australian pastoralism. We showed how moral economy was not only a result of societal ideals around how these markets should operate but was generated in the everyday interactions of bankers and clients. Close, long-term banker–client relationships generated in bankers a sense of care, which motivated more conservative lending decisions in ways that could be expected to reduce the extent of financialisation in these markets, without having been motivated by an intention to do so. This highlights the benefits of viewing financialisation as assembled by a range of this locally grounded and diverse work, which interacts with often unpredictable effects. Our evidence from northern Australian pastoral markets, assembled by local people with care, highlights the importance of people and place in the constitution of these markets.

Acknowledgements

This research was supported by: the Australian Research Council (DP 160101318); the Australian Government Research Training Program Scholarship; the Ministry of Education of the Republic of Korea and the National Research Foundation of Korea (NRF-2016S1A3A2924243); and the Norwegian Research Council (FORFOOD No. 220691).

References

Aitkin, D. (1985). *Countrymindedness: The spread of an idea. Australian Cultural History*, 4, 34–41.
Akhavein, J., Goldberg, L. G. & White, L. J. (2004). Small banks, small business, and relationships: An empirical study of lending to small farms. *Journal of Financial Services Research*, 26(3), 245–261.
Anderson, B., Kearnes, M., McFarlane, C. & Swanton, D. (2012). On assemblages and geography. *Dialogues in Human Geography*, 2(2), 171–189.
Athanasoglou, P P., Daniilidis, I. & Delis, M.D. (2014). Bank procyclicality and output: Issues and policies. *Journal of Economics and Business*, 72, 58–83.
Australian Government. (2015). *Our north, our future: White paper of developing Northern Australia*. Retrieved from www.industry.gov.au/data-and-publications/our-north-our-future-white-paper-on-developing-northern-australia.
Beck, T., Degryse, H., De Haas, R. & Van Horen, N. (2018). When arm's length is too far: Relationship banking over the credit cycle. *Journal of Financial Economics*, 127(1), 174–196.
Berg, G. & Schrader, J. (2012). Access to credit, natural disasters, and relationship lending. *Journal of Financial Intermediation*, 21(4), 549–568.
Bolton, P., Freixas, X., Gambacorta, L. & Mistrulli, P.E. (2016). Relationship and transaction lending in a crisis. *The Review of Financial Studies*, 29(10), 2643–2676.
Breger Bush, S. (2012). *Derivatives and development: A political economy of global finance, farming and poverty*. New York, NY: Palgrave Macmillan.
Burch, D. & Lawrence, G. (2013). Financialization in agri-food supply chains: Private equity and the transformation of the retail sector. *Agriculture and Human Values*, 30(2), 247–258.
Carrier, J.G. (2017). Moral economy: What's in a name. *Anthropological Theory*, 18(1), 18–35.
Cheshire, L. & Woods, M. (2013). Globally engaged farmers as transnational actors: Navigating the landscape of agri-food globalization. *Geoforum*, 44, 232–242.

Christophers, B. (2015). The limits to financialisation. *Dialogues in Human Geography*, 5 (2), 183–200.

Clapp, J. (2014). Financialization, distance, and global food politics. *The Journal of Peasant Studies*, 41(6), 797–814.

Clapp, J. & Isakson, S.R. (2018a). *Speculative harvests: Financialization, food and agriculture.* Rugby: Practical Action Publishing.

Clapp, J. & Isakson, S.R. (2018b). Risky returns: The implications of financialization in the food system. *Development and Change*, 49(2), 437–460.

Commonwealth of Australia. (2019). *Final report: Royal Commission into misconduct in the banking, superannuation and financial services industry* (Volume 1). Retrieved from https://financia lservices.royalcommission.gov.au/Pages/reports.aspx.

Ducastel, A. & Anseeuw, W. (2017). Agriculture as an asset class: Reshaping the South African farming sector. *Agriculture and Human Values*, 34(1), 199–209.

Ducastel, A. & Anseeuw, W. (2018). Facing financialisation: The divergent mutation of agricultural cooperatives in postapartheid South Africa. *Journal of Agrarian Change*, 8(3), 555–570.

Elders. (2020). *Rural services.* Retrieved 22 April 2020 from https://elders.com.au/.

Epstein, G. (2005). *Financialization and the world economy.* Cheltenham: Edward Elgar.

Fiordelisi, F., Monferrà, S. & Sampagnaro, G. (2014). Relationship lending and credit quality. *Journal of Financial Services Research*, 46(3), 295–315.

Ghosh, J., Heintz, J. & Pollin, R. (2012). Speculation on commodities futures markets and destabilisation of global food prices: exploring the connections. *International Journal of Health Services*, 42(3), 465–483.

Gunnoe, A. (2014). The political economy of institutional landownership: Neorentier society and the financialisation of land. *Rural Sociology*, 79(4), 478–504.

Hann, C. (2016). *The moral dimension of economy: Work, workfare, and fairness in provincial Hungary* (Working paper 174). Halle: Max Planck Institute for Social Anthropology.

Henry, M. (2017). Meat, metrics and market devices: Commensuration infrastructures and the assemblage of 'the schedule' in New Zealand's red meat sector. *Journal of Rural Studies*, 52, 100–109.

Henry, M. & Prince, R. (2018). Agriculturalizing finance? Data assemblages and derivatives markets in small-town New Zealand. *Environment and Planning A: Economy and Space*, 50(5), 989–1007.

Higgins, V. (2006). Re-figuring the problem of farmer agency in agri-food studies: A translation approach. *Agriculture and Human Values*, 23, 51–62.

Hilkens, A., Reid, J.I., Klerkx, L. & Gray, D.I. (2018). Money talk: How relations between farmers and advisors around financial management are shaped. *Journal of Rural Studies*, 63: 83–95.

Ho, K. (2009). *Liquidated: An ethnography of Wall Street.* Durham, NC: Duke University Press.

Hunt, L., Rosin, C., Campbell, H. & Fairweather, J. (2013). The impact of neoliberalism on New Zealand farmers: Changing what it means to be a 'good farmer'. *Extension Farming Systems Journal*, 9(1), 34.

Klerkx, L. & Jansen, J. (2010). Building knowledge systems for sustainable agriculture: Supporting private advisors to adequately address sustainable farm management in regular service contacts. *International Journal of Agricultural Sustainability*, 8, 148–163.

Konzelmann, S., Fovargue-Davies, M. & Wilkinson, F. (2013). The return of 'financialised' liberal capitalism. In S. Konzelmann & M. Fovargue-Davies (Eds), *Banking systems in the Crisis: The faces of liberal capitalism*. London: Routledge, 32–56.

Larder, N.Sippel, S.R. & Argent, N. (2018). The redefined role of finance in Australian agriculture, *Australian Geographer*, 49(3), 397–418.

Larder, N. & Sippel, S.R., Lawrence, G. (2015). Finance capital, food security narratives and Australian agricultural land. *Journal of Agrarian Change*, 15(4), 592–603.

Langford, A. (2019). Capitalising the farm family entrepreneur: Negotiating private equity partnerships in Australia. *Australian Geographer, 50*(4), 473–491. https://doi.org/10.1080/00049182.2019.1682320.

Langford, A. (2020). *Agri-food transformations in Northern Australia: The work of local actors in mediating financial investments.* [Doctoral dissertation, University of Queensland]. Espace. https//doi.org/10.14264/uql.2020.698.

Langford, A., Smith, K. & Lawrence, G. (2020). Financialising governance? State actor engagement with private finance for rural development in the Northern Territory of Australia. *Research in Globalization*, 2(100026), 1–9. https://doi.org/10.1016/j.resglo.2020.100026.

Langford, A., Lawrence, G. & Smith, K. (2021). Financialisation *for* development? Asset-making on Indigenous land in remote Northern Australia. *Development and Change*, 1–24. https://doi.org/10.1111/dech.12648.

Lapavitsas, C. (Ed.). (2012). *Financialization in crisis.* Chicago, IL: Haymarket Books.

López-Espinosa, G., Mayordomo, S. & Moreno, A. (2017). When does relationship lending start to pay? *Journal of Financial Intermediation*, 31, 16–29.

McGrathNicol. (2009). *Project Conserve: Financial due diligence* (Volume 1 – Final Report). Retrieved 22 April 2020 from https://financialservices.royalcommission.gov.au/public-hearings/Documents/exhibits-2018/25-june/EXHIBIT-4.8.3.pdf.

Magnan, A. (2012). New avenues of farm corporatization in the prairie grains sector: Farm family entrepreneurs and the case of One Earth Farms. *Agriculture and Human Values*, 29(2), 161–175.

Magnan, A. & Sunley, S. (2017). Farmland investment and financialization in Saskatchewan 2003–2014: An empirical analysis of farmland transactions. *Journal of Rural Studies*, 49, 92–103.

Martin, S. & Clapp, J. (2015). Finance for agriculture or agriculture for finance? *Journal of Agrarian Change*, 15(4), 549–559.

McMichael, P. (1984). *Settlers and the agrarian question: Foundations of capitalism in colonial Australia.* Melbourne, Australia: Cambridge University Press.

McMichael, P. (2012). The land grab and the corporate food regime restructuring. *The Journal of Peasant Studies*, 39(3–4),681–701.

Meat and Livestock Australia. (2020). *Farm survey data for the beef, slaughter lambs and sheep industries.* Retrieved 15 May 2020 from http://apps.daff.gov.au/mla/.

Moss, C.B., Kropp, J.D. & Bampasidou, M. (2018). The financial economics of agriculture and farm management. In G.L. Cramer, K.P. Paudel & A. Schmitz (Eds), *The Routledge Handbook of Agricultural Economics.* London: Routledge.

Ouma, S. (2015). Getting in between M and M' or: How farmland further debunks financialization. *Dialogues in Human Geography*, 5(2), 225–228.

Ouma, S. (2020). *Farming as Financial Asset: Global Finance and the Making of Institutional Landscapes.* New York, NY: Columbia University Press.

Pike, A. & Pollard, J. (2010). Economic geographies of financialization. *Economic Geography*, 86(1), 29–51.

Pritchard, B., Burch, D. & Lawrence, G. (2007). Neither 'family' nor 'corporate' farming: Australian tomato growers as farm family entrepreneurs. *Journal of Rural Studies*, 23, 75–87.

Rabobank. (2020). *Why Rabobank?*. Retrieved 22 April 2020 from www.rabobank.com.au/about-rabobank.

Rose, D.C. (2011). *The moral foundation of economic behaviour.* Oxford: Oxford University Press.

Royal Commission into Misconduct in the Banking, Superannuation and Financial Services Industry. (2018) [Transcript of Proceedings], 28 June 2018.

Ruddy, M. (2018). Royal Commission into the misconduct in the banking, super-annuation and financial services industry: Submission of Melville Ruddy. Retrieved July 2020 from https://financialservices.royalcommission.gov.au/public-hearings/Documents/Round-4-written-submissions/mel-ruddy-written-submission.pdf.

Schmidt, T. (2016). *The Political Economy of food and finance.* New York, NY: Routledge.

Sippel, S.R. (2018). Financialising farming as a moral imperative? Renegotiating the legitimacy of land investments in Australia. *Environment and Planning A*, 50(3), 549–568.

Tsing, A.L. (2004). *Friction: An ethnography of global connection.* Princeton, NJ: Princeton University Press.

Visser, O. (2017). Running out of farmland? Investment discourses, unstable land values and the sluggishness of asset making. *Agriculture and Human Values*, 34, 185–198.

Webb, J. (2019). New lamps for old: Financialised governance of cities and clean energy. *Journal of Cultural Economy*, 12(4), 286–298.

Williams, J.W. (2014). Feeding finance: A critical account of the shifting relationships between finance, food and farming. *Economy and Society*, 43(3), 401–431.

Wolford, W. (2005). Agrarian moral economies and Neoliberalism in Brazil: Competing Worldviews and the State in the struggle for land. *Environment and Planning A*, 37(2), 241–261.

8 Schools as marketsites

Making markets in New Zealand schools

Nicolas Lewis* and Donna Wynd**

*SCHOOL OF ENVIRONMENT, UNIVERSITY OF AUCKLAND
**INDEPENDENT ACTIVIST RESEARCHER

Introduction

In this chapter, we examine the marketisation of public schooling in Auckland, New Zealand. Schools are prime targets for economisation initiatives. They are sites where large populations assemble routinely on a daily basis. They are sites where significant sums of public and private money circulate, multiple social objectives are addressed, and cultural capital is renewed. Billions of dollars move through the compulsory schooling system each year. Today's schools are also markets for e-learning curricula and associated hardware, while every student pocket contains a mobile phone that is endlessly acquiring and selling data and consumer products. More peripherally markets for all manner of cultural products and social status are permanently in operation. However, schooling remains far from fully marketised, despite the presence of longstanding markets for objects such as textbooks, stationery, uniforms, desks and classrooms.

We explore two cases of market-making: the proliferation of privatised in-service teacher support services (professional learning development, PLD) and the economisation of public health objectives in schools in the form of school lunch provision. In a wider landscape of marketisation and quasi-market formation in New Zealand schooling (O'Neill, 2017; Gordon, 2016; Thrupp & Willmott, 2003; Robertson & Dale, 2013), we ask what it means that schools have become marketsites for delivering school lunches to children and selling emotional intelligence to teachers. Together the cases explore what the socio-technical focus of the market-making literature can add to a more established critique of marketisation as a key neoliberal governmentality. The cases highlight the entanglement of market-making in schooling with the making of markets for self-help, resilience, well-being and positivity associated with the rise of positive psychology (Purser, 2019). We argue that this entanglement has made schools sites for making markets for 'virtue'.

Both teacher learning and health objectives have long been part of routine practice in New Zealand schools and the governance of social life through schooling (Carusi & Niwa, 2020). Once a set of practices internalised within schools and complemented by periodic external inspection, in-service teacher support has been formalised in new public management reforms and broken up

DOI: 10.4324/9780429296260-8

and reassembled into a proliferating set of professional development products (O'Neill, 2011). Increasingly entangled in new public management technologies of control and the new expertise of human resources (HR) management, these 'products' are now largely delivered by external agents. Teacher practice and teacher bodies have become sites for accumulation by consultants, while schools have become key sites for targeting the delivery of health programmes to at-risk populations using private and charitable providers (Robertson, 2000; Ball, 2009).

Three observations have intrigued us about these processes of economisation. First, routine practices of schooling (teacher pedagogies and public health promotion) have now become sites for accumulation as well as for the fashioning of neoliberal subjects and the exercise of *state governance at a distance*. Second, the products being delivered have been given discursive form and affect by the tightening relations between discourses of resilience and well-being, the promotion of a certain form of happiness, and development of a new expertise of management. The markets we examine are framed by a concerted body of ideas drawn from positive psychology. Third, taken together, the two examples of economisation in schooling point to the significance of the public purse as a new source of accumulation in 'after'-neoliberal settings. It seems to us that market-making in this context is making available teacher and student bodies for simultaneous projects of accumulation, subjectification and *government*.

This chapter draws on an emerging geographies of market-making literature and the social studies of economisation and market-making that underlie it (Berndt et al., 2020; Berndt and Wirth, 2018; Berndt & Boeckler, 2009, 2011; Boeckler and Berndt, 2013; Callon, Méadel & Rabeharisoa, 2002). Borrowing language from debates about the inclusive, after-neoliberal state (Gill & Kanai, 2018; Higgins & Larner, 2017; Tronto, 2017; Rose, 2000) and the role of schools in fashioning the entrepreneurial yet caring subjects of its rule (O'Neill, 2016), we ask what this turn to markets tells us about the role of schooling. Our answer, referring also to the critique of neuroliberalism and positive psychology, is that marketsites for well-being, virtue, and self-improvement in schools are not only providing new spaces for accumulation and fashioning new subjects of rule, but that schools are being enrolled in an affective infrastructure that secures contemporary neoliberal government.

Market-making, marketisation and economisation

The market-making turn in economic geography begins from the observation that neither market advocates nor critical scholars have asked how markets come about, what they actually do, and how they work (Berndt & Boeckler, 2009; Berndt et al., 2020). Markets are fundamentally under-researched, given their centrality in social life and the weight placed on them in neoliberal governance. Instead commentators have tended to take them for granted as spontaneous, self-regulating and largely uniform institutions of economic exchange or social governance, even if they have argued about their ethics and political effects and the extent to which they require direction. Much follows from this. The variegated forms, practices and 'how' of markets, their placeness and their material specificities need to be addressed as a first principle of explanation. Materialised markets can be interpreted as assemblages of heterogeneous agencies and economic practices – unruly materialities, shifting relationalities and unintended consequences of the human and non-human agency assembled. Markets must be made, stabilised and maintained, and their messiness and unruly elements must be pacified.

The 'who', 'what' and 'where' of market-making is intricately bound up with the 'how', especially in education (Carusi, 2019). Markets are accomplishments *in place* – emergent, dynamic and held in temporary relation by the socio-technical arrangements that bring them about and stabilise their contradictions, which inevitably *overflow* efforts to contain them. The marketisation of schooling, for example, has been widely resisted by teachers unions, leftist political parties, and the public more generally, while the contradictions of market governance in terms of equity, access and uneven spatial development are widely criticised (Ball, 2012; Thrupp & Wilmott, 2003; Lauder *et al.* 1999). Market-making in schooling is, in practice, fraught and incomplete. Interest among geographers in market-making in education is growing (Williamson, 2020; Cohen, 2018; Cohen & Lizotte, 2015; Riep, 2017; Komljenovic & Robertson, 2016; Thiem, 2009).

Market-making ideas originate from a literature that talks more generally of 'economisation' defined as 'the processes through which activities, behaviours and spheres or fields are established as being economic' (Çalışkan & Callon, 2009). Kurunmäki *et al.* (2016, p. 496) describe economisation as the work performed by 'the ideas and instruments through which individuals, activities, organisations, nation states, regions, projects, and much else besides are constituted as economic actors and entities'. This involves much more than the discursive separation of economy from the polity performed by economics. It refers as much to the performative links between economising and governing, namely the measurement, quantification, metrology and subjectification that constitutes 'particular modes' of both governing and being (2016, p. 397). For Peetz (2019, p. 591), this link is particularly apparent at the level of organisations such as schools, where what is often critiqued broadly as neoliberalism might be better understood as organisational economisation ('a form of structural change in which organisations increasingly refer to economic problems, codes, programs or semantics'). It is in this broader sense of economisation that we mobilise the market-making literature in this paper. We draw four key insights.

First, the literature tends to emphasise *the socio-technical dimensions of markets*, filling a long-standing gap in economic geography and social economy literatures. These include the algorithms that guide financial markets, the social technologies of contracts, performance indicators, consumer surveys, and big data, the measurement devices and regimes that define qualities and values in perishable products, and the certification practices of green economies. The work of these devices makes the qualities of 'products' measurable, visible and commensurable and allows them to circulate and be exchanged. The socio-technological infrastructures and calculative metrologies into which devices assemble work to pacify relational agencies and stabilise economies. In the cases that we discuss here, market objects such as PLD courses or health programmes are qualified, or conspicuously not qualified, by registration and certification, branding techniques, and formal evaluation practices. Similarly, those delivering them are registered and certified. What emerges is a socio-technological architecture.

Second, authors demonstrate how market devices produce markets in place by prefiguring, performing and enabling new associations among market objects and actors, qualifying objects and subjectifying actors. Kear (2018), for example, uses the metaphor of the 'marketsite' to capture what he argues to be the inherent spatiality of the work of market-making devices and the socio-technical architecture of markets that emerges. Marketsites are sites where the heterogeneous elements that intersect to create a market materialise. They are sites where socio-technological devices are deployed, discourses are mobilised, calculations are brought to bear, market agencies go to work, and new subjects are summoned into being to create markets. They connect market-making to the institutions, discursive and socio-cultural formations, and 'mesh of practices and material arrangements' (Schatzki, 2005, p. 472) that constitute place and signal its mattering.

Third, the new emphasis on socio-technical devices is connected to the wider set of institutions (formal and informal), relations and knowledge (codified and tacit) that shape and govern relations among competitors, suppliers, and customers. Fligstein and Calder (2015) utilise the idea of a 'social architecture of markets' to capture the co-constitutiveness of this connectivity and the sustained social interaction beyond momentary and/or spontaneous exchange in sites that it produces, especially in place. Market architectures point to the organisation, co-ordination and stabilisation of exchange across multiple actors, space and time. They have been closely studied by economic geographers for at least 30 years, but commonly as context for economic process, an explanation for difference, a feature of competitiveness or a function of capitalism rather than as market-making (Berndt & Boeckler, 2009). Market-making ideas open-up this assemblage from the materialities of practice outwards to reveal much of what has to date remained hidden, including messiness, performativity, incompleteness and overflows (activities, relations and consequences that escape the framings put around them and refuse to be pacified).

Fourth, Berndt and colleagues have opened-up a productive line of tension between *market-making* (a process intrinsic to capitalist exchange) and *marketisation*, which is a central neoliberal strategy associated with privatisation and the use of quasi-markets to manage state activities through market technologies and disciplines. The contrast reminds us that the binary politics of 'more markets' versus 'more state' is more complex than often acknowledged. Critique needs to be sharper and to attend to markets and how they work. If focused on socio-technical devices, it needs to accommodate the politics brought to markets via their sites and the social relations that transcend specific sites. Markets are always embedded in place, and the overflows of their successes and failures are always present and widely contested (Berndt *et al.*, 2020).

Finally, a market-making perspective directs us to focus more attention on the politics that is always there to be practised (Lewis & Le Heron, 2020). It directs us to consider opportunities to make new and more just economic relations by targeting the incompleteness of apparently established markets or experimenting with new forms of market. Kear (2018), for example, argues that any world 'after markets' will only emerge on the terrain of 'markets' themselves, such that we need to understand how they take form in pivotal sites/institutions/practices of economy. The challenge is to ask what work any particular market actually does in relation to its defining material and ethical contradictions, and to identify potentially generative instabilities and points of intervention. It is the possibilities for initiating new experiments in economising social life from the messiness of that which will not be stabilised, the subjects who will not be pacified, and the unruly relations that will not be ordered, to which we should attend.

Making markets from (and for) positive thought and well-being

Positive psychology is a behaviouralist approach to the analysis of social change that emphasises the potential force of positive emotions for positive change in all contexts (Seligman, 2018). Its underlying premise is that positive emotional states drive individual well-being and positive change within the workplace and social organisations more broadly. Positive emotions are argued to derive from a set of 'social and emotional skills, ranging from empathy to resilience, adaptability, mental strength and delayed gratification and self-control' (Atkinson, Bagnall, Corcoran, South & Curtis, 2019). They are also argued to include mindfulness, coping strategies, and emotional intelligence (the ability to control one's emotions). Emotional intelligence (EI) can be cultivated, learned, measured (i.e. emotional quotient) and taught (e.g. mindfulness). A master concept of positive psychology as praxis, EI is argued to underlie optimism, adaptability, self-esteem, self-motivation and the ability to manage stress, stimulate happiness and control impulse; and to manifest in social settings as social competence, relationship skills, empathy, and emotional perception. Translated into leadership training or even social policy, the challenge is to accentuate positivity and strengths rather than identify and repair weaknesses (Peterson & Seligman, 2004). Widely read popular texts proclaim the transformative force of 'learned optimism' (Seligman, 2006) and the 'happiness revolution'.

At core, positive psychology builds on 'a version of the self as a largely independent, autonomous and intentional individual' (Atkinson *et al.*, 2019). Underpinned by neuroscience, big data and an unholy alliance between evolutionary economics and behavioural psychology, positive psychology takes conceptions of the self from the preference schedule and utility maximisation of neoclassical economics inside the body. The responsibility for behavioural failings, poor individual outcomes and uneven collective outcomes lie in emotional and precognitive inadequacies as much as poor choices and failures to accept individual responsibility. Methodologies such as biosensing of physiological responses associated with emotions, the analysis of social media posts, and random control behavioural trials open up internal processes of mind, emotion and pre-cognition as sources of explanation and targets for governance and corrective intervention. They define a new and interventionist science of the social that frames new realms for analysis, diagnosis, prophylactics, and treatment. At the same time, positive psychology has opened up a new psycho-scientific industrial complex ranging from focus groups to consultancy and from self-help markets from publishing to food. For Purser, it is best understood in terms of the cult of mindfulness, a new capitalist spirituality that is simultaneously a US$4 billion industry (Purser, 2019).

The approach is linked to neoliberal governance and market utopianism, a constellation of power and knowledge dubbed 'neuroliberalism' (Whitehead, Jones, Lilley, Howell & Pykett, 2018). It links brain structure, low positivity, weak resilience and poor self-esteem to anti-social behaviours, poor social wellbeing and negative social outcomes, imagineering a social world in which these pre-cognitive responses are presented as the most authentic account of experience, emotion, cognition and wellbeing. The redirection of intellectual, political and popular attention to the inner self rather than the external social context represents a direct challenge to social welfarism and its constitutive ideologies, policies and practices (Burman, 2018). As a knowledge assemblage, positive psychology provides bridges between a radical decentring of the social to the neural scale of the emotion and contemporary neoliberal statecraft, to which it adds legitimacy via concerns with positivity, empathy and well-being. Conceptions of inequality and social justice, however, are displaced by concerns with the failure to think positively and correctional interventions such as 'attitudinal' training for the individual management of wellbeing (Friedli & Stearn, 2015).

Burman (2018) addresses the truth *effects* of positive psychology embedded in policy. He identifies a new set of 'policy pedagogies' that seek to create the subjects of worlds of happiness by entangling social ethics with behavioural codes and notions of achievement and wealth creation. These pedagogies are linked to the transfer to state powers to business and advisory bodies, creating spaces for new forms of business, intermediaries such as consultancies, and philanthropy. Responsibility for social well-being is translated downwards to local organisations and the minds of individuals. All this is built on a new, self-reinforcing consensus about the productive and progressive values of well-being and resilience understood in terms of individual psychology rather than socio-political worlds. The consensus is formed around new 'voices' of authority, modes of reasoning, quantitative pseudo-scientific measurement and compliant subjects of schooling, health care and disasters. Social-psychological worlds are prepared for an essentially economic form of management. Burman (2018) argues that:

> the concatenation of character (education) with resilience thus performs a double occlusion of the social: individualising and responsibilising the precarity of current economic and political insecurities to render them as qualities (traits, characteristics) to be found within (primarily working class) children whereby, in so doing, that social context disappears.
>
> (p. 419)

Positive psychology has become an influential school of thought in educational, health and community research and in human relations practice and social policy (Pykett & Enright, 2016). Schools are one of the places where resilience, self-esteem, and positive social behaviours and well- being can be cultivated measured and learned, by students, teachers, and new generations of the wider population (Rappleye, Komatsu, Uchida, Krys & Markus, 2020; Williamson, 2019; Ecclestone, 2007; Pianta & Walsh, 1998). In the context of PLD, positive emotions are argued to be capable of inducing a self-reinforcing cycle of contagious and cumulative happiness, which will boost job performance. In the case of health programmes in schools, the links to well-being and positivity are even more direct. They bind growth mindsets as pedagogy for enterprise and student/school improvement directly to individual health. Small and simple interventions are deemed capable of having a major impact on organisations. All this performs markets into being at the same time as creating their possibilities. Pykett and Enright point to an infrastructure of ideology and practice that blends optimism with optimalisation. This infrastructure of self-improvement has in schools been grafted on to discourses of school improvement, which have for 25 years underpinned the managerialisation of schooling with the theory that enhanced school performance can be driven by models of management and leadership (Thrupp & Willmott, 2003). The mix of self-improvement (optimism) and school improvement (optimalisation) is a heady one (Miller, 2008; Purser, 2019).

Economising professional learning in New Zealand schools

The government owned and run *Aotearoa New Zealand Education Gazette* [1] is a bi-monthly online publication that describes itself as 'New Zealand's source of education news, articles and career development opportunities for education professionals'. It is in effect an industry or trade magazine, which government uses to inform the various quasi-markets of public schooling. The *Gazette* is a pivotal site of market-making in its own right. It provides a vast range of information, from formal Ministry announcements to advertising all manner of educational products and services from trade fairs and conferences to teaching jobs. It facilitates encounters among market actors, acts as a market development platform and mediates relations between schools, teachers, policy agencies and private purveyors of education. In the language of market-making, it facilitates and normalises the unbundling of schooling, categorises and qualifies activities for exchange, establishes commensurabilities among 'products', enables and encourages the formation of marketising agencies and collects user data to sell more precise consumer information.

The Gazette advertises a plethora of PLD services and opportunities for teachers and schools. One click away from its list of workshops planned for July 2019 takes website visitors to Learning Network New Zealand (LNNZ). It routinely carries links to activities facilitated by LNNZ, a not-for-profit trust that operates as a more focused PLD market intermediary, an events and conference manager, a renter of rooms for workshops and a provider of PLD courses. LNNZ is a marketising agency in the new assemblage of market agents that has emerged around public schools. It provides an additional, more focused infrastructure for many of the marketising activities performed by the *Gazette*, helping to establish, extend and mediate market encounters, set prices and establish qualities more directly through its organisational imprint. The *Gazette* and LNNZ, operating in and through it, make markets in PLD.

In the years since the disestablishment of the schools' inspectorate in the early 1990s and its replacement by the audit-based Education Review Office (Lewis, 2004), PLD has been contracted out to an increasingly marketised field of teacher support. At first, it was understood largely in terms of refresher courses delivered by colleges of education and later university-based schools of education as the colleges became absorbed into universities. Secondary school-level professional development was also delivered collaboratively and collectively by regional subject associations. PLD for teachers became unbundled from collective practice in schools as new managerial models reorganised schools. Experiments with bulk funding highlighted for the Ministry of Education the question of how to fund and deliver professional development in managerialised schools. At the same time, the professionalisation of HR in the corporate world cemented the logics of professional development for managing staff and career pathways within organisations. More generally, teachers' professional development became enmeshed in the reduction of education to learning for improvement and the production of the neoliberal individual, a process that Biesta (2013) calls learnification.

The Ministry's response was two-fold: to point out to schools that their funding made them largely responsible for the challenge; and to target particular schools and/or curriculum and expertise fields for interventions, which it contracted out. In recent years, contracting and delivery models have shifted from large, bulk delivery contracts with university providers to a current model in which schools compete for targeted PLD opportunities to be delivered by a set of roughly 600 providers nationally who each run a stable of certified facilitators. Schools either approach these providers directly to purchase facilitation services privately or apply for targeted state-funded programmes. Most recently, extra layers of competition and a proliferation of independent consultancies have been stimulated by requiring schools to request particular facilitators to deliver programmes. This has placed new emphasis on individual reputations in the making of PLD markets.

Mary-Anne Murphy and market-making

A LNNZ Notice placed in the July 2019 Gazette advertised a series of 'Emotional Intelligence for Leaders' (EIL) workshops provided by Murphy. On her own website, she promoted the workshops by claiming that they would provide 'dynamic emotional capital tools for leadership', adding that:

> Never before has the education profession seen a more critical time to invest in our own wellbeing; particularly our emotional wellbeing. With educationalists showing signs of PTSD, high rates of burnout and rethinking their commitment to the profession, the time is now to invest in

maintaining your emotional equilibrium … emotional competencies. … our roles require emotional agility, inner strength and deep relational skills … Emotional intelligence is the skill of the future of leadership.

These EIL workshops are one of a host of life-coaching, leadership, and PLD products that Murphy offered for sale (Table 8.1). Murphy describes EI as 'the secret sauce of leadership (chocolate sauce at that. Nom!)'.[2] She observes that without it 'we have managers, not leaders'. The advertising of this programme makes much of emotional intelligence and links Murphy's life coaching work to her school leadership PLD. Her promotion makes much of her accreditation as Roche Martin's Emotional Intelligence for Leadership lead coach, trainer and assessor for New Zealand. Her current website (30 November 2020) also lists her certifications as an Neuro Linguistic Programming (NLP) and 'mBraining' coach. Both extend emotional intelligence ideas into a set of models of behavioural excellence, tools and techniques designed to shift mindsets radically to produce quick, effective and consistent change and achieve specific life goals. mBraining is a particular package of NLP tools and techniques, and is argued to be the practical cutting edge of a new field that:

Table 8.1 Summarised menu of courses from Mary-Anne Murphy (available in mid-2019)

Individual courses	*Price, NZ\$*
Training events: Creating life by design; Cultivating connected agile teams; Crucial conversations for stinky situations; Creating and leading a culture of care Coaching and mentoring for growth; Taking the panic out of public speaking	1-day workshops \$397.50 + GST 2-day workshops \$795 + GST
Levelled up Leadership: Strategic and Systems thinking and planning for change leadership	\$385 + GST
Life coaching: Mistress Mind (six months in a curated online community of like-minded women who want to find their voice)	\$2,695+GST (if paid up front)
Coaching (Monthly one hour online or face-to-face mentoring sessions – with follow-up and support)	\$2,400+GST one-off payment
Training trainers: EI Training equip you with the qualifications and skills to deliver the world's most advanced Emotional Intelligence (Emotional Quotient) tools	3-Day Workshop (\$3,675+GST)
Teams	
Any training event for up to 20 people	2 days \$4,950 +GST
The \$45k 12-month sh*t-shifting package: any five of Mary-Anne's six training courses; 12 months of ongoing coaching for your team (including retreats, copies of Mary-Anne's books, online access to Mary-Anne between courses, etc.)	Over \$80k of value for just \$45k

synthesises neuroscience and behavioural psychology, combine ancient wisdom with the very latest in medical imaging..[to].. maximise the core competencies of the head, heart and gut ... evolve to a new level of being..[and open].. up new possibilities to live life differently.

(www.mbraining4success.com/what-is-mbraining)

Both mbraining and NLP have their own gurus and industries of promotional material, resources, courses, conferences, coaching and certifications. New Zealand, for example has a formal NLP Association, while the University of Auckland teaches an executive education course in NLP.

Across three years of website redesign, Murphy has talked much about her personal story and made much of her own positivity in overcoming adversity. She has grounded the qualities of her products in terms of a persona of self, which she has described as 'sassy', an 'adventurer at heart', 'known for kickin'-ass with kindness' and more recently as a configuration of 'superpowers', including 'strong back, soft front, agile feet, and wicked sense of humour'. Alongside accounts of her own personal history, testimonies from clients and details of her professional experience, qualifications and Roche Martin accreditation, Murphy's Twitter feed, LinkedIn profile and Facebook page make her very much the product. Bound together by sassiness and positivity, they define a certain performance of self that is very much the product, an approach common to entrepreneurialism in contemporary cultural and creative industries (Molloy & Larner, 2013; Martina & Vacirca, 2017).

In the period since we first started tracking Murphy's internet presence, she has restructured her website and rebranded her professional self twice. First, working up her initial defining image of strength and independence, she dialled up the colour of her earlier playful use of her initials MAM to reinvent her life-coach persona as the 'Whip-Cracking, Shit-Shifting Mistress of my own Destiny'. Lacing her promotional material with quotations from Anais Nin, she built a persona centred on liberating clients from the baggage of their established thinking. As she took this approach to life-coaching, Murphy began to draw a clearer line between her life coaching work and her work as a PLD facilitator. She launched 'Momentum Learning' (ML) in 2017 as a platform for seeking Ministry funding. While Murphy's own website came with click-bait to explore the 'censored, school-friendly version' of the programmes through a prominent click-through to ML, this created a different professional footing for her PLD work. Nonetheless, the 'Shit-Shifting Mistress' (SSM) persona was not entirely insulated from her PLD work. In late-2019, for example, she advertised a webinar in the Gazette[3] for aspiring school leaders, team leaders, deputy principals and principals behind the tagline that Mary-Anne is 'passionate about liberating people and organisations from their 'stinky-stuff' by building their emotional intelligence'. Albeit at the milder end of the SSM metaphorical register, the reference captured the continued co-development of PLD and life-coaching market-making.

As ML,[4] Murphy claims to provide 'powerful professional learning for the education sector' through a range of professional learning support programmes, from early childhood to tertiary-level organisations. The initial foundations of ML, as read through the early development of the website, included a set of resources categorised into articles, podcasts and videos. One of the articles (labelled 'levelled up leadership') highlighted her 'interactive e-book' by the same title and linked back to the MAM website. The other two linked to short articles written by Murphy, which were labelled 'White Papers': a set of definitions and claims about the gains to be had from student directed learning; and 'A Culture of Care', which assembled a set of claims about wellness, resilience and happiness backed by quotes from the World Economic Forum and material from a report commissioned by New Zealand primary teachers' union on the well-being of principals.

By mid-November 2020 reference to the SSM persona had disappeared from her website, replaced by the more sober tagline of 'soft, strong and unshakeable'. ML's website is now more complete. 'A Culture of Care' has been reconfigured as one of three spheres of PLD expertise now offered. While still light on product detail, Murphy assures purchasers that 'looking after staff wellbeing has been top of mind in recent times' and that future management of staff wellbeing 'requires a strategic, rather than hit-and-miss, or "fluffy" approach'. ML's two other areas of expertise involve leadership and resilience. The first is 'learning from the middle' – a focus on mid-level leadership that takes advantage of recent structural changes in the organisation of schooling that have focused on identifying teams and team leaders, often in new cross-school clusters. There is an accompanying white paper. The other is again targeted at making PLD markets from contemporary change, this time to do with resilience and well-being in relation to disasters. Labelled 'Unshakeable', this range of products links up with the resilience trope in well-being and positive psychology. It emphasises 'future proofing the emotional well-being of New Zealand's youth and school communities'. Earthquakes, the Christchurch Mosque attack, and Covid-19 are offered up as disruptions to be addressed and demonstration of a need to act strategically in advance of disruption. Again, there is a 'white paper', which includes an invitation to schools to utilise Ministry funding tagged for wellbeing to purchase ML products.

Market intermediaries and market failures

The September 2019 promotion of Murphy's exhumation of 'Stinky-Stuff' EIL webinar advertised in the *Gazette* was hosted by PepTalks. *PepTalks* was a new addition to the market architecture, an online delivery platform for PLD providers and other advisors and consultants to reach teachers through marketised provision of advice in the form of expert webinars. It organised its talks into four categories: Hauora (wellbeing), leadership, learning areas and pedagogy – a split between teaching practice and content on the one hand, and positive psychology on the other. They were delivered by a cast of entrepreneurial psychologists, teachers, researchers, private consultants and PLD facilitators whose offerings are well dressed in discourses of leadership, emotional intelligence and the future-focused educational techniques of happiness-making (Table 8.2). PepTalks advertised its services with the claim that 'teaching in a classroom can be lonely and teachers have to make difficult decisions every day with imperfect information. In our experience, the best advice often comes from the knowledge and experience of fellow teachers'. They claim that their webinars create magic for teachers because they are 'highly practical' and 'designed to get real conversations started'. Table 8.2 presents a selection of the 23 webinars that were available for purchase in mid-October 2019, as downloads from webinars already offered or as full-participants in upcoming events.

The PepTalks webinars reveal how actors are assembling PLD markets in relation to other market-making possibilities associated with positive psychology. The PepTalks story, however, was a brief one, closing for good in 2020. It helps to illustrate, however, the complexity and incompleteness of a market where products and qualities are only weakly defined and incommensurable.

A Professional Learning Development market

Mary-Anne Murphy introduces us to the making of PLD markets. Her story demonstrates how PLD is being assembled from the entrepreneurial activities of small, partly independent facilitators and consultants like herself; a mix of government funding programmes, the funding criteria attached to them and the measures behind these that target particular spheres of schooling; the claims and certifications of expertise made by market actors; the discursive formations and socio-technical devices of positive psychology; and the work of intermediaries and the connections and activities of marketising agencies that they facilitate, as well as the market infrastructure they provide. The account also exposes the extensive micro-level effort required to accomplish a market, its dynamics and its incompleteness of this market. MAM (as Murphy's professional persona) is in motion, as are Ministry of Education funding criteria, industry-positive psychology, the materialities of schooling and the actions of other enterprises and actors.

Read through these 'in the making' terms, the New Zealand 'market' for PLD comprises a complicated set of enterprises, purchasing arrangements, buyers, products, bottom lines and discursive framings, such as positive psychology and school improvement. It is framed by the hybridity generated by public-private arrangements in the provision of schooling. Murphy and other PLD providers must make markets in a complex relational assemblage, framed in distinctive ways. These might be understood in Callon's terms as: proliferation of marketising agencies, including intermediaries, the Ministry of Education and various hybrid competitors; pacifying goods (the repackaging of positive psychology and school improvement as webinars, workshops and white papers, the tools and models of positive psychology derivatives and the qualification processes of certification, reference to global gurus and so on); the market encounters facilitated by the intermediaries and the performative nature

Table 8.2 PepTalks advertised webinars (as at 15 October 2019)

Current primary occupation	Key reference to interests	Statement of expertise
Digital Circus, a Ministry of Education-accredited PLD provider	Online digital fluency academy for primary school students; podcast	Post Graduate Certificate in Digital and Collaborative Learning Google certified educator, innovator
Unclear – educational entrepreneur	Author of The Personality Puzzle card sort resources	Qualified MBTI practitioner recipient of award for outstanding achievement in education
Teacher	Play as learning	Advocate for play based learning
Research professor of psychology	Research on the role of play in human evolution	Founder director/president of two nonprofits
Education Facilitator at government agency	Empower/excite learners with agency / critical inquiry	Certified coach, accredited teacher of Critical Thinking USA, recipient of Creative Thinking Skills awards
Private speech and language therapist	Evidence-based speech language therapy	Founder and clinician of web-based speech language therapy service
Movement Skills Advisor (local gov't)	Sport coaching, leadership	Former lecturer at polytechnic
Children's, young adult author	Passion for writing for young people	Former youth support worker
Resource Teacher: Literacy	Reading recovery – change that will make a difference	Literacy teacher, facilitator and mentor to teachers, parents and children
Unclear	Hands-on, jargon-free learning approaches and resources	Accredited facilitator, teacher, 'leader' Creator of learning resources
Independent education consultant	Transforming education systems (marketing, innovation, ingenuity)	Global experience
Private facilitator, life coach	'Supporting others to create the incredible lives and workplaces they thought only existed in their dreams'	Certified facilitator, coach; Masters in Educational Leadership, accredited NZ seller of emotional intelligence products
Guru	Well-being	Author of *Being A True Hero: Understanding and Preventing Suicide in Your Community*
Guru	Positive psychology	25 years of neuroscience research Host of documentary series

Source: Assembled from https://peptalks.co.nz

of the products (webinars, workshops and white papers); and market design and maintenance — what we might better label the assembling and stabilising work revealed through the dynamics of Murphy's website redesigns. This market-making supports — and is based on — work to cultivate 'attributes' of resilience, self-esteem and positive social behaviours and well-being in students and teachers.

Markets for school lunches, virtue and poverty-reduction in schools

As with PLD, new private providers of health curriculum and related food provisioning schemes have proliferated in schools. Rounds of neoliberal reform have rendered state agencies unable or unwilling to provide direct support for children who turn up to school hungry. Resource constraints and the practicalities of hollowing-out (Rhodes, 1994) has left both policy and delivery gaps that have been filled in three ways. First, the poverty and educational issues associated with food deficits among school children have become entangled in public health concerns, especially with obesity and most notably among poorer social groups. Schools have become sites where the impact of diseases of poverty and their impact on education, public health and behaviour are addressed. Behaviour change is seen as the solution. Second, the Ministry of Health has funded health priority programmes in schools alongside the national Diabetes Foundation or indirectly through District Health Boards, which have turned to private, philanthropic and/or charitable providers to deliver programmes. These providers have now become the entrepreneurs of these spaces, moving not just to fill funding, policy and delivery gaps, but create the need for their service.

A range of actors doing 'good' have taken up the challenge, developed and established practical responses and have become actors in a marketsite for virtue. Most are registered charities. While the lines between charitable agencies and other private providers are commonly blurred in this marketsite, tax-free status and investment in the form of tax-deductible donations shape business models and public personae. Most also depend on public funding and leverage their activities off the delivery of formal, Ministry-funded health programmes. This funding provides a platform on which competing enterprises chase local government project funding, philanthropic trusts and foundations and corporate sponsorships from firms looking to demonstrate social enterprise credentials or sanitise their reputations. Their activities build on an entrepreneurialism that stitches together charity networks, social enterprise investors, celebrity endorsements, media attention, state funding programmes and interwoven public concerns about child obesity, 'healthy' eating and child poverty. Schools are key sites at which these concerns, relations and practices are assembled into public health messages about food and nutrition. They are also sites of potential intervention, which can range from universal to highly targeted forms.

A range of organisations provide food and food-related support to schools (Pluim, Powell & Leahy, 2018; Gray, Pluim, Pike & Leahy, 2018). Almost all build programmes on assumptions around whānau (extended family) need and how filling that need will help children to be 'healthy' and 'fit' and improve educational outcomes. Others help schools to establish and run gardens. These extend the underlying assumptions about deficit to capabilities associated with food production and preparation. From environmental and health-based perspectives, these programmes are entirely positive, and they come with the educational win-wins of children who are biologically more able to learn and engaged in new and positive forms of learning in food gardens. The food programmes are linked to food, health and physical exercise messaging provided by organisations such as the Heart Foundation, as well as the messages embedded in the New Zealand curriculum.

As the number of providers is proliferating, new entrants have adopted diverse strategies to secure a niche by differentiating their offering. Different enterprises offer different levels and types of support, market forms, conditionalities and precision of targeting, competing in part on reducing transactions costs for schools and funders. Food providers generally provide breakfast and/or lunch and vary in scale, business model and operating philosophy. They range from small church groups providing snacks to local schools to national organisations with sophisticated business approaches. They offer services from quasi-targeted provision to universal provision within the school. Established providers have secured 'first mover' advantages. KidsCan, for example, was founded in 2005. It built a market for its services early – performing the nature of the service into being and establishing KidsCan as the pre-eminent provider of free food, raincoats, shoes and so forth to schools in poorer neighbourhoods. In a market where capital comes from donations and partnerships (including partnerships with the state) brand recognition and trust are crucial.

The enterprises involved, including schools themselves and state actors (health programme managers, etc.) have established accepted modes of operation, stabilising a charity market that has operated for some 15 years and remained remarkably free of discriminatory behaviour and fraud. The enterprises involved have assembled a series of cultural elements and social institutions and established a standard performance of charity, which has pacified financial practice and set expectations of ethical behaviour. All those involved are subject to direct scrutiny from the state and to public scrutiny via the media, as well as the underlying legal architecture within which schools, charities and state agencies operate. The rules of the charity game are well recognised, whether written or unwritten.

Eat my Lunch

Eat my Lunch (EML) was established in 2014. Founder Lisa King is at pains to point out that it is 'a business not a charity' albeit a business whose mission is 'social good'. EML is a limited liability company. Although it relies on volunteers, it does not rely on donations. Instead EML appeals to corporate lunch buyers (it also offers a catering service) to buy a lunch from EML and at the same time buy a lunch for 'a Kiwi kid in need'. Socially aware businesses can also send staff to assemble sandwiches in the early morning alongside the volunteer force. EML appeals directly to mainstream New Zealand, which has led it to advertise in trade publications such as *Supermarket News,* the magazine of national supermarket chain Foodstuffs, which is a 26 per cent shareholder in EML. It also promotes itself in public places such as bus shelters, lifts and billboards in shopping malls, in addition to its social media promotion and use of celebrity ambassadors. Promotion relies heavily on virtue-signalling through images and tag-lines 'making a difference', 'making it easier for Kiwis to help Kiwis', 'freshly made yummy school lunch' and 'healthy lunches'. Buying a lunch for 'a kiwi kid in need' is simultaneously an act of kindness, social responsibility, charity, public health promotion and nationalism.

This all points to the question of which 'hungry kids' get a free EML lunch. The answer is a mix of strategic selectivity on the part of multiple actors. The key criterion is geography. Deliveries are restricted to poorer suburbs of Auckland and Wellington. If there is 'genuine need', schools will go on to a waiting list, although it is unclear how 'genuine need' is determined. Schools can also be nominated through the website, which lists schools that currently get lunches. These are predominantly, but not exclusively, schools in poorer neighbourhoods. There is no indication of how long the waiting list is, or how long schools can expect to stay there. In common with other in-school donors, EML does not dictate how schools should distribute their wares. Once lunches are delivered, schools decide how they are distributed and to whom.

EML has clearly tapped into a marketsite and middle New Zealand's nagging discomfort about child poverty. Its business model is astute – focusing on lunch shields it from direct competition with the well-established *KickStart* breakfast programme funded by Fonterra (New Zealand's largest company and the world's largest international trader of milk products) or the fruit pottles and muesli bars provided by charity *KidsCan.* While activist groups such as Child Poverty Action Group have long campaigned for funding and government policy to address both absolute and relative poverty in New Zealand, EML founder Michael Meredith has taken a personal ownership of the 'problem' and the investment opportunity it provides. He writes that 'I feel in my heart this issue needs to be addressed… it has to be somebody's problem' (Jennings, 2018). The recently appointed general manager, Kellie Burbridge, adds that the issue is: 'something that I'm passionate about and use those [corporate] skills to make a real difference' (Shaw, 2019). Of those who invested as part of the crowdfunding, King says that 24 per cent of sub-scribers opted to put all of their interest payments back into lunches. For the less financially adventurous, doing good is as easy as dialling up a lunch. Meredith credits Foodstuffs for investing 'because they want to be part of the social impact' (Jennings, 2018).

The 'buy-one, give-one' business model had yet to yield a paid-out financial dividend by September 2018, although it was still looking to break even by the end of that year. It extended its business model to seek funding via PledgeMe, offering 12 per cent return (6 per cent cash dividend and 6 per cent going back to buy lunches for children). It also opened a fully commercial 'grab and go' store in central Auckland in July 2019. The lack of profit has not deterred EML from seeking to expand its market. In October 2019 it announced that it had appointed a new general manager with a background in corporate banking and had plans to take on equity, open in other major cities around New Zealand and 'roll out the concept to Australia, Canada and the United States' (Shaw, 2019). The expansion proposal is as fascinating as it is ambitious. Not only does it signal a globalisation of social enterprise and a global market for social virtue, but also a market for its business model/methodology in and of itself! Significantly, it raises the challenge of place in market construction, and the capacity of EML to respond to very different structural conditions around funding and the nature of lunch programmes. A smooth deployment of markets from one place to another cannot be assumed.

Framing markets for virtue in schools

These new 'social' entrepreneurs are assembling health charity economies centred on the figures of the hungry and obese school child and the possibilities provided by remaking schools as post-welfare, self-governing 'marketsites' (Kear, 2018). A market for virtue is being assembled from a complex network of providers of differing legal and organisational forms, schools, funding programmes, donors, state agencies, charitable motivations, and discursive formations that shape incentives, motivations and political commitments. Charities and social enterprises such as EML make the market by assembling this complexity in particular ways. They reshape discourses of poverty and define legitimate and effective poverty action. They work closely with donors, investors, school managers, state agencies and teachers to create the marketsite (Gray *et al.*, 2018). They launch promotional initiatives that celebrate virtue, affirm the policy models and keep 'hungry kids' in the public gaze through posters in suburban shopping malls and billboards in transport hubs which help to pacify potentially unruly actors and sustain the market. Beyond the immediate realm of food in schools, they have a presence in circuits of socially responsible entrepreneurs, speaking in prominent arenas and commenting publicly. Being active and being visible are key strategies in creating and pacifying, as well as stabilising the objects, actors, connections and overflows that constitute the market.

Entrepreneurial actors such as EML create markets for virtue in relation to a hollowed-out state that is looking elsewhere for delivery and legitimation of policy and governance at a distance. The state funds the virtue market at both ends, through schooling and welfare, as well as directly through health programmes and indirectly through tax deductions. The donating public buys virtue and is spared the problem of contemplating larger-scale political change to reduce child poverty on a more sustained basis. In the terms of the economisation literature, this complexity stabilises the market, but it is still vulnerable – to its own overflows in terms of market failures and bad publicity, and in terms of redefinitions of the three products at stake: virtue, public health and poverty reduction. These products remain entangled in matters of concern and subject to shifts in public opinion, policy priorities or policy delivery models.

While celebrity endorsements and shiny advertisements of their 'hand-up, not hand-out' bootstrap capitalism might inoculate specific business models against these overflows in a post-welfare, post-charity discourse of socially responsible private action, the economy remains unstable and must be continuously remade.

Conclusion: Insights from economisation studies

This chapter has examined two cases to demonstrate how schools are becoming marketsites for ancillary educational products – professional learning development and a bundled-up configuration of public health, virtue and poverty reduction in the form of school lunches. Our account reveals how the economisation of public education is opening up public school spaces as marketsites where private enterprises are making and profiting by making markets for positivity, virtue, resilience, and well-being actually work. We focus on how this economisation is commodifying public goods, reordering the ethical and organisational structures of their delivery, capturing public funding and entangling schooling in market relations and the happiness-led values of positive psychology. PLD and virtue entrepreneurs, school principals and Ministry officials are assembling hybrid public-private marketsites by stitching together organisational networks – practices informed by discourses of school improvement, positive psychology and poverty reduction and socio-technical devices such as contracts, websites, webinars and white papers. They are making markets in schools. To conclude, we highlight five dimensions of these dynamics that help us to demonstrate the value of an economisation approach to research and issue two caveats and a final note of concern.

First, this critique adds new dimensions to the critique of the penetration of positive psychology into schooling (Pykett & Enright, 2016; Humphrey, Curran, Morris, Farrell & Woods, 2007). We point to an infrastructure of economisation that grafts the drive to happiness, well-being and self-improvement onto the neoliberal architecture of school improvement, which has for some 25 years underpinned the managerialisation of schooling. Positive expectations, growth mindsets and EI offer up codified expertise and affective managerial approaches for improved school performance in any setting. Borrowing Pykett and Enright's (2018) terms they align optimism with optimalisation.

Second, focusing on economisation has helped us to add detail to the critique of the neoliberal marketisation of schooling. We highlight elements of how school-based economies are actually being made. In doing so, we show how new agents of marketisation are actively reconfiguring schooling to make schools available for private profit from public funding. The markets we describe rely on public monies, which they direct into opportunities for private accumulation. Our account points to how the creation of new markets and spaces of accumulation is entangled with new public management and 'organisational economisation', especially when making markets for PLD. We also re-emphasise that neoliberalism is as much a cultural and governmental project as it is a political-economic project. By directing attention to how schools are being reconfigured as marketsites through material practice, we offer a fine-grained critique of the ongoing marketisation of public activities as neoliberalism is remade into new forms.

Third, our attention to practice informs a political economy reading of the marketisation of schooling. Murphy, EML, state agencies, philanthropists, social enterprises, and schools themselves are intricately entangled in formatting and framing schools as new sites of accumulation. They are creating exchange value from educational practice as well as poverty and insecurity and accumulating wealth, social status and moral capital by feeding from the public purse. For the state, their work reinforces managerial control and distracts attention from the challenges of the classroom and the entrenched spatial unevenness of schooling. The cases illustrate how states are governing at a distance through schools, which are again being put to work to serve the state in reproducing the political, economic and cultural subjects of new (well-being) times and to manage social unevenness legitimately (see Dale, 1989). Long critical sites of governmental programmes from colonialism to industrialisation and the welfare state, state schools are arguably being fashioned into key sites of a new socio-spatial fix.

Twenty-five years ago, Peck and Tickell (1995) asked whether neoliberalism required a socio-spatial fix and what it might look like. Reassembled as marketsite for production and sale of happiness, optimism, well-being, resilience and poverty reduction, state schooling has arguably become such a fix. More fluid, emergent, temporary, relational and cultural than any fix imaginable as 'after' to the collapse of the welfare state, it is better understood as an accommodation. That is, PLD and school lunch programmes are examples of the economisation of well-being, resilience, and continuous self-improvement that 'accommodate' neoliberalism. The school as marketsite is a hybrid state-private space where happy, positive, well and resilient selves are now being cultured in place of the competitive, acquisitive selves of an earlier reformist neoliberal moment, and where reparative work is performed on the losers of its defining competitions. The entrepreneurialism of Murphy, EML and their competitors are both the agents and embodiments of this accommodation. Along with school managers and state officials, they are assembling social enterprise, new informational infrastructures and the circulation of capital through the state, philanthropy and markets into new hybrid market forms and attending to the failures and overflows of matters of concern such as poverty-driven ill-health and hunger. Schools as marketsites and PLD and welfare intermediaries as entrepreneurs have displaced the state schools and bureaucrats of an earlier era.

Our account tells us, however, that this accommodation is neither stable and complete nor prior to the action of its agents, and it has a defining cultural dimension. Like the markets for well-being and virtue from which it is constituted, it is in the making, and it relies on the optimism/optimalisation double of positive psychology. The promise of equity and opportunity have been displaced by the seduction of happiness and the gospel of optimism. With one killer app, resilience makeover or emotional intelligence, happiness, wealth and self-improvement are but a website, social enterprise and public-private transfer away. There is something quintessentially neoliberal in such a fix, but also something reliant on an *affective infrastructure of stabilisation* (of school markets and schooling as governmental practice), which was unimaginable in 1994.

Fourth, there is little social in this accommodation. Resilience and well-being are aggregations of individual happiness, charity and optimism. They shift the contradictions of poverty, competition for success, and unrealised aspiration inwards to mindfulness, a full belly, and coping strategies; and outwards in space and time towards charity. It is in this light that we might see the appeal not just to the happy teacher and child and the social entrepreneur as the key economic figures of the new fix, but also to the emotional leader as its guardian figure. Murphy and EML assemble optimism (positivity) and optimisation (efficiency) and school improvement and social enterprise into a co-constitutive ethico-economic formation. Pykett and Enright insist that rather than a state of mind or a mood, optimism is, for positive psychologists, a 'state of explanation' or 'an appraisal of the situation'. It is an affective architecture, which, read from below, offers a fix that bypasses the social, drawing on it only as a source of funding and partial legitimation in relation to the claim on funding.

Fifth, despite our claim that these new public-private hybrids bypass the social as the space within which the political economy of marketisation requires a fix, they do speak to a material social world of affect. Here the fix lies in pre-cognitive realms. Murphy, EML and their like appeal to, draw and depend on and create a form of redemptive affect that transcends the individual. Individual caring and the mindful self have a moral economy beyond the act of individual care or concern with well-being. There are, as others have argued, strong links between positive psychology, well-being and cults of happiness to a vast economy of self-help and a fundamentalist rejection of the material social world as a structuring force. The point is far from trivial – schools are sites where social futures are overtly imagined and institutionalised and their subjects constituted in everyday social life. They are also supposed to be secular public spaces yet are becoming sites where this politics is being assembled and rolled out in practice, funded by the state and for private gain.

We need to end with two caveats. First, the fixing work of PLD and school lunches performs positive material work. Providing food for children who might otherwise go hungry is unimpeachably positive, whoever the provider and whatever the conditions might be. Similarly, affirmative forms of PLD release teachers and principals from workaday banality, excite and recharge them, and celebrate their professionalism. They can build community, connections and pedagogical knowledge, irrespective of the content of the sessions. Positive and emotionally attuned teachers are more than likely to be better teachers than negative teachers, while positivity is likely to reduce the attrition of teachers in schools (Gallant & Riley, 2017). Second, our research is not practice-based – we have not studied what actually happens in the rooms where school lunches are prepared or eaten or where teachers take their PLD classes. A more ethnographic approach would no doubt open up sharper insights about how lunches and PLD packages actually land in schools and affect the teacher and eater subjects that they prefigure. It is only at this level that we can safely shake off the 'time of movements, manifestoes, and best packages in education' to 'concentrate on the individual interventions that work best' (Kristjánsson, 2012, p. 103) and practice the enactive politics of possibility proposed by Lewis and Le Heron (2020), in the presence or otherwise of market-making.

Notes

1 See https://gazette.education.govt.nz.
2 See www.edgaz.nz/notices/1H9yx0-emotional-intelligence-for-leaders-webinar.
3 See www.edgaz.nz/notices/1H9yx0-emotional-intelligence-for-leaders-webinar.
4 See www.momentumlearning.ac.nz.

References

Atkinson, S., Bagnall, A., Corcoran, R., South, J. & Curtis, S. (2019). Being well together: Individual subjective and community wellbeing. *Journal of Happiness Studies*, 1–19.

Ball, S. (2009). Privatising education, privatising education policy, privatising educational research: Network governance and the 'competition state'. *Journal of Education Policy*, 24(1), 83–99.

Ball, S. (2012). *Global education inc: New policy networks and the neo-liberal imaginary.* London: Routledge.

Berndt, C., Rantisi, N.M. & Peck, J. (2020). M/market Frontiers. *Environment and Planning A*, 52(1), 14–26.

Berndt, C. & Boeckler, M. (2009). Geographies of circulation and exchange: Constructions of markets. *Progress in Human Geography*, 33(4), 535–551.

Berndt, C. & Boeckler, M. (2011). Geographies of markets: Materials, morals and monsters in motion. *Progress in Human Geography*, 35(4), 559–567.

Berndt, C. & Wirth, M. (2019). Struggling for the moral market: Economic knowledge, diverse markets, and market borders. *Economic Geography*, 95(3), 288–309.

Biesta, G. (2013). *Beautiful risk of education.* Boulder, CO: Paradigm Publishers.

Boeckler, M. & Berndt, C. (2013). Geographies of circulation and exchange III: The great crisis and marketization 'after markets'. *Progress in Human Geography*, 37(3), 424–432.

Burman, E. (2018). (Re) sourcing the character and resilience manifesto: Suppressions and slippages of (re) presentation and selective affectivities. *Sociological Research Online*, 23(2), 416–437.

Çalışkan, K. & Callon, M. (2009). Economization, part 1: shifting attention from the economy towards processes of economization. *Economy and Society*, 38(3), 369–398.

Callon, M., Méadel, C. & Rabeharisoa, V. (2002). The economy of qualities. *Economy and Society*, 31(2), 194–217.

Carusi, T. (2019). The ontological rhetorics of education policy: A non-instrumental theory. *Journal of Education Policy*, 1–21. https://doi.org/10.1080/02680939.2019.1665713.

Carusi, F. & Niwa, T. (2020). Learning not to be poor: The impossible position of teachers in Aotearoa New Zealand education policy discourse. *Asia-Pacific Journal of Teacher Education*, 48(1), 30–44.

Cohen, D. (2018). Between perfection and damnation: The emerging geography of markets. *Progress in Human Geography*, 42(6), 898–915.

Cohen, D. & Lizotte, C. (2015). Teaching the market: Fostering consent to education markets in the United States. *Environment and Planning A*, 47(9), 1824–1841.

Dale, R. (1989). *The state and education policy.* Milton Keynes: Open University Press.

Ecclestone, K. (2007). Resisting images of the 'diminished self': The implications of emotional well-being and emotional engagement in education policy. *Journal of Education Policy*, 22(4), 455–470.

Fligstein, N. & Calder, R. (2015). Architecture of markets. In S.M. Kosslyn & R.A. Scott (Eds), *Emerging trends in the social and behavioral sciences: An interdisciplinary, searchable, and linkable resource* (pp. 1–14). Retrieved from https://doi.org/10.1002/9781118900772.

Friedli, L. & Stearn, R. (2015). Positive affect as coercive strategy: Conditionality, activation and the role of psychology in UK government workfare programmes. *Medical Humanities*, 41, 40–47.

Gallant, A. & Riley, P., (2017). Early career teacher attrition in Australia: Inconvenient truths about new public management. *Teachers and Teaching*, 23(8), 896–913.

Gill, R. & Kanai, A. (2018). Mediating neoliberal capitalism: Affect, subjectivity and inequality. *Journal of Communication*, 68(2), 318–326.

Gordon, L., (2016). The sociology of education in New Zealand: An historical overview. *New Zealand Sociology*, 31(3), 168.

Gray, E.M., Pluim, C., Pike, J. & Leahy, D. (2018). 'Someone has to keep shouting': celebrities as food pedagogues. *Celebrity Studies*, 9(1), 69–83.

Higgins, V. & Larner, W. (Eds.). (2017). *Assembling neoliberalism: Expertise, practices, subjects.* New York, NY: Springer.

Humphrey, N., Curran, A., Morris, E., Farrell, P. & Woods, K. (2007). Emotional intelligence and education: A critical review. *Educational Psychology*, 27(2), 235–254.

Jennings, M. (2018). Eat my Lunch returns serve, *Newsroom*. Retrieved from www.newsroom.co.nz/2018/09/13/235500/eat-my-lunch-returns-serve-1.

Kear, M. (2018). The marketsite: A new conceptualization of market spatiality. *Economic Geography*, 94(3), 299–320.

Komljenovic, J. & Robertson, S. (2016). The dynamics of 'market-making' in higher education. *Journal of Education Policy*, 31(5), 622–636.

Kristjánsson, K. (2012). Positive psychology and positive education: Old wine in new bottles? *Educational Psychologist*, 47(2), 86–105.

Kurunmäki, L., Mennicken, A. & Miller, P. (2016). Quantifying, economising, and marketising: Democratising the social sphere? *Sociologie du travail*, 58(4), 390–402.

Lauder, H.*et al.* (1999). *Trading in futures: Why markets in education don't work.* Buckingham: Open University Press.

Lewis, N. (2004). Embedding the reforms in New Zealand schooling: After neo-liberalism? *GeoJournal*, 59(2),149–160.

Lewis, N. & Le Heron, R. (2020). *Postructuralist political economy. In A. Kobayashi (ed.) International Encyclopedia of Human Geography* (pp. 226–233). Oxford: Elsevier.

Martina, M. & Vacirca, S. (2017). The celebrity factory: new modes of fashion entrepreneurship. *ZoneModa Journal*, 7(1), 37–53.

Miller, A. (2008). A critique of positive psychology—or 'the new science of happiness'. *Journal of Philosophy of Education*, 42(3-4), 591–608.

Molloy, M. & Larner, W. (2013). *Fashioning globalisation: New Zealand design, working women and the cultural economy.* Chichester: John Wiley & Sons.

O'Neill, J. (2011). The privatisation of public schooling in New Zealand. *Journal of Education Policy*, 26(1), 17–31.

O'Neill, A. (2016). Assessment-based curriculum: Globalising and enterprising culture, human capital and teacher–technicians in Aotearoa New Zealand. *Journal of Education Policy*, 31(5), 598–621.

O'Neill, J. (2017). Marketplace or commodity progressivism and state schooling. *Teachers and Curriculum*, 17(1), 7–10.

Peck, J. & Tickell, A. (1995). Jungle law breaks out: Neoliberalism and global-local disorder. *Area* 26, 317–326.

Peetz, T. (2019). Neoliberalism or organizational economization? *Ephemera: Theory & Politics in Organization*, 19(3), 591–613.

Peterson, C. & Seligman, M. (2004). *Character strengths and virtues: A handbook and classification*. Oxford: Oxford University Press.

Pianta, R. & Walsh, D. (1998). Applying the construct of resilience in schools: Cautions from a developmental systems perspective. *School Psychology Review*, 27(3), 407–417. https://doi.org/10.1080/02796015.1998.12085925.

Pluim, C., Powell, D. & Leahy, D. (2018). Schooling lunch: Health, food, and the pedagogicalization of the lunch box. In S. Rice & A.G. Rud (Eds), *Educational dimensions of school lunch: Critical perspectives* (1st ed., pp. 59–74). Cham: Palgrave Macmillan.

Purser, R. (2019). *McMindfulness: How mindfulness became the new capitalist spirituality*. Watkins Media Limited.

Pykett, J. & Enright, B. (2016). Geographies of brain culture: Optimism and optimisation in workplace training programmes. *Cultural Geographies*, 23(1), 51–68.

Rappleye, J., Komatsu, H., Uchida, Y., Krys, K. & Markus, H. (2020). 'Better policies for better lives'?: Constructive critique of the OECD's (mis)measure of student well-being. *Journal of Education Policy*, 35(2), 258–282.

Rhodes, R. (1994). The hollowing out of the state: The changing nature of the public service in Britain. *The Political Quarterly*, 65(2), 138–151. https://doi.org/10.1111/j.1467-923x.1994.tb00441.x.

Riep, C.B. (2017). Making markets for low-cost schooling: The devices and investments behind Bridge International Academies. *Globalisation, Societies and Education*, 15(3), 352–366. https://doi.org/10.1080/14767724.2017.1330139.

Robertson, S. (2000). *A class act: Changing teachers' work, globalisation and the state* (Vol. 8). New York, NY: Taylor & Francis.

Robertson, S. & Dale, R. (2013). The social justice implications of privatisation in education governance frameworks: A relational account. *Oxford Review of Education*, 39(4), 426–445. https://doi.org/10.1080/03054985.2013.820465.

Rose, N., (2000). Community, citizenship, and the third way. *American Behavioral Scientist*, 43(9), 1395–1411. https://doi.org/10.1177/00027640021955955.

Schatzki, T. (2005). Peripheral vision: The sites of organizations. *Organization studies*, 26(3), 465–484. https://doi.org/10.1177/0170840605050876.

Seligman, M. (2006). *Learned optimism: How to change your mind and your life*. London: Vintage.

Seligman, M. (2018). PERMA and the building blocks of well-being. *The Journal of Positive Psychology*, 13(4), 333–335. https://doi.org/10.1080/17439760.2018.1437466.

Shaw, A. (2019). Eat My Lunch appoints former ANZ executive as new general manager. *New Zealand Herald*. Retrieved from www.nzherald.co.nz/business/eat-my-lunch-appoints-former-anz-executive-as-new-general-manager/4GMX5JFCKDZQJPNW7WBXPTCLUM.

Thiem, C. H. (2009). Thinking through education: The geographies of contemporary educational restructuring. *Progress in Human Geography*, 33(2), 154–173.

Thrupp, M. & Willmott, R. (2003). *Educational management in managerialist times*. Maidenhead: McGraw-Hill Education.

Tronto, J. (2017). There is an alternative: *Homines curans* and the limits of neoliberalism. *International Journal of Care and Caring*, 1(1), 27–43. https://doi.org/10.1332/239788217x 1486628168758.

Whitehead, M., Jones, R., Lilley, R., Howell, R. & Pykett, J. (2019). Neuroliberalism: Cognition, context, and the geographical bounding of rationality. *Progress in Human Geography*, 43(4), 632–649.

Williamson, B. (2019). Psychodata: Disassembling the psychological, economic, and statistical infrastructure of 'social-emotional learning'. *Journal of Education Policy*, 1–26. doi:10.1080/02680939.2019.1672895.

Williamson, B. (2020). Making markets through digital platforms: Pearson, edu-business, and the (e) valuation of higher education. *Critical Studies in Education*, 1–17. https://doi.org/10.1080/17508487.2020.1737556.

9 Mobile markets for meters

The connections between new electricity metering markets in New Zealand and Australia

Heather Lovell

UNIVERSITY OF TASMANIA

Introduction

Digital electricity meters are replacing traditional 'spinning disc' or analogue meters worldwide. Digital meters have several advantages over traditional meters, including the ability to be read remotely, much more frequent meter readings, and their provision of data to energy feedback devices, in order to give more in-depth information to households and other end consumers (Accenture, 2016). Digital electricity meters, also known as 'smart meters', are usually required if renewable energy generation is installed, such as household rooftop solar photovoltaic panels. Furthermore, digital meters have a number of advantages to electricity network utilities in terms of smooth electricity grid operation, including rapid response to outages, and voltage control (Deloitte, 2011).

In Australia and New Zealand there have been digital metering programs implemented within the past ten years, and these are the focus of this chapter. At first glance this might seem like a not very exciting topic of research, but the process of creating markets for electricity meters – and the international transfer of these markets – reveals much about the role of place within markets, and also the agency of technology. Internationally there have been two main approaches to implementing digital electricity meters: state-led mandatory implementation, wherein households and businesses have no or limited choice about whether to have a new meter installed; and market-based implementation, where consumer choice is celebrated and installing a new meter is voluntary, and organised by the utility retailer.

Australia is an instructive case study because it has done both: an initial mandatory programme in 2009–13 (in one State of Australia – Victoria), and then a shift in approach away from mandatory implementation to a voluntary market-led implementation, from December 2017 to present, across Australia's National Electricity Market. New Zealand has only had a voluntary market-based digital metering programme, which commenced in 2009. In this chapter I examine how the New Zealand market-based metering programme was invoked in Australia and played a key role in Australia's decision to switch to a voluntary market-led implementation

DOI: 10.4324/9780429296260-9

approach in the period 2015–17. I explore some of the key contextual differences between New Zealand and Australia, drawing on cultural economy and policy mobilities theory, outlining how an approach that takes the place-based nature of markets seriously (see for example Bunnell & Coe, 2001; Hébert, 2014) draws our attention to, and helps to provide an explanation for, why the New Zealand electricity metering market has not translated straightforwardly to Australia.

The methodology used for this chapter is qualitative and comprises a mix of research techniques including interviews with 20 key stakeholders (plus transcription, analysis and coding), analysis of policy documents, and participant observation at several workshops and conferences. The empirical research was conducted in the period May 2015 to November 2017.

The remainder of this chapter is structured as follows: first, a brief overview of relevant concepts and theory – policy mobilities and cultural economy (for more detail, see Chapter 1 of this volume); second, the core empirical analysis, including an exploration of the two cases – Australia and New Zealand; and third, a short summary and conclusion, reflecting on the core themes of the *Markets in their Place* book and how this case contributes.

Understanding markets in their place and their transferability

Markets in their Place is about the geographies of markets, and this chapter focuses on the international transfer of a market-based policy approach, using the case of electricity meters, from New Zealand to Australia. Policy mobilities scholarship is introduced here because its core ideas are sensitive to the particularities of place, and it has a particular focus on the international movement of policies (McCann, 2011; Peck & Theodore, 2010; Prince, 2012). The focus is on how policy concepts and practices (including markets) move and are transferred internationally, sometimes inappropriately. There are notable overlaps with cultural economy – the second area of scholarship briefly explored. The contributions in this book are about how place is pivotal to the making of markets; showing how markets are not abstract, they are always developed and operate in particular places. Other chapter contributions examine the particular place-based social, political, cultural, technical and material arrangements that give rise to markets. In my analysis here, the focus is on market connections and the transfer of markets (or elements of markets) from place to place. In the case of digital electricity meters, a better understanding of the particular context of electricity meters and the electricity market in New Zealand is central to understanding why the market-based mechanism for implementing smart meters worked relatively well in New Zealand, but thus far is struggling in Australia, as well as how and why it changed in the process of moving. The case also explores how place acts as a narrated entity, with the story – or particular representation – of metering implementation success in New Zealand being an important influence on its adoption in Australia. The chapter hence tackles one of the book's key themes (see Chapter 1), namely the way that superficially similar markets work out differently in different places, and why, by considering what enables and restricts market connections.

Policy mobilities

The concept of policy mobilities is relatively new, and builds on a tradition of analysis of the transfer and diffusion of policy within the political sciences from the 1960s onwards (Dolowitz & Marsh, 2000; Robertson, 1991). However, policy mobilities scholarship has much less of a focus on the nation-state than political science approaches, and instead primarily describes the movement of new policy initiatives from urban-to-urban areas, and gives greater priority to the role of corporate actors (Pow, 2014; Prince, 2014), in keeping with its focus on neoliberalism (Peck & Theodore, 2015). Policy mobilities scholarship is especially relevant to thinking about markets, and how markets move, because of its opening up of analysis to different types of organisation beyond the state, in particular corporations and other market actors. This is borne out by the several business, commercial and market-based empirical case studies within policy mobilities scholarship, including, for example, the international movement of university student recruitment strategies (Geddie, 2015), and policies to support the creation of business districts (Ward, 2006).

Policy mobilities scholarship is also relevant to the study of markets because of its interest in the material objects, ideas and institutions that constitute market-based policies. There are parallels here with cultural economy approaches to markets, which concentrate our gaze on the diverse multitude of things and people that make up markets. Hence both areas of scholarship are attentive to the role of place in generating both similarity and difference in policies and markets, as well as the mobilities and immobilities of policies and markets – how easily they travel and diffuse.

Cultural economy

Cultural economy is about the relationship between culture, the economy and society. Cultural economy approaches are interested in understanding the construction and operation of markets and economies in an holistic way, attentive to the social, cultural, political, technical and economic aspects of markets. There are many different definitions of cultural economy, stemming from a number of disciplines including economics and cultural geography, with the latter referring to cultural economy as a 'multivalent' term (Gibson & Kong, 2005). A cultural economy approach can refer to research on particular sectors of the economy (e.g film, music), particular modes of working (flexible, social), rethinking the economy as cultural, as well as the digitalisation of economies (Gibson & Kong, 2005).

A common thread linking cultural economy approaches is in seeing markets not as abstract, coherent entities, but rather as diverse, constantly evolving and 'overflowing' (Callon, 1998; Callon & Muniesa, 2007). In other words, cultural economy approaches take as their starting point an acceptance that markets are always changing, they are not static and robust, but rather fragile and contingent. Theories used within cultural economy studies are diverse, and include Foucault's governmentality, as well as Science and Technology Studies inspired accounts which also give attention to material things and objects (MacKenzie, 2008). The latter area of scholarship on the materiality of markets argues that non-human things – ranging from equations to computer software and perishable foods – are important influences in market design and operation. Such theories are not inherently sensitive to place (although with notable exceptions, see Hébert, 2014); instead the focus of material markets scholars is about how material things within markets act to stabilise the market across space. So, while there is recognition that markets are fragile in their geographical reach – they are prone to break down – the focus of analysis is about the holding together of single, uniform markets through stable material things, rather than their spatial differences (the operation of multiple markets). In the case of electricity meters, as explored below, there was an implicit assumption that the technology – the digital meter – could stabilise the new market in Australia and enable it to operate in the same way as in New Zealand.

Background to Australian and New Zealand electricity metering market cases

Before going into detail about the key findings of the electricity metering case study, a brief introduction is provided to electricity metering in New Zealand and Australia, including the timing of key initiatives, policy changes, and implementation approaches.

New Zealand

In New Zealand the digital metering programme commenced in 2009 and ran until 2013. It was a voluntary programme, so households and small businesses were not required to install a new digital meter. Rather, the emphasis was on the electricity retailers (who have responsibility for metering in New Zealand) making a persuasive case for new digital meters and encouraging uptake. The programme was seen as successful: more than three-quarters of New Zealand households and small businesses now have a digital meter, with a total of 1.3 million new digital meters installed since 2009 (NZ Parliamentary Commissioner for the Environment, 2013).

Retail competition was introduced in 1999 in New Zealand, so had been in place for ten years before the digital metering programme commenced. An objective of the digital metering programme was that the introduction of new digital meters would further increase retail competition in New Zealand, and this ambition appears to have been realised: many new retailers have entered the market (21 new retailers in the period 2011–16), and with new products based on digital meter capabilities and data. There are now just under forty retailers serving residential customers in New Zealand, indicating a high level of competition and customer choice.

Within the New Zealand context, the implementation of digital meters has taken a market-based approach – with relatively minimal government regulation and oversight. The main concern with the otherwise apparently successful

New Zealand digital metering programme is that only very simple or basic digital meters were installed, because of the light government regulation. There is concern that this may have been a significant lost opportunity for New Zealand, as for only a little extra cost, much higher specification digital meters could have been installed, with better functionality (Consumer NZ, 2015; NZ Parliamentary Commissioner for the Environment, 2013).

Australia

In Australia the original intention in the early to mid-2000s was to implement a mandatory metering programme across Australia's National Electricity Market (NEM). Note that the NEM covers most states in Australia, but not Western Australia or the Northern Territory. It was judged that a mandatory programme was a more efficient and cost-effective way of implementing digital meters (Department of Primary Industries, 2007; Essential Services Commission, 2004). In 2006 the State of Victoria, in south-eastern Australia, decided to proceed with a mandatory programme just within Victoria, called the Advanced Metering Infrastructure (AMI) Program. At the time a market-orientated method of implementing smart meters (as per the New Zealand model) was considered, but it was concluded that a market-based, customer-choice method of implementing digital meters was not as cost-effective or suitable as mandatory distributor-led implementation (see, for example, Ministerial Council on Energy, 2008; User Participation Working Group, 2004). The Victorian AMI programme officially commenced in 2009, and there was at the time the expectation that other NEM states would follow. It was the responsibility of the distribution and transmission utilities to implement the AMI Program (i.e. not the retailers, but the upstream 'poles and wires' utilities), although with strong initial direction and oversight by the Victorian state government. In the period 2009–13, some 2.3 million new digital meters were implemented across the State of Victoria, into 93 per cent of homes and small businesses (Victorian Auditor-General's Office, 2015).

However, despite the high implementation rate, the AMI Program had a lot of criticism. It was judged to be very expensive, and households and other key stakeholders (including the Victorian Auditor General's Office) raised significant concerns about the benefits (Victorian Auditor-General's Office, 2009, 2015; Victorian Energy Minister Michael O'Brien, 2011). Further, the state government was criticised for being too 'hands off' and allowing the utilities to escalate costs. Such was the level of criticism that other states in Australia began to say publicly that they did not wish to implement a mandatory metering programme like the Victorian AMI (Department of State Growth, 2015; Queensland Department of Energy and Water Supply, 2013). Consequently, in 2015 the Australian Energy Market Commission (AEMC) started a process of developing a new 'Competition in Metering' Rule Change – a voluntary, retailer-led programme.

The AEMC's new Competition in Metering Rule Change came into force in December 2017. As of December 2018 – a year later – a relatively modest 600,000 new digital meters had been installed across the NEM, including in 10 per cent of homes in the state of South Australia (Australian Energy Market Commission, 2018a, 2018b). Under the voluntary metering programme, electricity retailers have taken over responsibility for meters from the distribution network businesses. However, there are some provisions in the Competition in Metering Rule Change for mandatory installations in so-called 'new and replacement' cases where a new home or small business is created, or an old meter breaks down. In other words, the Australia market for electricity meters has been adapted a little from the New Zealand model, incorporating both voluntary and mandatory elements (see Chandrashekeran, Dufty & Gill, 2018 for further detail). There have been some problems with slow implementation of digital meters, and in early 2019 the AEMC introduced a new rule that electricity retailers must now provide new meters within a set time frame: 15 working days.

Key findings

In this section I explore what insights the New Zealand and Australian electricity metering cases provide about markets and their geographies, by exploring how and why the New Zealand metering programme came to be an example that Australia followed. The process of Australia examining the New Zealand market model and adopting it reveals much about how markets are conceptualised as abstract, and yet in practice are complex, place-based entities, and how tensions arise from this. Two empirical themes are briefly analysed, namely: the role of time *and* place; and why the New Zealand electricity metering market has not translated straightforwardly to Australia.

The role of time and place: explaining the appeal of the New Zealand case

Positive aspects of the New Zealand digital metering programme were circulating in policy forums around the same time as problems were emerging with the Victorian AMI Program. Thus, in very simple terms, there were two key factors at play here: time and space/place. With regard to timing, there was a metering policy crisis in Australia, with the original plan of having a mandatory metering programme across the NEM thrown into disarray by the upset in Victoria with the AMI Program not proceeding smoothly. The problems with the AMI Program were in large part attributed to its mandatory method of implementation. Another policy option had to be found quickly. Thus the New Zealand digital metering programme came to be celebrated and presented itself as a solution at the right time. As one interviewee clearly stated:

> New Zealand is largely seen as a positive example and Victoria as a negative one.
>
> (Australian State Government Manager, April 2015)

In other words, the existence of the New Zealand metering programme and early evidence of its success – using a different implementation mechanism (voluntary, retailer-led) – was an important influence on Australian smart metering policy at a particularly sensitive time when there was an active search for an alternative policy solution. Heavily influenced by the New Zealand metering market, a decision was made by the AEMC in 2015 to investigate a retailer-led voluntary metering programme across the rest of the NEM. There was particular attention to the mode of implementation of smart metering used in New Zealand: a voluntary market-led model, wherein customers had the choice of whether to accept a new meter or not, and with the electricity retailer as the organisation with responsibility for metering.

The empirical case fits with theories of policy mobility, introduced above, whereby there are always international policy flows (new knowledge, stories, learning) from elsewhere, with Australia positioned within international policy circuits in relation to digital metering (Lovell, 2016). When the Victorian AMI Program was found to not be proceeding well, the AEMC was already well-informed about New Zealand, having commissioned a study several years earlier on the New Zealand's smart metering programme (Murray & Black, 2008). This report gave some detail on the context for smart meters in New Zealand, including a comparison with the State of Victoria. The report noted that although there are general similarities between New Zealand and Victoria, for example in terms of population (1.9 million electricity customers in New Zealand and 2.4 million in Victoria) and electricity sector deregulation, there are notable differences in the organisational structure of the electricity sector with regard to meters. In New Zealand the retailers have had longstanding responsibility for, and experience with, electricity meters, whereas in Australia it is the distribution and transmission companies (the upstream network companies), who have until recently (December 2017) had responsibility for customer meters. The AEMC also maintained an ongoing interest in developments in New Zealand, for example through input at AEMC Public Forums (see, for example, Strata Energy Consulting, 2012) – a presentation in which the metering programme in New Zealand was cited as progressing well but with some concerns, for example around the metering technology guidelines being voluntary and the possibility of 'metering churn' (whereby if a customer switches retailer then a new meter is required). Individual state governments within Australia also researched metering in New Zealand, as one interviewee described:

> We went to New Zealand and had a look over there to see how they've done it there. That's been quite influential on the thinking here.
> (Interview, Manager, State government, April 2015)

This international review and 'horizon scanning' has also been actively occurring in New Zealand, notably including a detailed review of the Victorian AMI Program (Moore, 2015). This review was undertaken by an organisation called the New Zealand Smart Grid Forum – a public–private partnership of the New Zealand Ministry of Business, Innovation and Employment and the New Zealand

Electricity Networks Association (Moore, 2015). One of the rationales for the study was timing, in that:

> Both Jurisdictions have seen similar technology smart meters installed at the majority of electricity consumers' premises over broadly similar timeframes.
>
> (Moore, 2015, p. 4)

The New Zealand Smart Grid Forum report positions the Victorian AMI Program as a policy failure, stating that 'The Victoria Smart Meter Program has been widely reviewed and criticised' (Moore, 2015, p. 3) and noting further that '...the AEMC is working on rule changes to enable contestable metering service, partly as a result of the Victoria experience' (2015, p. 8). There are also insights from the Smart Grid Forum report about how learning about market function might be affected by differences in place:

> There are different ways to mandate and run a smart meter roll out; *some of the issues associated with the Victorian programme may not apply to other mandated programmes* but provide a useful comparison to the issues identified with market led investments in smart metering in New Zealand.
>
> (Moore, 2015, p. 12, emphasis added)

Thereby alluding to the unique confluence of place-specific issues associated with the AMI Program, which are seen as potentially separate – or able to be dissociated from – other mandated metering programmes. The author also notes the different place-based governance and organisational context in which the metering programs arose and were governed in New Zealand and Victoria:

> In New Zealand, the switch to smart meters was largely driven by electricity retailers seeking cost or service advantages and customers could opt out. In comparison, the smart meter roll out in Victoria was mandated by the state government.
>
> (Moore, 2015, p. 2)

In summary, when problems came to the fore in Victoria in the early 2010s, and a solution to the policy crisis provoked by the AMI Program failure needed to be found by the AEMC and other key stakeholders, there was an obvious allure of a policy approach that had been tested elsewhere and already 'packaged', namely the New Zealand example. Further, New Zealand had policy appeal because it was a clear change in direction for Australia: from a mandatory to a voluntary programme, from electricity network utility responsibility to electricity retailer, and from a state-led to a market-based programme. However, emerging evidence since the New Zealand model was implemented in Australia suggests that at least some of the initial optimism around this market model was misplaced.

Why the New Zealand electricity metering market has not translated straightforwardly to Australia

Close attention to the role of place in markets helps provide an explanation for why the New Zealand electricity metering market has not translated straightfor-wardly to Australia. It was anticipated that the New Zealand market could be moved unproblematically to Australia, i.e. it could be kept stable. However, evi-dence emerging in Australia since the AEMC metering contestability rule change in December 2017 suggests this is not the case.

First, there is the relatively modest overall rate of new digital meter installations, of just under 600,000 (as of December 2018), over a 12-month period, which represents only around 7% of the estimated total of 9 million NEM customers (Australian Energy Market Commission, 2018b). Note that there has been little data published about metering installation rates, and at the time of writing the 2018 installation numbers are the most recent ones released by the AEMC. This absence of data on the new electricity metering market has been criticised:

> There is no published framework for monitoring and evaluation of the market-led model within the AEMC. There is a lack of easily accessible aggregated data about the number of households that have received smart meters, their location and household characteristics. This makes it difficult for independent third parties to monitor the progress of the contestable metering approach.
>
> (Chandrashekeran *et al.*, 2018, p. 42)

Second, there has been criticism of the process for installing new digital meters, in particular an issue of long delays for households in waiting for a new meter. For example, in the State of NSW in December 2017 the average wait time was 60 to 72 business days (Independent Pricing and Regulatory Tribunal, 2018, p. 4). The main reason for the delays appears to stem from the transfer of metering responsibilities from the network utilities to the retailers, which hap-pened concurrently with the introduction of the New Zealand market-based model. It was subsequently realised that there were a host of tasks often asso-ciated with meter installation that the retailer was not licensed to complete, because they fall within the remit of the upstream network utility. As the NSW Independent Pricing and Regulatory Tribunal explains:

> While Metering Providers can install meters in most straightforward cases, they are restricted, through various regulations, from carrying out asso-ciated works in more complex cases. These include where there are service protection devices that require specialist equipment, live isolation, ripple load control devices or customers on a shared fuse. It is not always possible for the Metering Coordinator or Metering Provider* to determine whe-ther a case will be simple or complex before the site visit.
>
> (2018, p. 7)* now part of the electricity retailer

Thus the New Zealand market has met with a different context in Australia, in particular the lack of prior experience of retailers with metering. The ambition was that the digital meter — the technology — would do the work of stabilising the market and enable new organisational relations to be enacted in Australia, but a number of problems have emerged. The AEMC has acted to try to rectify the situation by putting in place a new 'Metering installation timeframes' rule change (from 6 December 2018), which requires retailers to provide small customers with new or replacement electricity meters within set timeframes (15 business days), or face penalties (Australian Energy Market Commission, 2019).

Further, it is also the case that the New Zealand approach to digital metering installation has not been straightforwardly transferred to Australia without changes and modifications being introduced. In Australia there are some subtle but important differences in how the retailer-led voluntary metering scheme has been implemented. From the Australian customers' point of view there are in fact three routes by which a digital meter can be installed: first, either by requesting one from the retailer or, second, by being offered one as part of a retailer implementation programme, and, third, a mandatory installation if the customer's meter fails or otherwise needs replacement (Chandrashekeran *et al.*, 2018). So, it has not been a wholesale transfer of the New Zealand model to Australia, but rather changes have been introduced as the digital metering policy has travelled from place to place. This is in keeping with findings from policy mobilities scholarship regarding the mutation of policies and initiatives, wherein:

> Policies, models, and ideas are not moved around like gifts at a birthday party or like jars on shelves, where the mobilization does not change the character and content of the mobilized objects.
>
> (McCann, 2011, p. 111)

In effect the transfer of markets (and policies) from place to place is never straightforward, because of place-based differences in people, objects, materials, institutions, regulations and governance structures that manifest in dynamic networks at specific locations.

Summary and Conclusion

This chapter has examined how markets move from place to place through investigating the case of digital metering, and how a particular market-based method of implementing new digital meters was adopted in Australia, having been implemented previously in New Zealand. Ideas from scholarship on policy mobilities and cultural economy have been used to explore the case. Key insights from the case include, first, the importance of timing as well as place, as there was a key moment of policy change in relation to digital metering in Australia which made the New Zealand market-based model attractive; and, second, the inherent difficulties of moving markets as the market object, in this case the electricity meter, was expected to do the work of enacting organisational changes, including in Australia shifting responsibility for meters from the network utility to the retailer. Here in conclusion I discuss each of these findings in more detail and with close reference to policy mobilities and cultural economies scholarship.

First, with regard to timing, as discussed above there was a rush to find a policy solution for metering in Australia and in the process some of the place-based particularities of the New Zealand metering market were overlooked, e.g. the passage of time since privatisation, and how retailers have had longstanding responsibility for meters, prior to the voluntary market being introduced. There was a willingness to overlook the details of the New Zealand market because it had already been discursively positioned in Australia as a successful market that was able to be transferred to Australia. The policy mobilities literature is helpful here because of its attentiveness to the mobilities of policies, differences between places and also the politics of the policy process (Lovell, 2019; Peck & Theodore, 2010; Prince, 2012; Wood, 2015). A cultural economy approach is less focused on the policy process and issues of change, so is in this instance less instructive. But both areas of scholarship have a blind spot with regard to timing issues; for example, they have little to say about what gets left out of market or policy transfer decisions when decisions are made in a hurry.

Second, with regard to the translation of markets from one place to another, in the New Zealand and Australian digital metering cases explored here the expectation was, on the part of the key actors involved, that the market would translate straightforwardly from one place to another. Furthermore, it was assumed that through the technology (the electricity meter) that new organisational arrangements would thrive and grow. However, too much expectation was placed on the digital meter to do this complex organisational work. There is a different organisational policy and regulatory context in Australia compared with New Zealand, and some of the more subtle differences were overlooked, e.g. tacit knowledge and organisational cultures. Cultural economy approaches are instructive here in showing us how markets are inherently cultural entities, and that their cultural aspects are often oversimplified and misunderstood (Hébert, 2014), as one interviewee described:

> Electricity network regulation is an inherently domestic issue…obviously, it's electrons going through copper wires and that's the same everywhere - and much of the technology is the same - but the regulatory ownership arrangements and the history of those and the political economy of those varies dramatically from country to country. Regulatory philosophy varies….
>
> (Interview, Australian Federal Government, June 2015)

Furthermore, cultural economies scholarship shows us how material things and objects such as electricity meters are important influences in market design and operation. However, several empirical cases also reveal how these objects often do not perform as intended – they break down and are misunderstood by users (Callon, 1986). In this case of electricity metering, there was an implicit underlying assumption that the digital meter could stabilise the new market (and its new relations in Australia) and allow it to operate in the same way as in New Zealand. This was shown not to be the case, and we see instead the fragility of markets as they move.

References

Accenture. (2016). *Realizing the full potential of smart metering*. Retrieved from www.accent ure.com/t20160413T230144__w__/us-en/_acnmedia/Accenture/Conversion-Assets/ DotCom/Documents/Global/PDF/Industries_9/Accenture-Smart-Metering-Report-Digitally-Enabled-Grid.pdf.

Australian Energy Market Commission. (2018a). *Industry workshop to help consumers upgrade to smart meters* [Media release]. Retrieved from https://www.aemc.gov.au/news-centre/media-releases/industry-workshop-help-consumers-upgrade-smart-meters.

Australian Energy Market Commission. (2018b). *Smart meter installations across the national electricity market update*. [Media release]. Retrieved from www.aemc.gov.au/news-centre/media-releases/smart-meter-installations-across-national-electricity-market-update.

Australian Energy Market Commission. (2019). *Metering installation timeframes Rule Change - 6th Dec 2018*. Retrieved from www.aemc.gov.au/rule-changes/metering-installation-timeframes.

Bunnell, T.G. & Coe, N.M. (2001). Spaces and scales of innovation. *Progress in Human Geography*, 25(4), 569–589.

Callon, M. (1986). Some elements in a sociology of translation: Domestication of the scallops and fishermen of St. Brieuc Bay. In J. Law (Ed.), *Power, action, belief*, (pp. 196–233). London: Routledge and Kegan Paul.

Callon, M. (1998). An essay on framing and overflowing: Economic externalities revisted by sociology. In M. Callon (Ed.), *The laws of the markets* (pp. 244–269). Oxford: Blackwell.

Callon, M. & Muniesa, F. (2007). Economic experiments and the construction of markets. In D. MacKenzie, F. Muniesa & L. Siu (Eds.), *Do economists make markets? On the performativity of economics* (pp. 163–189). Princeton, NJ: Princeton University Press.

Chandrashekeran, S., Dufty, G. & Gill, M. (2018). *Smart-er metering policy: getting the framework right for a consumer-focused smart meter rollout*. Melbourne: University of Melbourne.

Consumer NZ. (2015, August 14). *Smart meters: Have we missed a golden opportunity to make our electricity network really smart?* Retrieved from https://www.consumer.org.nz/articles/smart-meters.

Deloitte. (2011). *Advanced metering infrastructure cost benefit analysis*. Canberra, ACT: Department of Treasury and Finance.

Department of State Growth. (2015). *Tasmanian energy strategy: Restoring Tasmania's energy advantage*. Retrieved from www.stategrowth.tas.gov.au/__data/assets/pdf_file/0017/100637/Tasmanian_Energy_Strategy_Restoring_Tasmanias_Energy_Advantage.pdf.

Department of Primary Industries. (2007). *Victorian government rule change proposal - Advanced metering infrastructure Rollout*. Melbourne: Department of Primary Industries.

Dolowitz, D.P. & Marsh, D. (2000). Learning from abroad: the role of policy transfer in contemporary policy making. *Governance*, 13(1), 5–24.

Essential Services Commission. (2004). *Mandatory rollout of interval meters for electricity customers*. Melbourne: Essential Services Commission.

Geddie, K. (2015). Policy mobilities in the race for talent: competitive state strategies in international student mobility. *Transactions of the Institute of British Geographers* 40, 235–248.

Gibson, C. & Kong, L. (2005). Cultural economy: a critical review. *Progress in Human Geography*, 29(5), 2005.

Hébert, K. (2014). The matter of market devices: Economic transformation in a southwest Alaskan salmon fishery. *Geoforum*, 53, 21–30.

Independent Pricing and Regulatory Tribunal. (2018). *Retailers' metering practices in NSW.*

Lovell, H. (2016). The role of international policy transfer within the Multiple Streams Approach: the case of smart electricity metering in Australia. *Public Administration*, 94(3), 754–768.

Lovell, H. (2019). Policy failure mobilities. *Progress in Human Geography*. 43(1), 46–63.

MacKenzie, D. (2008). *Material markets: How economic agents are constructed.* Oxford: Oxford University Press.

McCann, E. (2011). Urban policy mobilities and global circuits of knowledge: toward a research agenda. *Annals of the Association of American Geographers*, 101(1), 107–130.

Ministerial Council on Energy. 2008. *Smart Meter Decision Paper - MCE 13 June 2008: Ministerial Council on Energy (MCE).* Retrieved from: www.efa.com.au/Library/MCESmartMeterDecisionPaper.pdf.

Moore, K. (2015). *Overview of the Victorian Smart Meter program – a mandated smart meter roll-out.* New Zealand Smart Grid Forum.

Murray, K. & Black, M. (2008). *Developments in the New Zealand market for advanced metering infrastructure and related services.* Report for the Australian Energy Market Commission, Sydney. Retrieved from www.aemc.gov.au/Media/docs/LECG%20Report%20On%20Developments%20In%20The%20New%20Zealand%20Market%20For%20Advanced%20Metering%20Infrastructure%20And%20Related%20Services%20-%2016%20July%202008-423f769e-117f-42fa-8956-08d21846d35d-0.pdf.

NZ Parliamentary Commissioner for the Environment. (2013). *Smart electricity meters: How households and the environment can benefit.* Retrieved from www.pce.parliament.nz/media/1230/pce-smart-meters-update-web.pdf.

Peck, J. & Theodore, N. (2010). Mobilizing policy: Models, methods, and mutations. *Geoforum*, 41(2), 169–174.

Peck, J. & Theodore, N. (2015). *Fast Policy: Experimental Statecraft at the Thresholds of Neoliberalism.* Minneapolis, MN: The University of Minnesota Press.

Pow, C.P. (2014). License to travel: policy assemblage and the 'Singapore model'. *City*, 18(3), 287–306.

Prince, R. (2012). Policy transfer, consultants and the geographies of governance. *Progress in Human Geography*, 36(2), 188–203.

Prince, R. (2014). Consultants and the global assemblage of culture and creativity. *Transactions of the Institute of British Geographers*, 39(1), 90–101.

Queensland Department of Energy and Water Supply. (2013). *The 30-year electricity strategy. Discussion paper – Powering Queensland's future.* Brisbane, Queensland Government – Department of Energy and Water Supply. Retrieved from www.dews.qld.gov.au/__data/assets/pdf_file/0005/187673/Final-paper-and-supporting-material-combined.pdf.

Robertson, D.B. (1991). Political conflict and lesson-drawing. *Journal of Public Policy*, 11(01), 55–78.

Strata Energy Consulting. (2012). *NZ metering arrangements – lessons for Australia?* [AEMC Public Forum presentation], Melbourne, 3 October. Retrieved from www.aemc.gov.au/getattachment/760a0c35-a460-404d-9f56-dc43c7e36b1a/Strata-Energy-Consulting.aspx.

User Participation Working Group. 2004. *Improving User Participation in the Australian Energy Market - Discussion Paper: User Participation Working Group – Ministerial Council* on *Energy Standing Committee of Officials*. Retrieved from www.efa.com.au/Library/MinCouncilonEnergyDiscPaperonUserParticipation.pdf.

Victorian Auditor-General's Office. (2009). *Towards a 'smart grid' – the roll-out of Advanced Metering Infrastructure*. Melbourne: Victorian Auditor-General's Office.

Victorian Auditor-General's Office. (2015). *Realising the benefits of smart meters*. Melbourne: Victorian Auditor-General's Office.

Victorian Minister of Energy, Michael O'Brien. (2011). *Smart meters here to stay despite cost blow-out*. Retrieved from www.abc.net.au/news/2011-12-14/smart-meter-roll-out-continues-despite-cost-blow-out/3730522.

Ward, K. (2006). 'Policies in motion', urban management and state restructuring: The trans-local expansion of business improvement districts. *International Journal of Urban and Regional Research*, 30(1), 54–75.

Wood, A. (2015). The politics of policy circulation: Unpacking the relationship between South African and South American cities in the adoption of bus rapid transit. *Antipode*, 47(4), 1062–1079.

10 Fields of dreams
Calculative practices and the New Zealand housing market

Laurence Murphy

SCHOOL OF ENVIRONMENT, UNIVERSITY OF AUCKLAND

Introduction

Houses and homes, although distinct, are inextricably linked. Houses are constructed from a hybrid of material and social practices, which affect a range of social and ontological/psychological outcomes (Smith, 2008; Cook, Davison & Crabtree, 2016). In housing systems dominated by home ownership and mortgage debt, housing has assumed a paradoxical role as both a commodity to be consumed and a financial investment (Smith, 2015). Within 'residential capitalism', the home is increasingly viewed as a financial asset that is assumed to generate wealth. Mortgage deregulation and financial innovation has transformed the home into a fungible asset (Smith, 2008) and resulted in the emergence of the 'investor figure'; someone too cautious to invest in the share market but wise enough to invest in property (Smith, 2015). In the context of economic austerity and social welfare reform, homeownership is politically, if problematically, constructed as a form of asset-based welfare and a potential pension (Murphy and Rehm, 2016). In addition, social rented housing has increasingly been subject to marketisation processes that have exposed tenants to market logics (Christophers, 2013; Clapham, 2018, 2019; Murphy, 2020a) and resulted in the poor being repackaged to make profits for a variety of property interests (Blessing, 2016). Significantly, housing has not only been shaped by financialisation, it is according to Aalbers (2016, 2017) an 'object of financialisation'. Thus, despite its mundane ubiquity, the humble house is a complex site of socio-material and financial entanglements. In addition, and significantly, housing is immobile and embedded in specific places and localities.

In contrast to this notion of housing as a site of complex socio-material entanglements, popular media and policy discourses represent housing in a more unambiguous fashion. Housing is predominately envisaged as a commodity that is made available via a 'thing' called the 'housing market'. The 'housing market' is normalised in everyday newspaper accounts of market trends, popular television programmes centred on buying or flipping houses, and governmental reports on housing market processes. It is difficult to conceive of a conversation about housing affordability or housing access that does not involve discussing the housing market. Significantly, much housing research has taken housing markets as given and proceeds to examine how house prices are formulated (Murphy, 2020b).

DOI: 10.4324/9780429296260-10

The housing market is not only normalised it is also externalised, viewed as an external constraint operating upon property actors such as housing developers, landowners, and mortgage agents. Indeed, these actors often defer to the power of the market in constraining their agency. Moreover, in much policy discourse the housing market is imagined as the outcome of a simplified (neo-classical economics) supply and demand model. Consequently, the housing market's failings (e.g. the rising housing affordability crisis) are not interpreted as a problem of market practices but of the constraints imposed on the market by the planning system (Austin, Gurran & Whitehead, 2014; Gurran, Austin & Whitehead, 2014). This discourse maintains that, left to its own devices, the housing market will reach an equilibrium price where demand equals supply.

While many Western housing markets share common overarching processes (e.g. mortgage deregulation, state support of homeownership) and even common tenure nomenclature (homeownership and social rented housing) (Smith, 2015), these markets are inherently place based. Housing markets consist of nationally constituted regulatory processes, construction traditions, labour practices and culturally inflected demand processes. Notwithstanding common discourses and shared ideologies, housing tenures are assembled via distinct locally embedded networks of actors and practices. Production, exchange, and consumption actors are entangled in myriad everyday taken-for-granted practices that in their totality reproduce local and national housing markets. In contrast to 24-hour global trading rooms, housing is fundamentally connected to land and land is immobile. Housing markets are emplaced.

Drawing on the work of Michel Callon (1998) and others, increasingly the notion of an externalised housing market has been subject to critique. This critique centres on the manner in which markets are made and operate as 'calculative devices' designed to produce market prices. This work highlights the ways in which socio-technical arrangements of human and non-human actants interact in discrete assemblage/agencement and how markets are performed (Smith, Munro & Christie, 2006; Murphy, 2020b). Increasingly attention has been given to research designed to examine "the beliefs and practices drawn into market-making" (Smith *et al.*, 2006, p. 82). This chapter examines two state-sponsored attempts to reconfigure the New Zealand housing market. These experiments in market-making centre on attempts to provide affordable housing (via the creation of special housing areas) and to expand the community housing sector (via the transfer of social rental housing stock). Both experiments involved an explicit attempt to operationalise an idealised and simplified economic model of the housing market and involved the application of new, if flawed, calculative practices. It shall be argued the relative failure of these experiments is reflective of the power of a 'locked-in' set of calculative practices (Lovell and Smith, 2010) that characterise housing markets (agencements) in the wild.

Performing housing markets

Smith et al. (2006) argue that housing economists have predominantly adopted an essentialist perspective concerning markets. Within this perspective markets are taken as given and research attention is focused on modelling price dynamics. Placing emphasis on market efficiency and the presumption that buyers and sellers are rational, attention is focused on the ways in which fundamental economic variables affect house prices. While it is acknowledged that markets are composed of various agents, rules and practices, these elements of markets are rendered invisible as attention is directed to understanding the role of 'market fundamentals' in driving market processes. More recently, drawing upon the work of Michel Callon and colleagues, geographers and housing researchers have increasingly shifted attention toward understanding the manner in which housing markets are made and performed (Smith et al, 2006; Christophers, 2014a, 2014b; Murphy, 2020b).

This emerging interest in housing 'market-making' mobilises the notion of markets as 'socio-technical arrangements or assemblages (agencement)' (Çalışkan and Callon, 2010, p3) to explore how particular socio-technical arrangements condition the operation of housing markets in different places. Agencements are socially and materially constructed assemblages, involving combinations of 'human beings (bodies) as well as material, technical and textual devices" (Çalışkan and Callon, 2010, p. 9) that have agency. Moreover, within this framework markets are viewed as collective calculative devices (Muniesa, Millo & Callon, 2007) employing various calculative tools and algorithms that "impose prices that these tools make it possible to calculate" (Çalışkan and Callon, 2010, p. 17). Significantly, the calculative tools and their outputs are not mere inputs into human decision making processes rather, these devices "... do things ... they act or make others act" (Muniesa *et al.*, 2007, p. 2).

Within the housing literature attention has been focused on the manner in which certain calculative practices become 'locked-in' and the ways in which calculative practices are inherently performative. Lovell and Smith (2010) examine the manner in which embedded calculative practices act to inhibit innovation in the British construction sector. Following Callon (1998), they maintain that the process of 'lock-in' is beneficial as it makes markets legible for actors. But once established, these accepted practices can act as a barrier to change. In particular, Lovell and Smith (2010) demonstrate how 'locked-in' financial calculative practices have been mobilised to support existing masonry construction methods over innovative prefabrication methods. Moreover, they maintain that "struggles over the assemblage and agencement of housing construction markets are the critical issues underpinning British resistance to prefabrication" (Lovell and Smith, 2010, p. 457). For Christophers (2014a), the calculative practices of valuers, housing financiers and consultants are inherently performative as these calculations "contribute to the reality that [they] describe" (Callon, 2007, p. 316). Examining how a particular private consultancy's development feasibility model has been incorporated into the English planning system, he argues that this calculative practice has effectively embedded developer profit in the not-for-profit affordable housing sector.

Moving beyond its role in the English planning system, the role of development feasibility analysis has been positioned as central in understanding the practices of developers in residential housing markets (Murphy, 2020b). Development feasibility analysis or residual land valuation (Atherton, French & Gabrielli, 2008; Havard, 2014) is a standard calculative practice operationalised internationally to calculate the expected profitability of a development and the value of land for the developer. Viewed within valuation theory and practice as a mechanism for estimating 'real' market prices (Mooya, 2016), development feasibility analysis is effectively a tool for producing market prices. It is a key 'valorimeter' (Çalışkan and Callon, 2010).

Development feasibility analysis, at its simplest, involves the calculation of either the residual value of the land or the profit of a proposed development (Atherton *et al.*, 2008; Havard, 2014; Henneberry, 2016). Residual land value is calculated by subtracting the developer's required profit (usually expressed as a percentage of either the gross development value (GDV) of the development or the total cost of development), plus the cost of development (including all finance costs) from the expected GDV. The residual is the amount that the developer should pay for the land in order to secure the required profit from a proposed development. Developer feasibility analysis is a key calculation and is required to secure development finance. In practice developers would use a discounted cash flow methodology (Henneberry, 2016; Wyatt, 2013), which takes account of the time value of money, to calculate a residual valuation and it is regarded as best practice to include scenario testing to take account of possible changes in interest rates and costs (Atherton *et al.*, 2008).

Development feasibility analysis is inherently performative (Ryan-Collins, Lloyd & MacFarlane, 2017; Murphy, 2020b). In contrast to the prevalent notion that developers are passively responding to externally generated market forces, the operationalisation of development feasibility has the effect of creating prices that need to be realised. Moreover, these calculations have site specific and sector wide implications.

At the level of the individual site, the assumptions and estimates employed in the developer's calculations need to be actualised. Recent analysis of large scale residential developments in the South East of England found that the rate of housing construction is "... organised around the expected 'absorption rate' for the kind of homes being sold by the house builder at *the price baked into the land value* [emphasis added]" (Letwin, 2018a, p. 14). In effect, house builders release or supply houses at a rate that accords with their development feasibility calculations set at the time they purchase the land and not in response to changing housing demand and supply interactions. Moreover, at the level of the sector, the application of residual valuation techniques ensures that development sites are secured by developers that generate the highest residual value. Thus when house prices are booming, it is argued that the "developer that makes the most bullish expectations of sale prices, and/or projects the lowest costs, will typically be able to offer the landowner the most and secure the site" (Ryan-Collins *et al.*, 2017, p. 98). In effect, rising house prices are translated into rising land values and successful developers are channelled into developing premium priced housing. Across the industry, during boom conditions the operation of residual valuation calculations is inimical to the production of affordable housing (Murphy, 2020b). In effect, left to its own devices, the housing market does not necessarily produce affordable new housing.

Notwithstanding the insights afforded by this literature, housing policy practice has been shaped by a pervading belief in a simplified economic model of housing demand and supply dynamics. Drawing on research that has challenged the value of urban growth boundaries (Bramley, 2013; Cheshire, 2008) and that argues that these boundaries result in house price increases, policymakers in the United Kingdom, Australia and New Zealand have emphasised the need to release housing supply to address housing affordability issues (Austin *et al.*, 2014; Gurran *et al.*, 2014). Within this policy construction, urban planning is viewed as a constraint on market process and policymakers often assume that minimising planning constraints will release housing supply and that an increase in housing supply will lead to a fall in house prices (Murphy, 2014, 2016). However, these policy prescriptions do not take account of the socio-technical processes shaping housing production. Developers will not supply housing at a rate that jeopardises the prices they need to realise their development feasibility models. To do so would result in bankruptcy.

At a broad level there is a striking incongruence between what is imagined as the operation of the housing market in policy discourses and the day-to-day practices of residential developers. In order to explore the consequences of this incongruence this paper will examine the nature and problems of housing policy introduced in New Zealand.

The New Zealand Housing Market and Housing Crisis

Arguably the New Zealand dream has revolved around the suburban notion of the 'quarter acre pavlova paradise' (Mitchell, 1972; Murphy, Friesen & Kearns, 1999). Strongly favoured by housing policy, homeownership has dominated the housing system. Homeownership rates peaked at 73 per cent in 1991; by 2013 the proportion of households that were homeowners had declined to a 60-year low of 65 per cent (Johnson, Howden-Chapman & Eaqub, 2018). Significantly, since the 1990s the rental sector has experienced considerable growth; approximately 33 per cent of households are currently renters (Johnson *et al.*, 2018) compared to only 23% in 1991 (Morrison, 2008). Social rented housing occupies a residual role in the housing system accounting for just 3.4 per cent of the housing stock (Johnson *et al.*, 2018). In 2017 the central government was the main supplier of social housing units (62,900), while local authorities (7,700 units) and community housing (12,700 units) made up the rest of the sector (Johnston *et al.*, 2018).

Given the dominant position of homeownership within the New Zealand housing system considerable media and political attention is focused on house price dynamics, issues of housing affordability and new housing supply. Since the early 2000s house prices have risen rapidly (Murphy, 2017). From 2002 until 2008 (the period up to the global financial crisis, GFC), house prices increased by 80 per cent (Murphy, 2011). In contrast to the situation in other countries, the impacts of the GFC were rather mild and short-lived. In particular, Auckland experienced a significant post-GFC boom. By 2014 average house prices in Auckland were 33 per cent above the pre-GFC crisis peak and were 51 per cent above the national average house price (Murphy, 2017). As house prices rose, housing affordability problems became more pronounced. In particular, considerable media attention was directed toward the plight of first-time homeowners and the rise of 'generation rent'. Significantly, while the GFC had little impact on house prices in Auckland it adversely affected housing production. New housing supply slumped to historically low levels (Johnson *et al.*, 2018) and by 2009 the number of housing consents declined by 54 per cent of the pre-GFC peak (Murphy, 2011).

Within the context of an emerging discourse of a housing affordability crisis, the New Zealand Productivity Commission (2012) released the findings of its 'Housing Affordability Inquiry'. While recognising the importance of mortgage markets and demand issues, the Productivity Commission placed considerable emphasis on the price effects of constrained housing supply. In particular, it argued that policies of urban containment, such as the use of a Metropolitan Urban Limit in Auckland, adversely affected housing supply and house prices. The Productivity Commission's analysis aligned with the then National government's interpretation of the housing crisis. Specifically, the housing crisis was seen as a crisis of supply and the slump in new housing supply was attributed to actions of an overly restrictive planning system. The then Deputy Prime Minister, Bill English, announced: "'What's stacked against first home buyers are planning laws that are explicitly designed to drive up house prices" (National Business Review, 2013).

The government's position on the origins of the housing crisis and its policy prescriptions for addressing the crisis illustrate the importance of understanding market-making processes and the role of calculative practices. In effect, the government's position was framed by an understanding of the market in terms of a simplified model of supply and demand. The crisis in new housing supply was not interpreted as a problem embedded in a particular 'socio-technical arrangement' of practices but in the external constraints of planners. The market was seen as the solution, not the problem. Consequently, the state turned to the market, or market-making processes, to address housing issues. In particular it embarked on legislative reforms designed to liberate the housing market.

Market-making and the New Zealand housing market

In order to examine issues concerning markets and place, this section examines two market-making experiments operationalised in New Zealand. The first centres on the government's attempts to promote the supply of new housing in the hope that an increased housing supply would reduce house prices, especially in Auckland. The second example considers the government's attempts to grow the community housing sector using large scale stock transfers. The relevant details of each experiment are presented first and then the implications of these experiments are discussed.

Unleashing housing supply?

In the wake of the GFC, the National Party government viewed a buoyant housing market as a measure of its successful management of a 'rock star' economy (Rotherham, 2015). In contrast to other nations New Zealand had escaped a prolonged housing crisis (Murphy, 2011). However, while buoyant house prices favoured existing homeowners and housing investors they also fuelled growing concerns regarding housing affordability; especially in Auckland, the country's largest and most expensive housing market. While ideologically predisposed to non-interventionist rhetoric, by 2013 the government faced increased public pressure to intervene in the housing market.

Three interrelated processes intersected to shape the government's housing policy at this time. First, a powerful discourse of a housing crisis emerged that was strongly aligned to the housing affordability analysis of a private international consultancy, Demographia (Murphy, 2014). Employing a simple but problematic measure of housing affordability, an average income to house price ratio, Demograhia positioned Auckland as one of the most expensive housing markets in the world. In addition, Demographia attributed Auckland's housing crisis to an overly restrictive planning system and in particular policies of urban containment. Significantly, leading members of the National Party agreed with Demographia's analysis and wrote introductions to its annual reports (Murphy, 2014). Second, the New Zealand Productivity Commission released its report in 2012 that specifically argued that urban containment policies were responsible for house price increases (Murphy, 2016). Third, the newly created Auckland Council was in the process of creating an urban plan that was designed to determine the future direction of urban development (Lewis and Murphy, 2015) and it was expected that the council would continue to pursue policies of urban containment (Murphy, 2014, 2016). Faced with the possibility of an enduring housing affordability crisis, the government felt compelled to act.

In 2013 the government announced a Housing Accord with the Auckland Council. The accord was designed to fast-track the residential planning consent process and release the production of 39,000 new houses (Murphy, 2014). To give effect to the accord the Housing Accords and Special Housing Areas Act 2013 (HASHAA) was passed. The HASHAAs primary objective was to address housing affordability by increasing the supply of land for residential development. Constructing the market as the solution to housing affordability, the HASHAA was deemed by the government as an appropriate vehicle to release housing production. In addition, the HASHAA was designed to curtail the power of local government in the housing market and to enhance central government's role in the residential consenting process (Murphy, 2016). In parliament, the Minister of Housing stated:

> We have got a constipated planning system bogging new residential construction, and this bill is a laxative to get new houses flowing … It makes plain that the Government's strong preference is to get this work done in partnership with councils, through housing accords, but it also provides that the Government can get on with the job if councils stand in the way of delivering an increased supply of affordable housing.
>
> (New Zealand Parliament Debates, 2013)

The HASHAA created the conditions for Local Authorities to fast-track the residential development consenting process by reducing public engagement in the planning process in designated areas. However, the Act did not mandate the production of affordable housing. Instead, it allowed for Local Authorities to require developers located in Special Housing Areas to supply up to 10 per cent of housing as affordable housing. Significantly, affordable housing was defined in terms of the market price in a locality and not in relation to household incomes. The affordable price was set at 75 per cent of the market average price of the preceding September (Murphy, 2017).

While the HASHAA was applied nationally, of the 213 Special Housing Areas (SHA) that were designated, 154 were located in Auckland (James, 2017). In effect, this legislation centred on addressing the Auckland housing crisis. In the three years that the SHAs were in effect in Auckland a total of 37,358 residential sections and dwellings were consented or 96 per cent of the government's target. In addition, the SHAs are expected to yield an additional 62,535 dwellings or sections in the next 20 years (Murphy, 2017). Reflective of the government's desire to address the perceived problem of urban containment, 68 per cent of the total future housing yield of SHAs is on greenfield sites and the SHAs resulted in an additional 1,660 hectares of Auckland's urban periphery being zoned residential (Murphy, 2017).

While the SHAs added to the number of dwellings and sections being consented, it is questionable if they contributed to a significant increase in housing supply or the provision of more affordable housing. In the three-year period to 2016, despite a considerable increase in the number of housing consents being issued, only 1,673 dwellings were completed in the Auckland SHAs (Murphy, 2017). In contrast to the simplified idea that, once released from the burden of planning regulations, development would respond rapidly to market demand, housing construction has been rather modest. In effect developers are performing in line with a set of calculative practices that have 'baked-in' high land valuations and house prices (cf. Letwin, 2018a, 2018b). Indeed, to actualise their development feasibility models developers need to restrict the rate at which they supply housing to the market (Murphy, 2020b).

In terms of the housing being supplied within the SHAs, considerable emphasis has been placed on producing premium priced houses. A 2017 analysis of house prices in Hobsonville, a flagship government supported development on the periphery of Auckland (20km from the CBD), indicated that three-bedroom detached houses were selling for between NZ$825,000 and NZ$950,000, and four-bedroom houses had advertised prices of NZ$1,349,000 to NZ$1,450,000 (Murphy, 2017). These prices were clearly aligned with above average prices in the metropolitan area and were not discounted as a consequence of being located within an SHA on the urban periphery.

The HASHAAs' direct attempt to provide 10 per cent of affordable housing was hampered by the manner in which affordable housing was defined. The legislation anchored the definition of affordable housing to the moving average market price. Consequently, as market prices rose, so too did the price of affordable housing. At the beginning of the accord period an affordable dwelling in Auckland was priced at NZ$386,250 but by September 2016, as the median house price in Auckland increased to NZ$825,000, the 'affordable house' price increased to NZ$618,750 (Murphy, 2017). This represented a 60 per cent increase in the price of so-called affordable units under the legislation.

Stock transfers to the community housing sector

At the same time that the government was attempting to reconfigure housing supply it also embarked on a social housing reform programme (SHRP). Building on the report of the Housing Shareholders' Advisory Group (HSAG, 2010), which advocated for a range of providers in the social housing sector, the government mapped out an ambitious programme of structural reform in the social rented housing sector. In 2013 the Social Housing Reforms (Housing Restructuring and Tenancy Matters Amendment) Act (SHRA) was passed. Key elements of the reforms included: the introduction of reviewable tenancies in the state housing sector, the extension of Income Related Rent Subsidies (IRRS) to community housing providers (CHP); and, stock transfers from the government's social housing provider Housing New Zealand (HNZ) to the community housing sector (Murphy, 2020a).

The SHRP had wide ranging impacts that fundamentally altered social tenants' security of tenure and shifted the administration of housing allocation from HNZ to the Ministry of Social Development. Underpinning the reform programme was a desire to establish a housing continuum which households were assumed to move across in response to their housing needs. The broad range of policies changes and their effects are examined elsewhere (Murphy, 2020a); this section focuses on examining the ways in which the government sought to establish a community housing sector that would be attractive to private investors.

Social housing providers around the world have increasingly been subjected to marketisation reforms that have resulted in them assuming increasingly hybrid market/non-market characteristics (Christophers, 2013; Jacobs & Manzi, 2019; Manzi & Morrison, 2018; Morrison, 2017). In the context of economic austerity and welfare retrenchment, CHPs have had to attract private funding. In New Zealand the small scale nature of the CHPs, combined with their focus on servicing households on below average incomes, made them unattractive for private investors. In reconfiguring the CHP sector the New Zealand Government focused on enhancing the sector's rental stream and asset base.

As part of the SHRP, the government extended the IRRS to CHPs. Under this new system the Ministry of Social Development publishes the number of IRRS that it is willing to fund and CHPs can apply for this funding. Successful CHPs are required to house tenants selected by the Ministry and can charge these tenants an income-related rent. In addition to this rent, the CHPs will receive an IRRS that will raise the rental stream to an assessed market rental. In effect, the CHPs receive a market yield and part of their rental income is guaranteed by the state. This increased guaranteed income is viewed as important in attracting new housing providers and new funders. Moreover, it is also assumed that an increased rental income will increase the ability of the CHPs to borrow from the private sector.

While the expansion of the IRRS to CHPs increased their income, the sector as a whole was constrained by its small asset base. In order to boost the size of the sector, the government initiated a stock transfer programme. Stock transfers have been employed internationally to grow third sector housing providers (Pawson & Gilmour, 2010). This programme offered the government two potential benefits. First, it reduced the stock of government managed social housing. Second, stock transfers have the potential to grow the community housing sector quickly and, in expanding its asset base, offers the potential for these CHPs to undertake borrowing to expand their activities.

To effect the transfers the government established a transfer team in the New Zealand Treasury. Its primary task was to ensure an appropriate market valuation for the housing being transferred and, given the value of HNZs housing assets as part of the government's balance sheet, that the transfers did not adversely affect the government's credit rating. In effect, Treasury was tasked with making a new market for a bulk social housing sell-off.

In 2015 Treasury announced that the regional centres of Tauranga and Invercargill had been selected for the first stock transfers under this new system. To facilitate the proposed transfers two new housing amendments acts had to be passed and a new methodology for valuing the social housing stock had to be established (Murphy, 2020a). Given that the purpose of the transfer was to expand the community housing sector and to ensure the continued provision of social rented housing, the nascent calculative practice involved pricing the housing stock and the government's retained interest in the housing being sold. In a complex tendering process CHPs were requested to bid for HNZ stock as an ongoing business. The state's retained interest in this social housing was defined as its Initial Capital Investment (New Zealand Government, 2015), the difference between the book (market) value of the houses and the discounted sale price.

Notwithstanding potential difficulties in calculating the appropriate discount to apply to the sale of state housing, there was an assumption that the existence of a price discount and the potential to secure a rental stream of income (supported by the IRRS) would be attractive to CHPs and investors. It was assumed that with the right incentives a market would emerge. However, in reality, the stock transfer programme proved problematic. In particular, while the tender process focused on the financial dimensions of the sale (i.e. the prospective rental yield for buyers) there was a lack of clarity concerning the material nature of the stock and related issues regarding the potential need for capital expenditures required for maintaining or upgrading the properties. In the absence of support for capital expenditures, potential buyers were exposed to considerable risk, especially as the sale required a long-term commitment to own and manage the stock. Reflective of the scale of this risk, and in a blow to the government's plans, the Salvation Army announced that it was withdrawing from the tendering process as the financial obligations were too onerous (Feek, 2015).

In 2016 it was announced that the Invercargill tender had been put on hold as a CHP withdrew from the process. In 2017 the government announced the sale of 1,140 HNZ properties in Tauranga to Accessible Properties, a community housing provider (Adams, 2017) that managed some 1,600 houses throughout New Zealand (Accessible Properties, 2019). Thus, despite the belief that an appropriate price discount would create a market for social housing, the programme faltered and was eventually stopped with the advent of a new Labour-led government elected in 2017.

Discussion

In combination these two examples demonstrate the place based nature of housing markets and market-making. It is clear that the New Zealand housing crisis has a variegated geography and housing problems are manifest in different ways and at different geographical scales. In response to national housing problems the state has adopted policies that are inherently place-based. The SHAs are predominantly located in Auckland and were established as a direct government response to the Auckland housing crisis (Murphy, 2014, 2016). In addition, the social housing stock transfer programme had a regional focus (Murphy, 2020a). The success or failure of these market interventions was clearly affected by the localities in which these policies were enacted.

Yet, notwithstanding the real estate trope of 'location, location, location', the state's housing policies were conceived within a market logic based on a simple construction of market-wide demand and supply impulses. The SHAs were envisaged as a supply response that would, once the market was liberated from urban planning constraints, result in price declines and improved housing affordability. The social rented housing stock transfers were part of a programme designed to make a new housing market. Stock transfers were intended to grow the CHP sector but also to position these enlarged providers as suitable recipients of bank lending or private investment funding. To operationalise these market-making strategies the state employed regulatory reforms (HASHAA, SHRA) and created new calculative practices (e.g. defining an affordable price, valuing social housing, etc.).

Significantly, the market-making processes involved in these case studies were not creation *ex nihilo* but 'modifications' to an existing assemblage/agencement. The reforms intersected with an existing agencement that operationalised distinct 'locked-in' calculative practices (Lovell & Smith, 2010). The SHA fast-track planning approval process, which was designed to reduce developer risks and promote housing supply, in effect enhanced the value of the land in these areas compared to surrounding sites. As sites within SHAs offered less risk to developers, these sites became more attractive to developers and competition for these sites resulted in rising land values (cf. Ryan-Collins et al., 2017). In effect, the locked-in practices of development feasibility analysis worked to transfer a change in planning practice into land value uplift. The government's imagining of housing market processes was frustrated by the mundane everyday calculative practices that are locked into the residential development sector. In addition, the government's ambition to create an enlarged CHP sector was frustrated. Simply valuing the social rented stock as a capitalised rental stream accorded with a certain financialised imagining of housing, but this 'market imagineering' failed to take cognisance of the materiality of the housing stock that was for sale. The stock was old and in need of maintenance and upgrading. In the absence of a capital grant or some form of government assistance, the cost and risk of taking on an aging housing stock was too high, and only one stock transfer eventuated.

Conclusion

Houses are actively produced and reproduced through complex entanglements of material, socio-cultural and financial processes and practices (Cook *et al.*, 2016). Under conditions of emerging 'residential capitalism' (Smith, 2015) and financialisation (Aalbers, 2016, 2017), it is possible to envisage housing markets as increasingly homogenised and reduced to a set of financial processes. Indeed, political and popular discourses around housing and housing markets centre on essentialised readings of the assumed benefits and problems of individual housing tenures. In addition, housing policy is often framed within a simplified economic model of demand and supply processes (Austin *et al.*, 2014; Gurran *et al.*, 2014) in which market actors (developers, mortgage agents, valuers, etc.) are rendered passive responders to wider and dominant market forces. In reality, housing markets are embedded in place. Not only are houses physically anchored in localities, they are (re)produced in nationally constituted housing markets characterised by distinct regulatory processes and building practices (Murphy, 2011).

In contrast to the idea that housing markets are simply given, increasingly attention has been directed towards understanding how markets are made (Smith *et al.*, 2006; Christophers, 2014a, 2014b; Murphy, 2020b). Markets, as sociotechnical agencements, operate as calculative devices producing prices and valuations. They are combinations of "material and technical devices, texts, algorithms, rules and human beings that shape agency and give meaning to action" (Berndt & Boeckler, 2009, p. 543). In order to explore the implications of market-making processes this chapter examined government-sponsored experiments in 'making' housing markets. It was argued that the New Zealand government mobilised a simplified abstract economic model of the housing market to implement a set of housing reforms designed to affect the production of affordable housing and expand the CHP sector. This mobilisation involved regulatory reforms and new calculative practices. In effect, this abstract model was performative. It was mobilised in ways that attempted to create or constitute a new housing market and it produced housing outputs. But, reflective of the contingent manner in which markets are formulated and the inherent power of 'locked-in' market (calculative) practices (Lovell & Smith, 2010), the reforms failed in their primary objectives. They did not address the housing affordability crisis (Murphy, 2016, 2017) and they did not produce large-scale social housing stock transfers (Murphy, 2020a). The government's dreams of fields of affordable housing did not eventuate.

Focusing on the manner in which housing markets are made renders visible the agency of calculative practices and market participants. The housing market is not the outcome of anonymous macro-level demand and supply impulses but is the product of the operation of a distinct agencement (encompassing people, rules and spreadsheets, etc.). Moreover, housing as a commodity is characterised by locational fixity. Houses are produced via local articulations of agencements that are inflected by local practices. To understand housing markets it is important to not only comprehend how housing markets are made but also how they are produced in place.

References

Aalbers, M.B. (2016). *The financialization of housing: A political economy approach*. London: Routledge.

Aalbers, M.B. (2017). The variegated financialization of housing. *International Journal of Urban and Regional Research*, 41(4), 542–554.

Accessible Properties. (2019). *Accessible Properties New Zealand Ltd*, Retrieved 26 July 2019 from www.accessibleproperties.co.nz.

Adams, A. (2017). *New landlord for 1140 Tauranga HNZ tenants, Minister of Social Housing* [Press release]. Retrieved 24 August 2018 from www.beehive.govt.nz/release/new-landlord-1140-tauranga-hnz-tenants.

Atherton, E., French, N. & Gabrielli, L. (2008). Decision theory and real estate development: a note on uncertainty. *Journal of European Real Estate Research*, 1(2), 162–182.

Austin, P.M., Gurran, N. & Whitehead, C.M. (2014). Planning and affordable housing in Australia, New Zealand and England: common culture; different mechanisms. *Journal of Housing and the Built Environment*, 29(3), 455–472.

Berndt, C. & Boeckler, M (2009). Geographies of circulation and exchange: Constructions of markets. *Progress in Human Geography* 33(4), 535–551.

Blessing, A. (2016). Repackaging the poor? Conceptualising neoliberal reforms of social rental housing. *Housing Studies*, 31(2), 149–172.

Bramley, G. (2013). Housing market models and planning. *Town Planning Review* 84(1), 9–35.

Çalışkan, K. & Callon, M. (2010). Economization, part 2: A research programme for the study of markets. *Economy and Society*, 39(1), 1–32.

Callon, M. (2007). What does it mean to say that economics is performative? In D. MacKenzie, F. Muniesa & L. (Eds), *Do economists make markets? On the performativity of economics* (pp. 311–357). Princeton, NJ: Princeton University Press.

Callon, M. (Ed.). (1998). *The laws of the markets*. Oxford:Blackwell Publishers.

Cheshire, P. (2008). Reflections on the nature and policy implications of planning restrictions on housing supply. Discussion of 'Planning policy, planning practice, and housing supply' by Kate Barker. *Oxford Review of Economic Policy*, 24(1), 50–58.

Christophers, B. (2013). A monstrous hybrid: The political economy of housing in early twenty-first century Sweden. *New Political Economy*, 18(6), 885–911.

Christophers, B. (2014a). Wild dragons in the city: urban political economy, affordable housing development and the performative world-making of economic models. *International Journal of Urban and Regional Research*, 38(1), 79–97.

Christophers, B. (2014b). From Marx to market and back again: Performing the economy. *Geoforum*, 57, 12–20.

Clapham, D. (2018). Housing theory, housing research and housing policy. *Housing, Theory and Society*, 35(2), 163–177.

Clapham, D. (2019). *Remaking Housing Policy: An International Study*. Abingdon: Routledge.

Cook, N., Davison, A. & Crabtree, L. (Eds). (2016). *Housing and Home Unbound: Intersections in economics, environment and politics in Australia*. Abingdon: Routledge.

Feek, B. (2015, May 23). Salvation Army rejects buying state homes: 'Housing NZ is making a mess'. *New Zealand Herald*. Retrieved from www.nzherald.co.nz/nz/news/article.cfm?c_id=1&objectid=11421462.

Gurran, N., Austin, P. & Whitehead, C. (2014). That sounds familiar! A decade of planning reform in Australia, England and New Zealand. *Australian Planner*, 51(2), 186–198.

Havard, T. (2014). *Financial feasibility studies for property development: theory and practice*. Abingdon: Routledge.

Henneberry, J. (2016). Development viability, in T. Crook, J. Henneberry & C. Whitehead (Eds). *Planning gain: Providing infrastructure and affordable housing* (pp. 115–139). Chichester: John Wiley & Sons.

HSAG. (2010). *Home and housed – A vision for social housing in New Zealand*. Wellington: The Housing Shareholders Advisory Group.

Jacobs, K. and Manzi, T. (2020). Neoliberalism as entrepreneurial governmentality: Contradictions and dissonance within contemporary English housing associations, *Housing Studies*, 35(4), 573–588.

James, B. (2017). *Getting the housing we say we want: Learning from the Special Housing Area experience in Tauranga and the Western Bay of Plenty – Paper 1*. Working paper prepared for Building Better Homes Towns and Cities SRA The Architecture of Decision-making. Retrieved from www.buildingbetter.nz/publications/SRA1/James_2017_getting_the_housing.pdf.

Johnson, A., Howden-Chapman, P. & Eaqub, S. (2018). *A stocktake of New Zealand's housing*, Wellington: New Zealand Government.

Letwin, O. (2018a). *Independent review of build out rates: Draft analysis*. London: Ministry of Housing, Communities and Local Government, UK.

Letwin, O. (2018b). *Independent Review of Build Out Rates: Final Report*. London: Ministry of Housing, Communities and Local Government, UK.

Lewis, N. & Murphy, L. (2015). Anchor organisations in Auckland: Rolling constructively with neoliberalism? *Local Economy*, 30(1), 98–118.

Lovell, H. & Smith, S.J. (2010). Agencement in housing markets: The case of the UK construction industry. *Geoforum*, 41(3), 457–468.

Manzi, T. & Morrison, N. (2018). Risk, commercialism and social purpose: Repositioning the English housing association sector. *Urban Studies*, 55(9), 1924–1942.

Mitchell, A. (1972). *The half-gallon quarter-acre pavlova paradise*. Christchurch: Whitcombe & Tombs.

Mooya, M.M. (2016). *Real Estate valuation Theory*, Berlin: Springer.

Morrison, N. (2017). Selling the family silver? Institutional entrepreneurship and asset disposal in the English housing association sector. *Urban Studies*, 54(12), 2856–2873.

Morrison, P. (2008). *On the falling rate of home ownership in New Zealand*. Wellington: Centre for Housing Research Aotearoa New Zealand.

Muniesa, F., Millo, Y. & Callon, M. (2007). An introduction to market devices. *The sociological review*, 55(2), 1–12.

Murphy, L. (2011). The global financial crisis and the Australian and New Zealand housing markets. *Journal of Housing and the Built Environment*, 26(3), 335–351.

Murphy, L. (2014). 'Houston, we've got a problem': The political construction of a housing affordability metric in New Zealand. *Housing Studies*, 29(7), 893–909.

Murphy, L. (2016). The politics of land supply and affordable housing: Auckland's housing accord and special housing areas. *Urban Studies*, 53(12), 2530–2547.

Murphy, L. (2017). Housing affordability, urban planning and Auckland's special housing areas. In P. Howden-Chapman, L. Early & J. Ombler, (Eds), *Cities in New Zealand: Preferences, patterns and possibilities* (pp. 66–78). Wellington: Steele Roberts.

Murphy, L. (2020a). Neoliberal social housing policies, market logics and social rented housing reforms in New Zealand, *International Journal of Housing Policy*, 20(2), 229–251. https://doi.org/10.1080/19491247.2019.1638134.

Murphy, L. (2020b). Performing calculative practices: residual valuation, the residential development process and affordable housing, *Housing Studies*, 35(9), 1501–1517. https://doi.org/10.1080/02673037.2019.1594713.

Murphy, L. & Rehm, M. (2016). Homeownership, asset-based welfare and the actuarial subject: exploring the dynamics of ageing and homeownership in New Zealand. In N. Cook, A. Davison & L. Crabtree (Eds), *Housing and home unbound: Intersections in economics, environment and politics in Australia* (pp. 53–69). Abingdon: Routledge.

Murphy, L., Friesen, W. & Kearns, R.A. (1999). Transforming the city: people, property and identity in millennial Auckland. *New Zealand Geographer*, 55(2), 60–65.

National Business Review. (2013). *Planning laws stacked against first time buyers.* NBR. Retrieved from www.nbr.co.nz/article/planninglaws-stacked-against-first-home-buyers-englishck-140343.

New Zealand Government. (2015). *Transfer of Tauranga Social Housing* [Information Memorandum]. Retrieved from www.chapmantripp.com/publication%20pdfs/PUB%20Client%20Alert%20-%20Final%20Information%20Memorandum%20Transfer%20of%20Tauranga%20Social%20Housing%20-%20Aug%2015.pdf.

New Zealand Parliament Debates. (2013). *Housing Accords and Special Housing Areas Bill – Third Reading.* [Hansard Debates]. Retrieved from www.parliament.nz/minz/pb/debates/debates/50HansD_20130905_00000016/housingaccords-and-special-housing-areas-bill-%E2%80%94-third.

New Zealand Productivity Commission. (2012). *Housing Affordability Inquiry.* Wellington: New Zealand Productivity Commission.

New Zealand Treasury. (2017). *History of Social Housing Transfers- April 2010 to December 2017.* Retrieved from https://treasury.govt.nz/publications/history-social-housing-transfers-%E2%80%93-april-2010-december-2017.

Pawson, H. & Gilmour, T. (2010). Transforming Australia's social housing: Pointers from the British stock transfer experience. *Urban Policy and Research*, 28, 241–260.

Rotherham, F. (2015). NZ still has 'rock star economy', says HSBC economist, *National Business Review*, Retrieved from www.nbr.co.nz/article/new-zealand-still-has-rock-star-economy-says-economist-bloxham-bd-171205.

Ryan-Collins, J., Lloyd, T. & MacFarlane, L. (2017). *Rethinking the economics of land and housing.* London: Zed Books with the New Economics Foundation.

SHRA. (2013). *Social Housing Reform (Housing Restructuring and Tenancy Matters Amendment) Act 2013.* Retrieved from www.legislation.govt.nz/act/public/2013/0097/latest/DLM5200608.html.

Smith, S.J. (2008). Owner-occupation: At home with a hybrid of money and materials. *Environment and Planning A*, 40(3), 520–535.

Smith, S.J. (2011). Home price dynamics: A behavioural economy? *Housing, Theory and Society*, 28(3), 236–261.

Smith, S.J. (2015). Owner occupation: at home in a spatial, financial paradox. *International Journal of Housing Policy*, 15(1), 61–83.

Smith, S.J., Munro, M. & Christie, H. (2006). Performing (housing) markets. *Urban Studies*, 43(1), 81–98.

Wyatt, P. (2013). *Property Valuation* (2nd ed.). Chichester: John Wiley & Sons.

11 Fictive places in wine markets

Winemaking and place-making in New Zealand

John Overton* and Warwick E. Murray*

*VICTORIA UNIVERSITY OF WELLINGTON

Introduction

Wine has made and transformed places in Aotearoa/New Zealand. The considerable growth and expansion of the industry since the mid-1980s has radically changed rural landscapes, particularly in Marlborough and parts of Hawke's Bay, Central Otago and North Canterbury; it has remoulded the character of rural towns such as Martinborough; it has significantly transformed the economies of regions such as Marlborough and Central Otago; and it has created new 'wine places' (Gimblett Gravels, Bannockburn, Waipara/North Canterbury), where the public conception of these places is inextricably linked with vineyards and wine. To a large extent, these transformations have resulted from the reconfiguring of the rural economies of existing regions and place names. Yet we have also seen the emergence of new places, actively constructed and promoted in the public imaginary, in order to sell the idea that these places produce higher-quality (and therefore higher-priced) wine.

Such place-making processes have been driven by the way the New Zealand wine industry has attached itself to global markets; to its norms, fads, styles and techniques of production, promotion and consumption. In particular, we have seen the adoption of wine quality narratives: notions of 'vintage', *'terroir'*, and 'classic' varieties have become embedded in the way New Zealand wine is made and consumed. Global cultures of wine consumption and global conceptions of what is 'fine' or 'quality' wine have shaped the trajectories of New Zealand wine industry development and left a marked imprint on the New Zealand landscape. Overwhelmingly, this transformation has been centred on a single variety – Sauvignon Blanc – and, largely, on a leading region – Marlborough (Hayward & Lewis, 2008; Stewart, 2010; Moran, 2016; Lewis, 2014; Howland, 2020). It is this wine that has found a significant place in the global wine market, and it dominates the country's wine exports and total production. It has also attracted considerable interest from global beverage corporations, which have invested in the New Zealand industry in order to add Marlborough Sauvignon Blanc to their product portfolios. This is the 'behemoth' of the New Zealand industry (Overton & Murray, 2014b).

Yet place-making in the New Zealand wine industry involves much more than just a single region. We can see processes at work at various spatial and economic scales. Global beverage companies, such as Pernod Ricard and

DOI: 10.4324/9780429296260-11

Constellation Brands, might dominate total production, but medium- and small-scale companies, right down to family-run enterprises, are also active in defining, promoting and protecting wine place-makers throughout the country (Overton & Murray, 2016b; Lewis & Le Heron, 2018).

In this chapter we seek to explore the ways in which wine and wine markets have made and reshaped places. We are interested in the complexities of the industry, seeing how different markets have been read and tapped and manipulated through the narrative of place, and seeing how different forms of capital are engaged in place-making strategies. This leads us then to consider how wine places feed back into wine markets and wine consumption. What we suggest is that there is a complex and multi-scaled landscape of place-making in the wine industry – one that sees different relationships between capital and place and between different fragments of capital. Furthermore, we not only see place as malleable and contested, but we also see it as a conspicuous component of the product that is wine – perhaps even a factor in its production and sale – that is actively constructed.

Fictive place

The idea of place, specifically place of origin, is deeply embedded in wine markets. Although many other products – cheese, tequila, coffee, apples, even potatoes (Bowen, 2010; Dogana & Gokovali, 2012) – have adopted narratives of place-specific qualities, it has been the wine industry (and the European industries in particular) that have adopted and actively promoted the notion that wine grapes derive particular characteristics from where they are grown. This is manifested in the French concept of *terroir*. This is a term that defies satisfactory translation into the English language. It encompasses a holistic view of a place: its soils, climate, topography, landscape, flora, aspect, underlying geology and its history, culture and traditions. It helps to establish the identity of wines, their character and taste profiles, because grapes, perhaps more than any other agricultural product, are supposed to reflect their *terroir* in the way that they are grown and their flavours. *Terroir*, in practice, is particularly linked to claims about the way in which soil types affect flavours, and climate, aspect, slope and geology are also prominent narratives (Demossier, 2020). In some regions, *terroir* also embraces stories of how wine-making traditions have become established over long periods of time and have become an essential feature of a region's wine (Ulin, 1995; Moran, 2001).

Building on this idea that *terroir* creates distinctiveness in wines from different places are the claims made that some places are more favoured than others, and that *terroir* can be a marker of quality (Vaudour, 2002; Sommers, 2008). Thus, some soils, such as those derived from limestone, might be said to produce 'better' wines than those from heavy clays; or particular regimes of temperature and sunshine are said to imbue grapes with particular – and desired - sugar and acid characteristics (Wilson, 1998; Fanet, 2004; Dutton, 2020).

The idea of 'quality' in wine is critical in wine markets. Supermarket shelves and wine outlets worldwide display a huge array of wine brands, varieties, places of origin, vintages, styles and, critically, prices. For the consumer, there is confusion and a baffling array of choice. Price is the critical factor, although there is not a simple direct and inverse relationship between price and demand. For many consumers, low-cost wines are sought, and a cheap bottle of wine will be seen as delivering a pleasant drinking experience. But for others, wine is seen as a commodity with status value: a more expensive wine is one that can be consumed conspicuously, perhaps in the hope of indicating the wealth or taste of the consumer. Wine consumption cultures vary greatly (Demossier, 2004; Dutton, 2020), but there is much to suggest that imagined quality is positively related to price. Expensive wines can be luxury items, and some consumers – perhaps most – will be prepared at times to pay much more than the low end of the market for a wine that they believe will taste better.

Thus, we see in the global wine industry a wide range of production and marketing strategies. There is clearly a considerable segment of the market that competes on the basis of low prices. Here we see, in effect, Fordist wine production techniques. Economies of scale are sought in grape-growing (very large vineyards and low cost land, mechanisation and/or low-cost labour, yield maximisation) and industrial techniques of winemaking are used to produce wines that vary little from year to year or place to place (and juice from different regions and vintages can be blended to achieve this and even out spatial and temporal variations in yield and character). They might also seek to satisfy tastes for particular styles of wine (e.g. sweeter) that consumers come to expect from a particular brand. Overall, low-cost production is the vital objective – a 'race to the bottom' strategy – as that makes the wines competitive on global markets.

At the other end of the market, however, we see wines that are deliberately higher-cost, lower-volume and with distinctive flavour characteristics that can vary markedly from vintage to vintage. Also, in employing narratives of *terroir* and artisanal production (emphasising winemaking traditions, the skills of particular winemakers or higher-cost techniques, such as the use of oak barrels or bottle-ageing), these wines are promoted as unique, rare and even collectable. Wine competition results and reviews from putative authorities and arbiters of quality – such as Robert Parker (McCoy, 2005) – are used to reinforce such claims to distinctiveness and quality.

While these opposite ends of the wine market spectrum present quite contrasting production and marketing strategies, it is inbetween that we see the bulk of the market and a very complex interplay of these two factors: the need to present wine that is affordable for most consumers, but that simultaneously engages in claims regarding quality. Qualitative differentiation in the wine market is based on several dimensions that are promoted as markers of desirability: grape variety is prominent, there is visible indication of the year of harvest, and some brands become associated with quality positions in the markets (whether as a reliable producer of reasonably priced wines, or as a top chateaux in Bordeaux). However, it is place (country, region, locality or vineyard of origin) that has become one of the key markers of differentiation and, in many aspects, a surrogate indicator of quality (Goodman, 2010; Bowen, 2011; Charters, 2020; Overton & Murray, 2013; Pedersen, Persson & Sharp, 2019).

Because of the importance of place in wine, there have been significant – and contested – strategies to define, regulate and protect places. European wine producers have adopted a variety of regulatory schemes to undertake this. The French appellation d'origine contrôlée (AOC) system is the most prominent, and it has influenced the evolution of systems elsewhere. French laws have progressively demarcated certain regions – and localities within regions – within which rules have been applied to standardise not only the use of place names (Champagne, Bordeaux, Burgundy, etc.) but also viticultural and winemaking techniques within them (Barham, 2003; Charters, 2006). Designated regions are thus associated with wines of particular styles, and place of origin has come to be an indicator of the grape varieties used, the character of the wine and, through a long process of narrative-building, of quality. Not only has the French system been mirrored in Spain, Italy and elsewhere in Europe, these national schemes have received a higher level of regulation with European Union (EU) laws further protecting and standardising the way places are used in and attached to wine production and marketing.

Although this system is often portrayed as a fixed marker of place and quality (often in contrast to supposed new, experimental and innovative New World winemaking), in practice it has been subject to political squabbles: it has seen changes in boundaries, and quality designations have shifted over time as some producers (and localities) are elevated in status, while others have slipped down the scale (Moran, 1993b; Lewis, Moran, Perrier-Corne & Barker, 2002; Barker, 2004; Kelly, 2007). Nor does the AOC system have a monopoly in terms of French wine production. Traditionally, wine has long been produced as *vin ordinaire* for cheap daily consumption, without any major indication of place of origin or claim for quality, alongside the emerging 'fine wine' sector. In addition, the contemporary French (and wider European) wine industry has proved to be highly flexible. Exports of wine from Europe compete not only with AOC wines at the high end, but it is now common to see mid-range and cheaper French wine from outside established and prestigious appellations now utilising marketing strategies and winemaking techniques common in the New World, such as explicit branding of the grape variety. Furthermore, the *garagistes* movement has seen French winemakers producing wine on a small-scale and in higher price brackets but outside the AOC rules and place designations.

Nonetheless, the AOC system and its other European variants have proved to be influential in the wider trading environment. In global trade negotiations since the 1990s, the strong push for trade liberalisation was met with resistance, particularly by European negotiators. One concession they were able to secure was the recognition of place names of origin – Geographical Indications (GIs) – as 'intellectual property' (Moran, 1993a). In this way, GIs have become an element of product differentiation and a powerful instrument to define and protect place names (such as Champagne, Bordeaux, etc.). GIs have spread well beyond the wine sector and now protect a very wide range of agro-commodities globally (Goldberg, 2001; Hughes, 2006; Josling, 2006). GIs have meant that *terroir* narratives have become embedded in many markets for many products (Bowen, 2010; Bowen & Valenzuela Zapata, 2009).

With this power of the place name now established in wine and other markets, we have seen various agents devise strategies to delimit and register place names. To a large extent, this has involved merely taking existing place names (such as Burgundy) and having their association with a particular product (wine) codified and protected by law. However, in practice, this process of recording place names has been complex and sometimes contested. Delimiting a region involves drawing lines which include some and exclude others. Thus, we have seen in Australia, for example, how the Coonawarra wine region, as originally defined, was challenged and altered to accommodate wine producers on the margins (Banks & Sharpe, 2006).

Furthermore, we have suggested that there have been active and deliberate strategies to invent places; to make up new names, draw new boundaries and, in particular, craft various environmental and historical narratives in order to build new imaginaries of particular places. In the New Zealand wine industry, this has been evident in the creation of the Gimblett Gravels winemaking region – a name that was invented and protected by a trademark (Overton & Heitger, 2008). It is also seen in Martinborough, where an original attempt to define a New Zealand wine 'appellation' on the Martinborough Terrace has been amended to include new areas nearby in Te Muna, and the 'terrace' notion has been weakened and virtually withdrawn (Howland, 2008; Overton & Murray, 2014a; Murray & Overton, 2011; Moran, 2016).

These place-making processes we have referred to as 'fictive place' (Overton & Murray, 2016a). We see these actions to construct new places, to build new imaginaries of place and to codify places as deliberate economic strategies to secure new market niches, based on notions of *terroir* and with the aim of differentiating a mass product on the basis of place. Such place-making is an active strategy. Wine places are discovered and tested (to see if they can produce good quality wine grapes reliably and profitably) but then such favoured places are embellished with stories and meanings promoted through wine. This involves promoting places and their characteristics – their soils, climate, history, etc. – and this has an economic function: the enhanced value of place is realised through hoped-for higher prices for bottles of wine (Overton, 2010). Fictive place, we suggest, is a result of a new economic strategy that is facilitated by GIs: there is a 'race for place' (the efforts to define, register and promote new GIs) which can be seen as a means to secure new economic values through place (and putative quality) differentiation as an alternative to Fordist 'race to the bottom' strategies to gain profitability by cutting costs, producing uniformity and pursuing economies of scale. The importance of place as an economic strategy has been revealed in cases where some wine producers have been found guilty of fraudulently labelling wine with regard to its place of origin, in order to gain a premium. A recent example of this is Southern Boundary Wines in Waipara, which was caught passing off wine as being from a single vineyard, with claims to its particular *terroir*, when it contained juice from other regions (Van Beynen, 2019).

Place, scale and capital: two hypotheses

The concept of fictive place offers us some insight into the way in which places are constructed and reconfigured as part of economic processes of accumulation. Capital in various forms – and often in intense landscapes of competition – is engaged in (re)making, demarcating and protecting places. The GI mechanism provides a framework of regulation that defines places as forms of intellectual property attached to particular commodities that then are able pursue marketing strategies that seek to persuade consumers that those places are markers of quality and, hence, market premium.

But how does this work in practice? What is the role of different forms of capital? And what about the spatial resolution of place – what scales and layers of place are manifested through these processes of place-making in the wine industry? In addressing these questions, we posit two hypotheses with regard to capital and scale.

The first hypothesis is that ***the granularity of place is directly related to the price/quality of wine.***

We suggest that the 'granularity' of place is not only uneven, but also related to different marketing strategies for wine. At one end of the scale in the global wine industry, we see, particularly in France, systems for defining wine places to a very fine level of detail. In wine maps of Bordeaux or Burgundy, for example (e.g. Johnson & Robinson, 2013), we see very fine-grained definitions of place, often down the level of an individual vineyard, and these detailed wine places are explicitly linked to the putative quality of the wine produced from these tightly defined and closely protected places. At the other end of the market, cheap bulk wines often appear without an indication of their vintage or variety, let alone even their region of origin (or with wine mixed from different countries). In this segment of the wine market, price is the critical factor. In order to keep costs down, producers seek economies of scale and industrial production methods. It is a Fordist production strategy, for not only is it based on minimising the cost of production, it also depends on delivering a uniform product year in, year out that customers can recognise and return to. The blending of wines from different places is a key element of these strategies, for it can help to iron out variations in yields from one place to another (a poor vintage in one region can be balanced by using grapes from another), it can be used to obtain the cheapest suitable fruit available, and blending is used to produce wines that have a uniform style (rather than one that varies based on year, place and variety).

The New Zealand wine industry does not have these extremes in terms of its 'placing' itself in the wine market: high labour and land costs preclude raw 'race to the bottom' strategies; and there is little chance to construct deep historical (or even environmental) narratives about particular hillsides, villages or traditions. Yet there are strong elements of granularity in the country's wine landscape. Marlborough Sauvignon Blanc is characteristically produced from very large vineyards on the extensive plains and valley floors of the Wairau and Awatere Rivers. Although there have been some attempts to promote sub-regions here, for example based on the north-facing lower hills of the Wairau and tributary valleys, the 'Marlborough' designation remains dominant, as do the large wine companies. Elsewhere, we see these same companies in Hawke's Bay (and formerly in Gisborne), where the wider regional name tends to be employed more than the sub-regional designations. In Hawke's Bay, for example, Pernod Ricard has its Church Road brand. In 2019 this brand produced 18 different wines. Fifteen of these used only 'Hawke's Bay' as their designated place of origin on the label (and without any accompanying narratives of origin from particular locations within the region). Only its 'One' premier label went beyond the 'Hawke's Bay' name to list 'Gimblett Gravels' as its source, and this was part of a sub-brand strategy which, unusually for Church Road, promoted 'One vineyard, one craftsman [sic], one wine' (www.church-road.com/en-nz/our-wines accessed 5 July 2019). Pernod Ricard's main New Zealand brand, Brancott Estate (formerly, in effect, Montana), also has two red wines in its stable (a little down the market range from Church Road) from Hawke's Bay, and again, these use only the regional name.

However, wine from New Zealand comes with many different regional descriptors. One indicator of this is the New Zealand Winegrowers labelling guide of 2013, which lists some 90 New Zealand wine GIs to be used in the EU (New Zealand Winegrowers, 2013), and these cover a wide range of spatial scales from the national ('New Zealand') to the very specific (Martinborough: a 'Defined winegrowing area in Martinborough Ward'). Interestingly, in these and later guidelines from New Zealand Winegrowers (the Labelling Guide of 2017 for example – New Zealand Winegrowers, 2017), some small wine-producing areas, such as Clevedon or Matakana, are listed explicitly as a 'grape growing region or locality', while others, such as Gimblett Gravels, are not. The 2017 guidelines suggest regional names 'may be accompanied by the name of a geographical sub-unit' (p. 34), and some examples are given, but these seem to fall short of formal codification and protection. There is, then, still a rather confused and complicated array of place names used in New Zealand wine, from the very large-scale (e.g. North Island) to small localities, the latter often with little official recognition (Overton & Murray, 2017). Our hypothesis is that these small regions and districts are associated with smaller-scale enterprises and, with their higher costs of production, they seek to compete at the higher end of the market. So finer-grained place designation is, we suggest, associated with strategies to produce supposedly higher-quality and higher-priced wine.

This first hypothesis can be depicted as in Figure 11.1 as a relationship between scale of place definition and quality/price of wine. Here we take price per bottle as a surrogate for the perception of quality of wine. On the horizontal axis, we see a gradation from 'course' place granulation (no designation of place or only at a very large scale, such as country of origin) to 'fine' (a specific definition of a relatively small area, such as a hillslope or a particular vineyard). Operationally, granularity is difficult to quantify, so we employ a classification of place definition as follows:

In New Zealand, these categories can be illustrated with the following:[1]

1 **Multi-country:** e.g. 'product of Chile and New Zealand' (also place not specified).
2 **Single country:** e.g. 'New Zealand'
3 **Large-scale or multi-region:** e.g. 'East Coast', 'South Island', 'New South Wales'
4 **Single region:** e.g. 'Marlborough', 'Hawke's Bay', 'Central Otago', 'Wellington', etc.

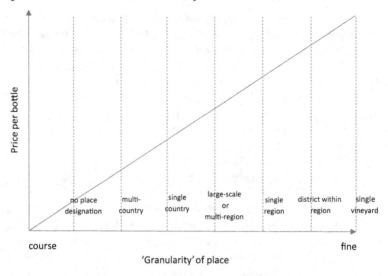

Figure 11.1 Wine price and place granularity

5   **Sub-region/district:** (mostly contiguous wine district) e.g. 'Gladstone', 'Martinborough', 'Waitaki Valley', Gimblett Gravels', 'Bannockburn'
6   **Single vineyard:** a named vineyard (c.f. unspecified 'single vineyard')

Thus, we suggest that there might be a relationship between quality claims (and price demands) for wine and the fineness of place definition. So the way in which places are shaped is related to how place is positioned in wine markets.

The second hypothesis is that *different fragments of capital are engaged in different – and conflicting – place-making strategies.*

We have argued previously (Overton & Murray, 2017) that, in New Zealand's stuttering attempts to institute a GI scheme for wine (and other commodities), we can discern a tension between those large-scale agro-commodity producers who use largely Fordist-type production methods to export bulk commodities (milk powder, cheese, butter, lamb, etc.) and those smaller-scale producers who struggle to establish market niches and added value. The former align with often US-led attempts to resist forms of trade protectionism – and GI mechanisms are seen as such (Josling, 2006; Goldberg, 2001). These producers, such as Fonterra in the dairy industry, seem to be happy to promote a national brand in global markets, but they are not keen to support forms of sub-national geographical indications that would protect producers of specialist and regionally-specific products. Perhaps the case of cheese is illustrative: most New Zealand cheese exported is in bulk and without a regional brand, beyond appropriated foreign place-based terms such as Cheddar, Gouda or Parmesan. This pits it against largely European-led attempts to protect place brands such as Parmesan (Parmigiano-Reggiano), feta or Camembert. So support for GI regulations would go against trade liberalisation strategies and leave the country's largest cheese exporters at a competitive disadvantage. However, smaller-scale producers, who cannot achieve economies of scale and 'race to the bottom' production strategies, seek to survive and prosper by securing niches in the market based on claims to higher quality (and price). Place of origin – association of those places with particular and distinctive or unique quality characteristics – is one of the most common strategies in this regard. Thus, these producers align themselves with attempts to protect GIs as forms of intellectual property. In global trade negotiations, this has broadly pitted US-led and often New World producers against established European producers and negotiators (Josling, 2006).

In the New Zealand wine industry, we can see elements of this tension and schisms based on source of capital and scale of operation, although it is not as stark as in, say, the cheese industry. As we have seen, Marlborough Sauvignon Blanc dominates the New Zealand wine industry in terms of total production and share of exports; and this wine and its marketing is largely in the hands of the global corporations (Pernod Ricard and Constellation Brands in particular) and, to a lesser extent, the larger New Zealand companies (e.g. Villa Maria, Delegats). For these wine producers, their success on the global wine market depends on the establishment and maintenance in effect of only two place names: 'New Zealand' and 'Marlborough'. For the former, they are aligned well with the exporters of other commodities (cheese, butter, lamb, and perhaps we could include tourism) who combine to promote 'brand New Zealand' with its particular iconography (the use of black and the silver fern, together with images of snow-capped mountains and pristine lakes and forests) and motifs ('clean and green', '100 percent pure'). For the latter, Marlborough is associated with wine and narratives linked to the characteristics of Sauvignon Blanc (crisp, fruit-driven, clean, etc.). Any finer definitions of place – for example, to define sub-regions within Marlborough or other Sauvignon Blanc-producing regions in New Zealand, would be seen as counter-productive, obfuscating and confusing consumers.

However, wine producers who are based in regions outside Marlborough or who produce some of the many other wine varieties, position themselves rather differently in terms of how places are defined, promoted and protected. In New Zealand, there are many examples of the way clusters of producers have formed in particular regions and worked to collectively define and promote their places.[2] Beginning in Martinborough in 1991, there were attempts to demarcate a small and distinct wine region – an *appellation* – so that winemakers there could promote a *terroir* narrative about how the distinctive environmental qualities (temperatures, sunshine, soils) of the area that supposedly imbued the wines with certain qualities that made them 'better' (Howland, 2014; Moran, 2016). Elsewhere, the Gimblett Gravels Association succeeded in demarcating a wine district (of about 800 ha), again with claims to do with a unique regime of climate and soils, Waipara was able to separate itself from the rest of the Canterbury wine-producing region, and a collection of sub-regions, such as Bannockburn, the Bridge Pa Triangle, Te Awanga, and Waiheke Island, have promoted themselves as having a special place in the New Zealand wine environment (Tipples, 2007; Overton & Murray, 2014a; Overton, Banks & Murray, 2014; Howland, 2014; Baragwanath & Lewis, 2014). It is apparent that in these appellation initiatives, the lead agents have been regional winemaker associations. They characteristically comprise small and medium-sized wine enterprises, they are based in the place (or nearby), and they have involved local individuals closely associated with the locale's wine development. In general, the large wine companies have not been a part of these initiatives, although we might see the presence of some of the larger companies in one or two such places (such as Pernod Ricard in Waipara, or Villa Maria and Delegats in Gimblett Gravels).

Therefore, this hypothesis seems to be borne out, at least in part, by the way in which large producers, if not resisting geographical specification and protection entirely, seem to gravitate towards large-scale and simple place associations: the New Zealand and Marlborough place brands in particular. By contrast, the multiplicity of place-making activities at finer geographical resolution – different regions and districts within regions – seems to be driven by smaller-scale producers. Capital, then, is very unevenly engaged in the making of places in the wine industry and is sometimes in different camps with regard to the scale of place definition and promotion.

Place-making in the New Zealand wine industry

Each of our hypotheses is difficult to prove or disprove empirically. It is very difficult, for example, to analyse systematically and quantify the nature of capital involved in the New Zealand wine industry. Data on the scale of operation, let alone revenue and profit generation, are not available, and it is a difficult task to unravel the complexities of ownership behind the multiplicity of wine brands available in markets. Second, in attempting to link price/quality with definition of place, we face the difficulty that 'quality' remains such a subjective and elusive concept (Murdoch, Marsden & Banks, 2000; Moragues-Faus & Sonnino, 2012; Garcia-Parpet, 2008).

However, we can gain some insights into both hypotheses by analysing the way in which wine is labelled in terms of place of origin and relating this to both price per bottle and the nature of the winemaking enterprise (Banks, Kelly, Lewis & Sharpe, 2007; Banks, 2014), despite the difficulty of using wine labels as a sometimes inaccurate indicator of the wine and its source (Saker, 2017). We chose to analyse one particular variety, Chardonnay, on the New Zealand wine market. This is a commonly available variety that spans a wide range of styles and prices and places of origin. Chardonnay wine can be produced fairly simply and cheaply, or it can come from lower-yielding vines or clones and receive expensive treatment in oak. It is found at the lower end of the market but can also be among the most expensive white wines available. It is grown in most major wine-producing regions, with some apparent differences in characteristics from *terroir*. There is a plethora of Chardonnay wine brands on the market. We chose two major outlets to constitute a sample of wine available (those listed as 'Chardonnay' and in 750ml bottles).[3] The first was Countdown supermarket, through their online listing of wines, and Advintage, a liquor importer, wholesaler and retailer in Hawke's Bay but with an established online national marketing presence.[4] In early July 2018 these two outlets had very similar number of offerings: Advintage had some 100 New Zealand-made Chardonnay wines available and about 20 imported wines; Countdown had 97 New Zealand Chardonnay wines and 24 imported ones. Despite these similar total numbers, there was surprisingly little duplication. When there were instances of the same wine (same brand and vintage) available in both outlets, we removed from analysis the more expensive option. In this way, we removed 13 from the Countdown list (mostly more expensive wines that were cheaper at Advintage) and eight from the Advintage list. Our total number of wines for analysis was therefore 218: 176 from New Zealand and 42 imported.

First, we examined the labels to see what place descriptor was used. We took the main place name, usually on the front label (e.g. Hawke's Bay), even if the back label might have contained a story about the grapes having come from a particular location (e.g. the location of the winery). In this way, we were interested primarily in how the wine was presented in a geographical sense in the most prominent way. In some cases, there was no regional descriptor on the front label, usually when the country of origin was only given on the back label. In no cases in our sample was there no indication of place of origin, and there were no instances of mixed-country origin (although we know that this practice of blending does exist).

The result of our initial analysis is presented in Table 11.1 and Figure 11.2. First, we can see that by far the most common regional descriptor used for place of origin was 'region' (Hawke's Bay, Marlborough, etc.). This covered the full price range from (just) below NZ$10 per bottle to the most expensive wine at over NZ $160. We can also see initially that imported wines were mainly in the lower price ranges, and these tended to use larger-scale descriptors: either the country only category (2) or the large-scale region (3 – for example, Southeast Australia, California or Western Cape). However, the most important impression to be gained from these data is that there does seem to be a relationship, as suggested in the first hypothesis, that the more fine-grained place descriptors do command higher-priced segments of the market. Thus, no wine with just a country of origin (1) used was on sale for more than NZ$17 a bottle (and an average of NZ$10.81), and the large-scale regions (2) mostly occupied the sub-NZ$20 per bottle shelves. Once we move into the categories with finer resolution, prices rise. Thus, with the exception of a small number of expensive bottles,[5] the region category (3) dominated the mid-range price categories. The defined sub-region (category 4 – e.g. Waiheke Island, Martinborough, Gimblett Gravels, Waipara, etc.) then moved upwards in prices, none being under NZ$15 per bottle and with an average at just under NZ$30 a bottle. However, it was the named single vineyard category (6 – e.g. Taylor's Pass Vineyard, Kidnappers Vineyard, etc.) that demanded the highest average price and occupied the NZ$30–$60 range.

Table 11.1 Analysis of Chardonnay sample by price and place designation

Place designation	Number of wines	Average price per bottle
Country	16	NZ$10.06
Large or multiple region	19	NZ$15.81
Region	132	NZ$23.03
Sub-region/district	34	NZ$29.73
Named vineyard	17	NZ$45.35

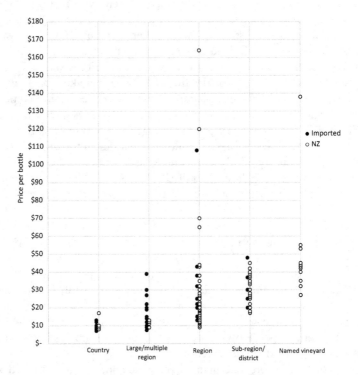

Figure 11.2 Price and place designation in the Chardonnay wine sample

Therefore, we suggest that these data confirm the first hypothesis, albeit with some wide variations and overlaps. More detailed place of origin is associated with higher price and, it could be suggested, consumer perceptions of higher quality. However, the predominance of the 'region' category (4) and its use by some comparatively very expensive wines might suggest that this category of place is effective in the market, particularly on more global markets. Thus, while some buyers might have an awareness of a particular district such as the Bridge Pa Triangle, this level of spatial detail will be lost on many consumers, particularly outside of New Zealand. Here, perhaps the only New Zealand regional appellation that has widespread recognition is 'Marlborough', or perhaps even 'Hawke's Bay'. Place-branding strategies, then, are conditioned by the nature of the market. Different markets have different levels of place recognition, and thus different resolutions of place either 'stick' in these markets or do not.

To examine our second hypothesis, we attempted to categorise the producers of the Chardonnay wines on sale to gain some indication of the different forms of capital in the wine industry. This is an imperfect analysis, for the underlying ownership and source of capital in wine-producing companies is often quite opaque. For example, while we might be able to know what New Zealand wine brands exist in the portfolio of a large company, such as Pernod Ricard, or we can see who owns a small winery, there are many instances where winemaking is conducted by complex business relationships: one winemaker might sell surplus production to another on the condition that its specific origin is obscured (to protect the initial brand); some winemaking companies buy grapes on contract, and this can differ from year to year, so we do not know how a particular brand or company is attached to a particular place; and wine companies use many different brands in different markets. However, we were able to trace the following general categories of producers:

a **Small to medium-sized producers.** This is a large category that spans small single-family operations with their own vineyards operations up to quite large producers (such as Palliser Estate or Clearview) who might make wines from more than one region, but who maintain an identity linked to a particular region.

b **Medium to large producers:** This category (in practice overlapping with the first) includes companies that have expanded to operate across several regions and, in many cases, produce wine under more than one brand. In New Zealand, this category includes companies such as the Villa Maria Group (including Esk Valley and Vidals), Delegats (including Oyster Bay), and Foley Family Wines (Te Kairanga, Vavasour, Grove Mill).

c **Wine processors and wholesalers:** This category is similar in some way to the *négociant* model, where merchants assemble wines from grapes grown and wines made by smaller producers and sell these under their own brand. In New Zealand and Australia, we see several instances of operations similar to this, although they tend to target the supermarket outlets with cheaper products. Thus, Woolworths has several associated brands (which we see in Countdown supermarkets) such as Seven Degrees, Cat Among the Pigeons or Nature's Harvest. The Poulter Group also has a stable of wine brands (including Goldridge, Makaraka and Duck Point) and these could be mainly wines from New Zealand grapes but could also include wine from Australia. Also in the category are various 'cleanskin' labels (or unspecified brands) where wine is obtained from established producers who could be sitting on surplus wine or cancelled orders and who wish to get some return without oversupplying the market and adversely affecting their own product and the price that it receives.

d   **Multinational beverage corporations:** These companies and their
    brands are visible in the New Zealand wine industry. They include the
    largest global beverage corporations, such as Pernod Ricard (Brancott
    Estate, Montana), Constellations Brands (Selaks, Kim Crawford), Treasury
    Wines (Matua, Shingle Peak), Accolade (Waipara Hills, Mud House) and
    Lion Beer (in turn owned by Kirin Holdings – Wither Hills, Corbans,
    etc.). We also include here the luxury brand corporation, LVMH which
    has Cloudy Bay in its portfolio. Thus, the brands in this sector span the full
    range of the market.

The analysis of these producers in relation to our sample of Chardonnay
wines for sale is presented in Figures 11.3a and 11.3b. Figure 11.3a shows
the number of wines from the different categories of producers across the
spatial descriptors. Here we see the dominance numerically of the small-
medium enterprises and the 'region' category (4). Figure 11.3b expresses
these data by percentage of each regional category. Here the differences are
marked. The course regional descriptors (2 and 3) are dominated by the
large corporations and the *négociants*. All are involved in marketing wines
from regional category 4 but, once the spatial resolution gets finer, we see

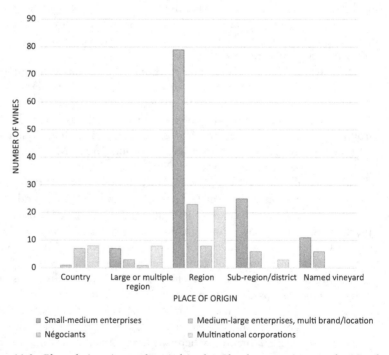

Figure 11.3a Place designation and capital in the Chardonnay wine sample: Number of
wines by place designation and type of enterprise

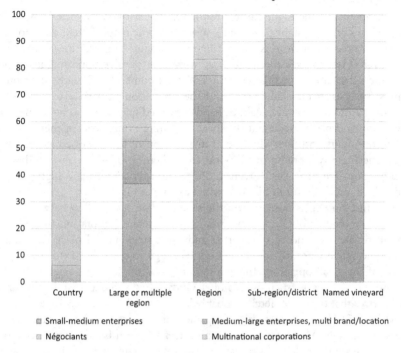

Figure 11.3b Place designation and capital in the Chardonnay wine sample: Share of place designation by type of enterprise

the smaller and medium-sized companies becoming more prominent. It is noticeable that the big corporation brands span the full range, except the single vineyard category, and they are not prominent in the smaller defined districts (such as Gimblett Gravels).

Conclusion: Place and markets

Our results suggest that place-making is occurring in the New Zealand wine industry. In particular, our analysis of the two hypotheses indicates that the processes involved show some interesting aspects of the role of place in wine markets. Our first hypothesis − that the granularity of place is directly related to the price/ quality of wine − seems to be largely confirmed, although with some qualifications. Certainly, at the lower end of the market, cheaper wine is associated with vague or large-scale place designation of origin, while the more expensive wines are found to come from named single vineyards or smaller wine-producing localities. Being able to specify a particular and favoured location seems to allow some winemakers at least to collect a premium on claims about the quality characteristics of wine from that small place. However, the relationship is not straightforward. Larger-scale regional names, such as Hawke's Bay and Marlborough, appear to have an established place in the market that allows some of their wines to command among the highest prices in the market, at the same time that much of the region's output might target the lower-to-middle range. There does not seem to be a simple linear process of upscaling by moving to more fine-grained place definition. Here we see that producers of more expensive wine might use place definition, but only at a broader scale and then combine this with other quality claims (such as 'hand-made' wine and the reputation of particular winemakers, and/or the use of expensive oak, or hand-harvested grapes and so on). Fine spatial resolution and place-making at the local level might only work if there are sufficient consumers with knowledge and imagination of the places concerned and a willingness to pay a premium for wines from them. Not all attempts to designate wine regions are successful (Overton, 2020), and reputations and high prices are difficult to maintain in the highly competitive wine market.

This first finding is mirrored by the second. The relationship between capital and place is evident but, again, uneven. Large beverage corporations and *négociants* dominate the low end of the market and the coarse-grained place designations, while the single vineyard and small boutique regions seem to be much more the arena of the small operators. Indeed, it seems as if the biggest companies eschew the boutique regions (such as Gimblett Gravels or Waiheke Island), despite the high prices that the wines fetch, probably because land is very expensive (Overton & Murray, 2016b). Yet these big companies can operate at different points on the spatial scale. Villa Maria, for example, produces a 'North Island' wine, yet also has in its range some single vineyard wines. However, in general, it is hard for smaller operators to function at lower price points, being hampered by access to supermarket shelves and the inability to gain economies of scale. For them, fictive place strategies are important for finding a place in the market.

Beyond these initial relationships between capital and place, however, we see a more complex and symbiotic relationship at a more macro level. The production and marketing of 'fine' wine from 'fine' regions helps to promote the overall quality image of wine and maintains an artisanal imaginary of the industry. Small wine producers are critical here, for they have some legitimate claims to artisanal and 'crafty' winemaking narratives. Big companies can leverage off this and notions of craft and *terroir*, for it not only reinforces the higher market segments they do work in (albeit in competition with smaller producers); it also promotes and adds richness to the overall public imagination of wine as a product. Thus, paradoxically perhaps, the smaller-scale and locally-oriented part of the industry helps to promote wine as a mass product – one that is often relatively cheap and produced on a large, industrial scale, but one that has connotations of prestige and associations with place (compared with many other alcoholic beverages). However, small producers might gain from the way in which large enterprises engage with *terroir* and place. Big companies, with marketing resources and scale of production, help to establish places in the market and thus open up opportunities for smaller producers. Without such substance and volumes on retail shelves, it is unlikely that many place names would gain public recognition: whether Marlborough Sauvignon Blanc in British supermarkets or Gimblett Gravels Syrah in Auckland wine shops.

Wine markets are large and complex. They are highly competitive, and there is a plethora of brands and products at many different price points and from many different parts of the world. The seeming diversity is bewildering for consumers, and buying decisions involve weighing up price, perceived quality, variety, vintage, origin and the aesthetic appeal of a certain label. Behind the complexity, however, lies the fact that most wine is produced by very large corporations, each with a wide portfolio of brands, and most is produced on an industrial scale. Wine markets are also diverse, with loyalty for national or local wines present in many places, but, again, most markets are driven by both global competition and global wine styles.

Such competition in global markets creates impulses for place-making strategies at different scales – and for tensions and contests for place. There is a 'race for place' to define and promote places of origin as points of difference in the market and to secure a premium. This is evident in the New Zealand wine industry. Although heavily dominated by a single region and variety – Marlborough Sauvignon Blanc – the past 30 years have seen not only a very large increase in grape and wine production but also a proliferation of 'place brands', with new wine-producing districts appearing and gaining varying degrees of traction in local and global wine markets. These new places of origin have enlarged and complicated the geography of New Zealand wine. However, the way in which such places are created and embraced (or rejected) in turn sends ripples back into markets. Through complex channels of capital, through layered markets and through various marketing strategies, the idea of place, constructions of place and imaginations of place have become key elements of wine markets.

Notes

1　We have not included a 'no place designation' in our analysis, as by law all wines in New Zealand must have at least an indication of country of origin.
2　We can see strong parallels here with the way in which strategies have been developed in wine and other rural industries in New Zealand to form develop a 'relationships economy' (Pawson & Perkins, 2017; also Perkins, Mackay & Espiner, 2015) and move from mass commodity production.
3　Some of these might have included another variety blended, although all were simply listed as 'Chardonnay'. We excluded wines that might have been made from Chardonnay, such as sparkling wine or ones with only a regional descriptor, such as Chablis, and no explicit indication of variety.
4　We thought that these two outlets provided a reasonably balanced indication of wines available. Both were large-scale retailers. The supermarket stocked high turnover brands, particularly for the cheaper end of the market (under NZ$12 a bottle), although it also stocked many mid-priced (NZ$12–$20) and some high-end brands. Advintage also had some cheaper brands available, but relatively it seemed to target the middle bracket and had relatively more wines in the over NZ$20 a bottle segment.
5　These very expensive wines, such as Clearview Estate Endeavour or Elephant Hill Salome, used only Hawke's Bay on their front label, although interestingly they might indicate on the back label that the grapes were from 'selected' vineyards or from a particular property (however, these place names were not prominently displayed).

References

Banks, G. (2014). What's in a name? Labels and branding in the New Zealand wine industry. In P. Howland (Ed.), *Social, cultural and economic impacts of wine in New Zealand* (pp. 120–136). Abingdon: Routledge.

Banks, G. & Sharpe, S. (2006). Wines, regions and geographic imperative: The Coonawarra example. *New Zealand Geographer*, 62(3), 173–184.

Banks, G., Kelly, S., Lewis, N. & Sharpe, S. (2007). Place "From one glance": The use of place in the marketing of New Zealand and Australian wines. *Australian Geographer*, 38(1), 15–35.

Baragwanath, L. & Lewis, N. (2014). Waiheke Island. In P. Howland (Ed.), *Social, cultural and economic impacts of wine in Zealand* (pp. 211–242). Abingdon: Routledge.

Barham, E. (2003). Translating terroir: the global challenge of French AOC labelling. *Journal of Rural Studies*, 19(1), 127–138.

Barker, J.P.H. (2004). *Different worlds: Law and the changing geographies of wine in France and New Zealand.* [Unpublished doctoral dissertation], University of Auckland.

Bowen, S. (2010). Embedding local places in global spaces: Geographical indications as a territorial development strategy. *Rural Sociology*, 75(2), 209–243.

Bowen, S. (2011). The importance of place: Re-territorializing embeddedness. *Sociologia Ruralis*, 51(4), 325–348.

Bowen, S. & Valenzuela Zapata, A. (2009). Geographical indications, terroir, and socioeconomic and ecological sustainability: The case of tequila. *Journal of Rural Studies*, 25(1), 108–119.

Charters, S. (2006). *Wine and society: The social and cultural context of a drink.* Oxford: Elsevier Butterworth-Heinemann.

Charters, S. (2020). Terroir wines in Champagne: Between ideology and utopia. In J. Dutton & P.J. Howland (Eds), *Wine, terroir and utopia: Making new worlds* (pp. 111–125). London: Routledge.

Demossier, M. (2004). Contemporary lifestyles: The case of wine. In D. Sloan (Ed.), *Culinary taste: Consumer behaviour in the international restaurant sector* (pp. 93–107). Oxford: Elsevier Butterworth-Heinemann.

Demossier, M. (2020). Burgundy's *climats* and the utopian wine heritage landscape. In J. Dutton & P.J. Howland (Eds), *Wine, terroir and utopia: Making new worlds* (pp. 75–92). London: Routledge.

Dogana, B. & Gokovali, U. (2012). *Geographical indications: the aspects of rural development and marketing through the traditional products Procedia - Social and Behavioral Sciences*, 62, 761–765.

Dutton, J. (2020). The four pillars of utopian wine: Terroir, viticulture, degustation and cellars. In J. Dutton & P.J. Howland (Eds), *Wine, terroir and utopia: Making new worlds* (pp. 24–41). London: Routledge.

Fanet, J. (translated by F. Bruton). (2004). *Great wine terroirs.* Los Angeles, CA: University of California Press.

Garcia-Parpet, M.-F. (2008). Markets, prices and symbolic value: Grands crus and the challenges of global markets. *International review of Sociology*, 18(2), 237–252.

Goldberg, S.D. (2001). Who will raise the white flag? The battle between the United States and the European Union over the protection of geographical indications. *University of Pennsylvania Journal of International Economic Law*, 22(1), 107–151.

Goodman, D. (2010). Place and space in alternative food networks: Connecting production and consumption. In M.K. Goodman, D. Goodman & M. Redclift. (Eds), *Consuming Space: Placing consumption in perspective* (pp. 189–211). Farnham: Ashgate Publishing.

Hayward, D. & Lewis, N. (2008). Regional dynamics in the globalising wine industry: The case of Marlborough, New Zealand. *The Geographical Journal*, 174(2), 124–137.

Howland, P.J. (2008). Martinborough's wine tourists and the metro-rural idyll. *Journal of New Zealand Studies*, 6–7, 77–100.

Howland, P.J. (2014). Martinborough: A tourist idyll. In P. Howland (Ed.), *Social, cultural and economic impacts of wine in New Zealand* (pp. 227–242). Abingdon: Routledge.

Howland, P.J. (2020). Plain-sight utopia: Boutique winemakers, urbane vineyards and terroir-torial moorings. In J. Dutton and P.J. Howland (Eds), *Wine, terroir and utopia: Making new worlds* (pp. 235–252). London: Routledge.

Hughes, J. (2006). Champagne, feta, and bourbon: The spirited debate about geographical indications. *Hastings Law Journal*, 58, 299–386.

Johnson, H. & Robinson, J. (2013). *The world atlas of wine*. (7th ed.). London: Mitchell Beazley.

Josling, T. (2006). The war on *terroir*: Geographical indications as a transatlantic trade conflict. *Journal of Agricultural Economics*, 57(3), 337–363.

Kelly, S.C. (2007). Constructing and mediating spatial relationships in French winegrowing: The Burgundian example. [Unpublished doctoral dissertation], University of Auckland.

Lewis. N., Moran, W., Perrier-Corne, P. & Barker, J. (2002). Territoriality, réglementation in industry governance. *Progress in Human Geography*, 26(4), 433–462.

Lewis, N. & Le Heron, E. (2018). New Zealand wine: Seeking success beyond growth. In E. Pawson and Biological Economies Team (Eds), *The new biological economy* (pp. 116–136). Auckland: Auckland University Press.

Lewis, N. (2014). Beyond the flawed narratives of a crisis of oversupply: A conceptual fix for New Zealand wine. In P. Howland (Ed.), *Social, cultural and economic impacts of wine in New Zealand* (pp. 86–102). Abingdon: Routledge.

McCoy, E. (2005). *The emperor of wine: The rise of Robert M. Parker, Jr., and the reign of American taste*. New York, NY: Harper Collins.

Moragues-Faus, A.M. & Sonnino, R. (2012). Embedding quality in the agro-food system: The dynamics and implications of place-making strategies in the olive oil sector of Alto Palancia, Spain. *Sociologia Ruralis*, 52(2), 215–234.

Moran, W. (1993a). Rural space as intellectual property. *Political Geography*, 12(3), 263–277.

Moran, W. (1993b). The wine appellation as territory in France and California. *Annals of the Association of American Geographers*, 83(4), 694–717.

Moran, W. (2001). Terroir – the human factor. *Australian and New Zealand Wine Industry Journal*, 16, 32–51.

Moran, W. (2016). *New Zealand wine: The land, the vines, the people*. Auckland: Auckland University Press.

Murdoch, J., Marsden, T. & Banks, J. (2000). Quality, nature, and embeddedness: Some theoretical considerations in the context of the food sector. *Economic Geography*, 76(2), 107–125.

Murray, W.E. & Overton, J. (2011). Defining regions: The making of places in the New Zealand wine industry. *Australian Geographer*, 42(4), 419–433.

New Zealand Winegrowers. (2013). *New Zealand winegrowers labelling guide* (22nd ed.). Retrieved 11 March 2016, from www.nzwine.com/assets/sm/upload/5l/ep/ut/un/NZW_labelling_guide_Aug2013.pdf.

New Zealand Winegrowers. (2017). *New Zealand winegrowers labelling guide* (26th ed.). Retrieved 18 June 2019, from www.wine-marlborough.co.nz/wp-content/uploads/2018/04/Labeling-guide.pdf.

Overton, J. (2010). The consumption of space: Land, capital and place in the New Zealand wine industry. *Geoforum*, 41(5), 752–762.

Overton, J. (2020). Landscapes of failure: Why do some wine regions not succeed? In C.C. Myles (Ed.), *Fermented landscapes: Lively processes of socio-environmental transformation* (pp. 57–82). Lincoln, NE: University of Nebraska Press.

Overton, J., Banks, G. & Murray, W.E. (2014). Waipara. In P.J. Howland (Ed.), *Social, cultural and economic impacts of wine in New Zealand* (pp. 243–252). Abingdon, UK: Routledge.

Overton, J. & Heitger, J. (2008). Maps, markets and merlot: The making of an Antipodean regional wine appellation. *Journal of Rural Studies*, 24(4), 440–449.

Overton, J. & Murray, W.E. (2013). Class in a glass: Capital, neoliberalism and social space in the global wine industry. *Antipode*, 45(3), 702–718.

Overton, J. & Murray, W.E. (2014a). Finding a place for New Zealand wine: Terroir and regional denominations. In P.J. Howland (Ed.), *Social, cultural and economic impacts of wine in New Zealand* (pp. 41–57). Abingdon, UK: Routledge.

Overton, J. & Murray, W.E. (2014b). Boutiques and behemoths: The transformation of the New Zealand wine industry 1990–2012. In P.J. Howland (Ed.), *Social, cultural and economic impacts of wine in New Zealand* (pp. 25–40). Abingdon: Routledge.

Overton, J. & Murray, W.E. (2016a). Fictive place. *Progress in Human Geography*, 40(6), 794–809.

Overton, J. & Murray W.E. (2016b). Investing in place: Articulations and congregations of capital in the wine industry. *Geographical Journal*, 182(1), 49–58.

Overton, J. & Murray W.E. (2017). GI Blues: Geographical indications and wine in New Zealand. In W. van Caenegem and J. Cleary (Eds), *The importance of place: Geographical indications as a tool for local and regional development* (pp. 197–220). Cham: Springer.

Pawson, E. & Perkins, H.C. (2017). New Zealand going global: The emerging relationships economy. *Asia Pacific Viewpoint*, 58 (3), 257–272.

Pedersen, M.U., Persson, K.G. & Sharp, P. (2019). The cost of ignorance: Reputational mark-up in the market for Tuscan red wines. *American Association of Wine Economists (AAWE)*, (Working Paper No. 243). Retrieved from www.wine-economics.org/dt_catalog/aawe-working-paper-no-243-economics.

Perkins, H.C., Mackay, M. & Espiner, S. (2015). Putting pinot alongside merino in central Otago, New Zealand: Rural amenity and the making of the global countryside. *Journal of Rural Studies*, 39(1), 85–98.

Saker, J. (2017). Wine labels and what they're not telling you. *Cuisine*. Retrieved 15 July 2019, from www.stuff.co.nz/life-style/food-wine/drinks/93715607/wine-labels-and-what-theyre-not-telling-you.

Sommers, B.J. (2008). *The Geography of Wine*. New York, NY: Plume.

Stewart, K. (2010). *Chancers and visionaries: A history of wine in New Zealand*. Auckland: Godwit Press.

Tipples, R. (2007). Wines of the farthest promised land from Waipara, Canterbury, New Zealand. In G. Campbell and N. Guibert (Eds), *Wine, society and globalization: Multidisciplinary perspectives on the wine industry* (pp. 241–254). New York, NY: Palgrave Macmillan.

Ulin, R.K.C. (1995). Invention and representation as cultural capital: Southwest French winegrowing history. *American Anthropologist*, 97(3), 519–527.

Van Beynen, M. (2019). Southern Boundary Wines – deceit and dishonesty in the wine industry. *Stuff*. Retrieved 5 December 2019, from www.stuff.co.nz/business/better-business/117606090/southern-boundary-wines–deceit-and-dishonesty-in-the- wine-industry.

Vaudour, E. (2002). The quality of grapes and wine in relation to geography: Notions of terroir at various scales. *Journal of Wine Research*, 13(2), 117–141.

Wilson, J.E. (1998). *Terroir: The role of geology, climate, and culture in the making of French wine*. London: Mitchell Beazley.

Afterword
The Place of Markets

Russell Prince, Carolyn Morris, Matthew Henry, Aisling Gallagher and Stephen FitzHerbert

SCHOOL OF PEOPLE, ENVIRONMENT AND PLANNING, MASSEY UNIVERSITY

The aim of this book was to deepen geographical engagement with markets, emphasising the role of place. Much more broadly, we suggested in the introduction that this engagement should contribute to the project of, as Peck (2012) has it, rethinking economy. If this collection is to make a contribution, and not just be a set of particular, individual, quirky case studies of little interest beyond the scope of their own subject matter, what lessons does it impart?

Lesson 1: Places shape markets and markets shape places

The clearest lesson, and perhaps the least surprising, is that places shape markets and markets shape places. For example, housing markets shape the built form of urban places, and they have important national and even international dimensions. But Murphy shows how different theories and practices of land valuation get put to work in places with particular planning laws and housing stock to produce localised housing markets with particular spatial and social dynamics. The material qualities of place have long been fetishised in the wine market, and, as Overton and Murray demonstrate, they provide the basis for the production of different quality market segments. These market logics are folded back onto places through the geographically defined rules and marketing programmes constructed at different scales around wine-making places, changing the latter in the process.

While the interaction between markets and places is clear, collectively the chapters illustrate a point we made in the introduction to this volume: markets are integrated into places. Location, locale and sense of place are not just shaped by markets and vice versa, they are partly constituted by them (and vice versa). The networks, institutions, ideas and technologies that are struggled over to enable exchange (Cohen, 2018) are also networks, institutions, ideas and technologies that constitute place.

Markets are worked out in existing social and community relations, as Langford and her colleagues illustrate with the morally inflected relational work conducted by bankers in Australia's small and isolated Northern Territory farming industry. Lewis and Wynd also link the moral economies of place to market making, where ideas about the role of schools in making happy and productive citizens and inadequacies in the local funding system create a space

DOI: 10.4324/9780429296260-12

for market-making actors to do their work. Equally, the material and social infrastructures of a place can confound market making efforts, as Lovell demonstrates in the work undertaken to try and make an electricity meter market in Australia. Recognising that markets are integrated into place means rethinking or abandoning the conceit that markets are about rationality clashing with culture. Laeis and Morris pick this apart in their chapter, showing how narratives about culture stymying a market are less accurate than recognising that markets will often exist where they can be put at the service of local cultural and social relations. Market rationalities are not outside of culture, but embedded in it, a point also made by Gallagher. These community *networks*, educational *institutions*, cultural *ideas* and metering *technologies* are all constitutive of markets and of place. Even location, which is seemingly the most inconsequential aspect of place, matters to markets in place. As Henry demonstrates, the location of New Zealand on the opposite seasonal cycle to the United Kingdom allowed for the construction of a set of temporal-material linkages that drew New Zealand farms and Smithfield market into alignment and made off-season lamb possible for British consumers. The spatial and temporal topologies of this market are also the topologies of place.

What might this mean for rethinking economy? Markets produce, enact and realise uneven relations of power. Speaking from a political economy perspective, Christophers (2015) has argued that alternative forms of exchange to capitalist markets may make the latter seem fragile, but they will only survive so long as they are not a threat to capital accumulation. As soon as alternative forms of exchange become a threat to the functioning and expansion of capitalist markets, the power of capital and the state will work to close them down. This recognition of structural power is important, and clearly advocating for or implementing alternative forms of exchange to the dominant capitalist market form will not lead to the former simply overthrowing the latter. But power is central to place – and the politics of place – as well. The topographies and topologies of place are buttressed, shaped and marked by power relations, some of which stretch across space. Studying markets in place means studying the link between power in place and the power of markets. What is their relationship? How did this relationship come to pass? And what does it mean for the future of the place and the market? These questions are vital to understanding our place in a world of markets.

Lesson 2: Places have multiple market ontologies

Another aspect of this collection that surprised us as the editors points to a second lesson. Half of the cases surveyed in this volume are about, in one way or another, failures in 'the market'. The idea of market failure is a technical term in economics, describing an 'inefficient distribution of goods and services in the free market',[1] meaning that actors cannot produce the optimum market-clearing outcome through rationality. In more day-to-day terms, market failure simply describes markets that collapse or result in unsatisfactory outcomes for those with a stake in it, and it is in this latter sense that market failure is apparent in at least half of the chapters. Murphy's discussion of the Auckland housing market reveals a situation of house prices getting out of reach for many looking to buy, even with interventions intended to provide affordable housing. The Māra Kai experiment described by FitzHerbert lasted just a few years before being shut down and dismissed as a failure by the state actors that had supported it. The market for local produce in the Fijian hotel industry development experts had high hopes for, which is discussed by Laeis and Morris, never eventuated in a significant way. Lovell points out that the failure to institute a market-based solution for smart-meter rollout in Victoria became a lesson for other states in their own infrastructure projects. Gallagher's example of state-led marketisation in childcare has failed to provide for the values of a significant, both numerically and politically, minority of the population.

It is clear that these failures are of quite different types. Sometimes the market continues on, despite its failings. Other times it collapses. Sometimes the failure of the market, as FitzHerbert argues, is the least important thing about its existence. Some participants in these markets would not necessarily regard them as failures, and this is the point. In all these cases, market failure is contextual. The lesson is that markets have their meaning and their role in place, and it is in place that its success or failure is judged. The study of failure is always an opportunity to reveal certain aspects of various political projects that were hidden or obscured (Lovell, 2017; Perrons & Posocco, 2009). In the case of markets, it is an opportunity to consider what it reveals about the place that the failure occurs, and what new arrangement, market or otherwise, emerges to replace it. Moreover, market failures, rather than a rebuke, have, according to Frankel and his colleagues (see Frankel, Ossandón & Pallesen, 2019; Ossandón & Ureta, 2019), become central to ongoing neoliberal forms of governing as it has morphed into a set of practices that deal with those failures and try to maintain market forms. The way that place-bound actors try to contend with ongoing market failures will demonstrate how place continues to throw grit in the gears of neoliberalism, forcing its ongoing variegated reconstruction across space (Larner, 2003; Peck, 2010).

This relatively simple lesson points to a deeper one regarding the political ontology of markets (see Mol, 1999). What had to be done to make markets possible in a place? And what does this mean for how markets might be different? These questions emerge most clearly in those chapters in which indigeneity is part of the story, and highlights one of the most valuable contributions 'southern scholarship' could make in this space (Connell, 2007). In her reading of the Treaty of Waitangi claim which forced the recognition that market making interventions are culturally specific interventions in their own right, Gallagher showed how the ontological stakes of markets are revealed when they clash with other ontological claims. In FitzHerbert's study, although the state was pushing for a particular form of market-led economic development, for those involved marketisation was not the only goal, with a range of diverse cultural aspirations and relations being worked out through the economic experiment. And Hikuroa, Le Heron and Le Heron demonstrate how horizons of what can be known are opened up by indigenous forms of knowledge, allowing for a rethinking of production, consumption and regulatory relations. New practices of ownership, regulation and enterprise could be imagined which could underpin future markets.

These cases, which are all drawn from the particular forms of indigenous and state-capital relations that pertain in Aotearoa New Zealand, make a number of points. Markets are often treated as clearing houses in market studies, where buyers and sellers, however they are conceived and/or constructed, come together to exchange and then depart. However they are conceptualised, exchangeable 'objects' are separated from their context. They are commodified. But in any particular place, multiple relational ontologies might be present that disrupt this understanding of market exchange. These cases are marked by an insistence from indigenous Māori that this separation not occur, and that certain things are kept together and are accounted for in the exchange – kinship, ecology and relationship to the land are all present. While Gallagher shows that this is a challenge to more conventionally conceived markets, both FitzHerbert and Hikuroa and his colleagues demonstrate how it could profoundly reshape markets to come. While there is a certain specificity about the Aotearoa New Zealand case for reasons that we outlined in the introduction, they signal how relations that are generative of different kinds of markets are possible in other places. While they are subject to the procrustean aspirations of certain actors, markets as practiced in place remain resolutely ontologically protean.

These examples point to a space where markets may be theorised differently. As Roscoe and Loza (2019) argue, there is more than one kind of market, and markets founded on different ontological underpinnings to capitalist markets regarding key aspects like enterprise, regulation, ownership, care, and social relations may produce different outcomes. Markets are objects of knowledge, not just in the sense that we can study them, but in the sense that they are a product of ontological and epistemological work that constructs and stabilises the various relational agencies required for exchange. Accounting for the situation of markets in place is one way that we can narrate diverse kinds of markets.

Lesson 3: Study places, not (just) markets

So perhaps the main lesson is methodological. When we study markets, we need to understand that we are studying places too. This is not to decry market studies that situate them in global capitalism, or link them to variegated shifts to 'market societies' in a Polanyian sense, or that trace out the aggregate shifts of money and commodities across space. Markets undeniably have multiple spatialities that can be explored. But this collection, which is written from a part of the world that has a particular history and offers insights that draw directly upon its history and geography, demonstrates what a deep engagement with place offers. Studying markets in their place is more than carbon-copying techniques of analysis and applying them in different places: it is recognising and accounting for the way that generative, as opposed to merely contextual, aspects of place like location, locale, sense of place, topography and topology deeply frame how the market operates there. Markets are always somewhere, and wherever they are, they are not separate from that somewhere, but a part of it.

Note

1 www.econlib.org/library/Topics/College/marketfailures.html, accessed 12 December 2020.

References

Christophers, B. (2015). Constructing and deconstructing markets: Making space for capital. *Environment and Planning A*, 47(9), 1859–1865. https://.doi.org/10.1177/0308518x15604971.

Cohen, D. (2018). Between perfection and damnation: The emerging geography of markets. *Progress in Human Geography*, 42(6), 898–915. https://doi.org/10.1177/0309132517729769.

Connell, R. (2007). *Southern theory: The global dynamics of knowledge in the Social Sciences.* London: Routledge.

Frankel, C., Ossandón, J. & Pallesen, T. (2019). The organization of markets for collective concerns and their failures. *Economy and Society*, 48(2), 153–174. https://doi.org/10.1080/03085147.2019.1627791.

Larner, W. (2003). Neoliberalism? *Environment and Planning D–Society & Space*, 21(5), 509–512.

Lovell, H. (2017). Policy failure mobilities. *Progress in Human Geography, 43(1), 46–63.* https://doi.org/10.1177/0309132517734074.

Mol, A. (1999). Ontological politics. A word and some questions. *The Sociological Review*, 47(S1), 74–89. https;//doi.org/10.1111/j.1467-954X.1999.tb03483.x.

Ossandón, J. & Ureta, S. (2019). Problematizing markets: Market failures and the government of collective concerns. *Economy and Society*, 48(2), 175–196. https://doi.org/10.1080/03085147.2019.1576433.

Peck, J. (2010). *Constructions of Neoliberal reason.* Oxford: Oxford University Press.

Peck, J. (2012). Economic geography: Island life. *Dialogues in Human Geography*, 2(2), 113–133. https://doi.org/10.1177/2043820612443779.

Perrons, D. & Posocco, S. (2009). Globalising failures. *Geoforum*, 40(2), 131–135. https://doi.org/10.1016/j.geoforum.2008.12.001.

Roscoe, P. & Loza, O. (2019). The –ography of markets (or, the responsibilities of market studies). *Journal of Cultural Economy*, 12(3), 215–227. https://doi.org/10.1080/17530350.2018.1557730.

Index

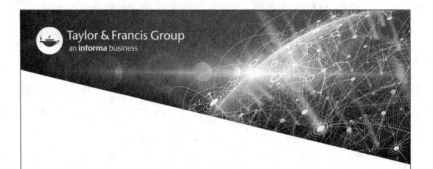

Printed in the United States
by Baker & Taylor Publisher Services